T0214673

Lecture Notes in Business Information Processing   419

Series Editors

Wil van der Aalst 🆔
  RWTH Aachen University, Aachen, Germany

John Mylopoulos 🆔
  University of Trento, Trento, Italy

Michael Rosemann 🆔
  Queensland University of Technology, Brisbane, QLD, Australia

Michael J. Shaw
  University of Illinois, Urbana-Champaign, IL, USA

Clemens Szyperski
  Microsoft Research, Redmond, WA, USA

More information about this series at http://www.springer.com/series/7911

Peggy Gregory · Casper Lassenius ·
Xiaofeng Wang · Philippe Kruchten (Eds.)

Agile Processes in Software Engineering and Extreme Programming

22nd International Conference
on Agile Software Development, XP 2021
Virtual Event, June 14–18, 2021
Proceedings

Springer

Editors
Peggy Gregory
University of Central Lancashire
Preston, UK

Casper Lassenius
Aalto University
Espoo, Finland

Xiaofeng Wang
Free University of Bozen-Bolzano
Bolzano, Italy

Philippe Kruchten
University of British Columbia
Vancouver, BC, Canada

(cc) (i) BY

ISSN 1865-1348 ISSN 1865-1356 (electronic)
Lecture Notes in Business Information Processing
ISBN 978-3-030-78097-5 ISBN 978-3-030-78098-2 (eBook)
https://doi.org/10.1007/978-3-030-78098-2

© The Editor(s) (if applicable) and The Author(s) 2021. This book is an open access publication.

Open Access This book is licensed under the terms of the Creative Commons Attribution 4.0 International License (http://creativecommons.org/licenses/by/4.0/), which permits use, sharing, adaptation, distribution and reproduction in any medium or format, as long as you give appropriate credit to the original author(s) and the source, provide a link to the Creative Commons license and indicate if changes were made.

The images or other third party material in this book are included in the book's Creative Commons license, unless indicated otherwise in a credit line to the material. If material is not included in the book's Creative Commons license and your intended use is not permitted by statutory regulation or exceeds the permitted use, you will need to obtain permission directly from the copyright holder.

The use of general descriptive names, registered names, trademarks, service marks, etc. in this publication does not imply, even in the absence of a specific statement, that such names are exempt from the relevant protective laws and regulations and therefore free for general use.

The publisher, the authors and the editors are safe to assume that the advice and information in this book are believed to be true and accurate at the date of publication. Neither the publisher nor the authors or the editors give a warranty, expressed or implied, with respect to the material contained herein or for any errors or omissions that may have been made. The publisher remains neutral with regard to jurisdictional claims in published maps and institutional affiliations.

This Springer imprint is published by the registered company Springer Nature Switzerland AG
The registered company address is: Gewerbestrasse 11, 6330 Cham, Switzerland

Preface

This volume contains the research papers presented at XP 2021, the 22nd International Conference on Agile Software Development, held online during June 14–18, 2021, due to the COVID-19 pandemic.

XP is the premier Agile software development conference combining research and practice. It is a unique forum where Agile researchers, practitioners, thought leaders, coaches, and trainers get together to present and discuss their most recent innovations, research results, experiences, concerns, challenges, and trends. XP conferences provide an informal environment to learn and trigger discussions, and welcome both people new to Agile and seasoned Agile practitioners.

XP 2021 marked the 22nd edition of the "First Conference in Agile." Our theme was "Agile Turns Twenty While the World Goes Online" as this year we marked both the 20th anniversary of the publication of the Agile Manifesto and the global move to remote working as a result of the COVID-19 pandemic. After the challenges of the past year and during these times of great change we continue to provide a space for academics and industry practitioners to come together and share what they have learnt over the last year. We elicited a wide range of contributions addressing all Agile approaches, theoretical viewpoints of Agile, applications of Agile in a wide range of areas including DevOps, FinTech, AI/ML, and IoT, and empirical studies exploring how Agile approaches are used and the impact they have in different settings.

The XP 2021 conference invited submissions on eight tracks: research papers, research workshops, experience reports, industry and practice sessions, empirical studies (on-site research), Agile gamification and facilitation, posters, and lightning talks. We ran a slightly reduced conference because of the pandemic and received 215 submissions, demonstrating that the XP community remains strong even in difficult times.

For the research paper track, we invited submissions of unpublished high-quality research papers related to Agile and lean software development. Submissions addressing topics across the full spectrum of Agile software development, on issues of concern to practitioners, researchers, or both, were welcomed.

The XP 2021 research paper track received 38 submissions. Each paper was reviewed by three members of the Program Committee. Based on the reviews, 11 full papers and 2 short papers were accepted for publication in these proceedings. The papers cover a wide range of topics, including Agile practices, assessment of agility and delivery performance, and large-scale Agile.

The success of the XP 2021 conference should be attributed to the passionate and hard work of many people. We greatly appreciate the contributions of the authors, the Program Committee, and the volunteers. Finally, we would like to express our gratitude to the XP Conference Steering Committee and the Agile Alliance for their ongoing support.

April 2021

Peggy Gregory
Casper Lassenius
Xiaofeng Wang
Philippe Kruchten

Organization

Conference Chair

Peggy Gregory   University of Central Lancashire, UK

Program Co-chairs

Xiaofeng Wang   Free University of Bozen-Bolzano, Italy
Casper Lassenius   Aalto University, Finland

Publication Chair

Philippe Kruchten   University of British Columbia, Canada

Program Committee

Noura Abbas   Colorado Technical University, USA
Ademar Aguiar   University of Porto, Portugal
Craig Anslow   Victoria University of Wellington, New Zealand
Hubert Baumeister   Technical University of Denmark, Denmark
Marthe Berntzen   University of Oslo, Norway
Jan Bosch   Chalmers University of Technology, Sweden
Frank Buschmann   Siemens AG, Germany
Fabio Calefato   University of Bari, Italy
Noel Carroll   National University of Ireland Galway, Ireland
Daniela S. Cruzes   Norwegian University of Science and Technology,
                          Norway
Torgeir Dingsøyr   Norwegian University of Science and Technology,
                          Norway
Yael Dubinsky   StepAhead, Israel
Jutta Eckstein   IT communication, Germany
Steven Fraser   Innoxec, USA
Ilenia Fronza   Free University of Bozen -Bolzano, Italy
Juan Garbajosa   Universidad Politécnica de Madrid, Spain
Alfredo Goldman   University of São Paulo, Brazil
Eduardo Guerra   Free University of Bozen-Bolzano, Italy
Orit Hazzan   Technion - Israel Institute of Technology, Israel
Helena Holmström Olsson   University of Malmö, Sweden
Fabio Kon   University of São Paulo, Brazil
Philippe Kruchten   University of British Columbia, Canada

Ville Leppänen	University of Turku, Finland
Lech Madeyski	Wroclaw University of Science and Technology, Poland
Sabrina Marczak	PUCRS, Brazil
Frank Maurer	University of Calgary, Canada
Tommi Mikkonen	University of Helsinki, Finland
Alok Mishra	Atilim University, Turkey
Nils Brede Moe	SINTEF, Norway
Parastoo Mohagheghi	Norwegian Labour and Welfare Administration, Norway
Jürgen Münch	Reutlingen University, Germany
Maria Paasivaara	IT University of Copenhagen, Denmark, and Aalto University, Finland
Ken Power	Independent Consultant, Ireland
Rafael Prikladnicki	PUCRS, Brazil
Pilar Rodríguez	Universidad Politécnica de Madrid, Spain
Darja Šmite	Blekinge Institute of Technology, Sweden
Simone V. Spiegler	University of Stuttgart, Germany
Viktoria Stray	University of Oslo, Norway
Stefan Wagner	University of Stuttgart, Germany
Hironori Washizaki	Waseda University, Japan
Eileen Wrubel	Software Engineering Institute, USA

Steering Committee

Hubert Baumeister	Technical University of Denmark, Denmark
François Coallier	Ecole de technologie supérieure, Canada
Jutta Eckstein	IT communication, Germany
Steven Fraser	Innoxec, USA
Juan Garbajosa (Chair)	Universidad Politécnica de Madrid, Spain
Peggy Gregory	University of Central Lancashire, UK
Ellen Grove	Agile Alliance, USA
Casper Lassenius	Aalto University, Finland
Michele Marchesi	University of Cagliari, Italy
Maria Paasivaara	IT University of Copenhagen, Denmark, and Aalto University, Finland
Viktoria Stray	University of Oslo, Norway
Xiaofeng Wang	Free University of Bozen-Bolzano, Italy

Sponsoring Organization

Agile Alliance, USA

Contents

Large-scale Agile

Short Contributions

Agile Practices

From Collaboration to Solitude and Back: Remote Pair Programming During COVID-19

Darja Smite[1,2(✉)], Marius Mikalsen[2,3], Nils Brede Moe[1,2], Viktoria Stray[2,4], and Eriks Klotins[1]

[1] Blekinge Institute of Technology, Karlskrona, Sweden
{darja.smite,nils.b.moe,eriks.klotins}@bth.se
[2] SINTEF, Trondheim, Norway
{darja.smite,marius.mikalsen,nils.b.moe,
viktoria.stray}@sintef.no
[3] Norwegian University of Science and Technology, Trondheim, Norway
[4] University of Oslo, Oslo, Norway

Abstract. Along with the increasing popularity of agile software development, software work has become much more social than ever. Contemporary software teams rely on a variety of collaborative practices, such as pair programming, the topic of our study. Many agilists advocated the importance of collocation, face-to-face interaction, and physical artefacts incorporated in the shared workspace, which the COVID-19 pandemic made unavailable; most software companies around the world were forced to send their engineers to work from home. As software projects and teams overnight turned into distributed collaborations, we question what happened to the pair programming practice in the work-from-home mode. This paper reports on a longitudinal study of remote pair programming in two companies. We conducted 38 interviews with 30 engineers from Norway, Sweden, and the USA, and used the results of a survey in one of the case companies. Our study is unique as we collected the data longitudinally in April/May 2020, Sep/Oct 2020, and Jan/Feb 2021. We found that pair programming has decreased and some interviewees report not pairing at all for almost a full year. The experiences of those who paired vary from actively co-editing the code by using special tools to more passively co-reading and discussing the code and solutions by sharing the screen. Finally, we found that the interest in and the use of PP over time, since the first months of the forced work from home to early 2021, has admittedly increased, also as a social practice.

Keywords: COVID-19 · WFH · Remote · Distributed · Pair programming · Agile

1 Introduction

Contemporary software engineering has become more social than ever [1]. The popularity of collaborative practices, such as pair programming (PP), have continuously grown along with the growing interest in implementing agile software development

© The Author(s) 2021
P. Gregory et al. (Eds.): XP 2021, LNBIP 419, pp. 3–18, 2021.
https://doi.org/10.1007/978-3-030-78098-2_1

methodologies. The increased interest in PP has been linked with that joint problem solving outperforms individual capabilities [2] and that developers enjoy pairing more than working solo [3].

PP emerged as a collocated practice, sometimes even facilitated by specially dedicated work areas, i.e., open space with groups of workstations for PP [4], and relies on constant communication and collaboration. This is why, when the worldwide COVID-19 pandemic in 2020 has forced many software companies to send their employees to work from home (WFH), many of the collaborative practices that used to depend on physical collocation, were, obviously, disrupted. An interesting research question is then: **What happened to the PP practice in the forced WFH regime?**

We know that collaborative practices are more challenging in virtual teams [5]. The use of digital communication tools due to physical distance brings challenges, such as reduced communication quality due to poor network and meaning, tone, and emotion being lost and misunderstood over digital media [6]. Furthermore, facilitation of remote pair programming (RPP) requires specific tool support. Existing literature suggests that although several tools developed for RPP exist, there is very little empirical evaluation [7]. Even though distributed work is challenging, RPP has been shown to have benefits similar to collocated pairing [8]. However, there are not many studies on RPP in industry settings, and most are investigating students from a teaching perspective [7]. Further, there are no studiesof teams that suddenly need to change from being collocated to working full-time remotely. All these research gaps motivated our study.

2 Background and Related Work

2.1 Pair Programming

Pair programming (PP) is a key collaborative agile practice that is believed to improve team performance. In PP, two developers sit side-by-side at one computer, continuously collaborating on the same design, algorithm, code, or test [10]. In its original form, one developer takes a leading role (called the driver) while another (called the navigator) observes and actively provides feedback, asks questions and makes suggestions to ensure high quality of the produced code [11]. While the roles of the navigator and drivers are widely accepted, pairs often take on both responsibilities at the same time instead of having an explicit division of labor. Chong and Hurlbutt [12] found in their ethnographic study that having a strict separation of roles inhibits the natural way of working and that both developers having imminent access to the keyboard enabled rapid switching and made the developers more engaged. Further, Wray [13] reports additional scenarios of how two developers can collaborate on jointly improving the same code, for example, by jointly reviewing and discussing issues and potential solutions without any explicit roles.

The processes of PP relate to key processes of effective agile teamwork [9], which are monitoring, feedback, and backup behavior [14]. Since the pair might constantly change the driver and the navigator, or work without separating the roles, PP can help exercising backup behavior and establishing it in teams when missing [15]. PP is also found to be an efficient practice for education, and consequently a good practice when onboarding new people [2, 16]. Pairing involves shared decision making, therefore the practice supports self-management [17]. Further, recent research reports that PP is effective in terms of raising coding quality [16]. Last but not least, PP has also been found to be a practice that developers enjoy. Williams et al. [3] found that more than 90% stated that they enjoyed collaborative programming more than solo programming.

2.2 Remote Pair Programming

There are not many studies on remote pair programming (RPP) in industry, and most focus on students from a teaching perspective [7]. From existing studies we know that RPP provides benefits similar to colocated pairing such as increased productivity, code quality, and knowledge transfer in addition to the benefit of promoting communication between distributed team members [8]. At the same time, it is evident that RPP can be more challenging to initiate and perform compared to collocated PP. Initiation can be challenging because team members cannot just swivel their chairs around to the person sitting close to them. As such, it is important to have social software that can show who is available for pairing in distributed teams [5, 18]. In colocated PP, you work on the same code and frequently switch roles. In a distributed setting you need technology to support this [19]. Further, pairs also need to make voice and video calls and share screens during the coding activity. Because many tools exist, developers often have their own preferences on how to perform RPP, which sometimes leads to frustration within a team [20]. Therefore, having the right tools accepted by all team members is a success criterion for RPP to work, along with a list of important functions. The main requirements are [7, 19, 20] that pairs must be able to: 1) access, edit and synchronize the same files, 2) coordinate and fulfill the driver and observer roles, 3) point to different parts of the code, 4) know about the presence of their partner (text or video).

3 Empirical Cases and Research Method

3.1 The Case Study Design

In this paper, we report our findings from studying RPP forced by the COVID-19 pandemic in two companies. We chose a multiple longitudinal case study design [21] to understand what happens to distributed PP using digital collaboration tools. The case study is multiple, as we study engineers in two different companies. Our unit of study is individual engineers and their perceptions of and experiences with RPP. The study is longitudinal (see Fig. 1) as we have inquired the same people at different points of time. The cases are selected by convenience sampling, based on the availability of access to the company data and personnel and the interest of the companies in understanding the PP practice. The interviewees and survey respondents have volunteered to participate.

It is worth mentioning that we initially had access to a third company, in which PP was neither practiced systematically before transitioning to working from home, nor during the COVID-19 pandemic. Therefore, we decided not to include this case.

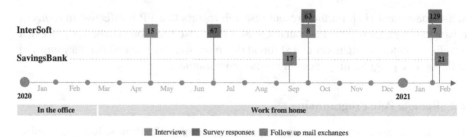

Fig. 1. Longitudinal data collection in each company

3.2 InterSoft and SavingsBank and Their Transition to WFH

The two companies we study are InterSoft and SavingsBank (both anonymized).

InterSoft is an international software company with development offices in Sweden, the UK, and the USA. In March 2020, InterSoft sent all employees in all locations to work from home, prohibiting access to the office spaces. The decision was initially set for two weeks with following extensions, which at the moment of our publication has reached September 2021. Thanks to the geographic distribution, the company has had the facilitating conditions, infrastructure and tools enabling distributed work before the pandemic. At the same time, InterSoft is an advanced agile company that promotes collaboration and teamwork, and agile practices, such as PP, are commonplace. Company culture seems to highly depend on intensive collaboration and collocation, this is why we were curious to study InterSoft's ability to transit into WFH. To support the employees, InterSoft has acquired various remote collaboration software licenses and launched a program for reimbursing office equipment in the early weeks of WFH and supported the transition to WFH through various experience sharing activities.

SavingsBank is a Norwegian software development company owned by an alliance of banks. In March 2020, its employees went from predominantly on-site work to 100% distributed work from home. Company sites were closed, and initially, employees were not allowed to be at the office at all. During the summer of 2020, because of a lower spread of the virus, the offices were open with restrictions (number of simultaneous employees at the office and in meeting rooms, and distance between employees). During the fall of 2020, the increased spread of the virus led to the offices being shut down again, which is still the case at the time of writing. Employees with a particular reason for being at the office (such as the need to run tests on a particular network or particularly problematic situation at home), are allowed to use the office. Notably, four of the 24 development teams in the company were partially distributed before, working across two different Norwegian cities, this is why SavingsBank also had facilitating conditions and infrastructure when moving into the WFH. The studied unit was described by practitioners as a leading agile environment in Norway, using state-of-the-art collaboration methods and technologies. Similar to Intersoft, SavingsBank had the technical infrastructure and tools that enable distributed work and a program for getting equipment from work. Through the year, employees were encouraged to keep their practices, and experiment with new practices and forms of digital collaboration.

3.3 Data Collection

This study is a part of a larger study of WFH experiences in each of the companies. PP emerged as one of the practices that changed, and thus became a candidate for a detailed analysis. Here, we report our findings from 38 interviews and 17 follow up inquiries from 30 engineers from the two companies, and a corporate tool satisfaction survey in one company. Our data collection is longitudinal, aiming at collecting experiences from same interviewees at different points of time to see changes in their experiences.

In InterSoft, we conducted 15 interviews in the first round of in April/May 2020. Interviewees were selected by convenience sampling, at the same time aiming at having representatives from the main locations (in Sweden and USA), age groups and family situations. The interviews were 45–60 min long and focused on the details of a typical day under WFH, reflections on the changes in the daily routines (schedule, tasks, meetings, teamwork, ceremonies, including PP), on what works and what does not work in the WFH mode, home office, and hopes for the future. We conducted follow up interviews with eight of the informants in September/October 2020. In the second round, the interviews were 30 min long and focused on the changes in routines and practices since the last inquiry. All interviews were semi-structured, conducted by two researchers in English via Zoom and audio-recorded with the consent of the interviewees. One of the interviewers led the interview, while the other took detailed notes (close to transcription). After the interview, notes were refined and complemented by cross-checking with the recording.

In SavingsBank, the interviews were conducted in September 2020. The interviewees were selected by tech leads to achieve a representative set of engineers. All interviews were 45–60 min long, conducted via MS Teams. Ten of the interviews were conducted by two researchers, and seven by one. The interviews were semi-structured, and focused on daily work practices using digital collaboration, interruptions, and internal open source. All interviews were audio-recorded with the consent of the interviewees and later transcribed. Notes were also taken during the interview. The interviews were conducted in Norwegian, the quotations from the interviews are thus translations.

For both companies we followed up interviewees with emails to aim at having multiple data points for each interviewee and to detail the RPP practices. The follow up inquiry was done in January/February 2021. We asked "Do you do RPP now?", "How often do you do RPP?", "Do you use any special tools for RPP?", "What do you think about RPP while working from home?". We received 21 answers (7 in InterSoft, and 14 in SavingsBank). As a result, we had four interviewees inquired (interviewed or emailed) three times, 22 inquired twice and only four inquired just once.

Additionally, we used results from an internal engineering satisfaction survey from InterSoft. We analyzed three survey rounds (Jul 2020, Oct 2020 and Jan 2021). We include responses regarding PP support: 67 responses from the first round, 63 responses from the second round and 129 responses from the third round. In the survey, respondents were asked to rate and comment on their satisfaction with the PP tools on a 5-point Likert scale (no support, poor support, moderate support, good support, great support). The survey was designed, ran, and analyzed independently from our study, qualifying it as secondary analysis of the secondary data [22].

3.4 Data Analysis

Our data analysis was conducted in several steps. First, we conducted interviews with a broad scope of inquiry to help companies understand how to cope with the new situation of working from home. After completing two rounds of interviews in InterSoft, and the first round of interviews in SavingsBank, the researchers involved in the interviews reflected on what emerged as the topics of interest for more detailed analysis.

Second, we presented preliminary findings to the companies and received their feedback. During the feedback session we took notes and later adjusted our interpretation of the findings based on the comments received.

Third, we analysed the written material, focusing on PP experiences. In the InterSoft case, we went through the written notes and partial transcripts from 23 interviews and found 21 references particularly relating to PP. In the SavingsBank case, the transcriptions were first coded in a bottom-up fashion, and 80+ codes were created, across 7 categories using the NVivo software for qualitative data analysis. Categories included concepts such as "new challenges during COVID". After this initial, close-to-the-text coding, we specifically looked for data on PP, and we found 15 references in the data.

Fourth, we started comparing the material for the two cases. Based on our initial understanding of the data, two of the researchers created an excel sheet in order to organize the data. The excel sheet had the following categories: "Whether or not PP is done", "How is PP done", "How often is PP done", "How often was PP done before working from home", and "Interesting quotes". The final category was used to capture interesting insights on the PP practice as experienced by the interviewees. These categories form the basis of the findings. In particular, we found the majority of the interviewees practiced PP before the pandemic, with the exception of few interviewees who did not; that the frequency of the use of RPP in WFH could vary between not at all, occasionally, regularly but less frequently than in the office, and more frequently than in the office; and for the way to perform RPP we ended up with two categories: Using special tools or Calling in & sharing screen. When the interview material was insufficient to answer the questions, we then sent follow up emails to inquire about more details. The feedback received was used to fill the gaps and enrich the findings.

Finally, the data from InterSoft was supplemented by the material from the tool satisfaction survey for triangulation and to seek explanations for the emerging findings.

3.5 Limitations and Threats to Validity

First, it's worth mentioning that our data collection initially was not focusing on the pair programming as the main topic of inquiry and the interview guides used in the two cases, although overlapping, were not fully aligned. We have mitigated this in the later follow-up inquiries, aligning the questions sent to the interviewees to mirror the data collected from the two cases.

Further, interviews as the data collection method have certain limitations. According to [21], interviews is one of the most important sources of case study information and should be considered "guided conversations rather than structured queries". And although interviews are insightful and provide perceived causal inferences and explanations, it is vital to be aware of the weaknesses of interviews as evidence. Interviews are likely to be biased, when it comes to poorly defined questions and responses. If the informant does not recall the past correctly, their answers are inaccurate, and they can be reflexive in the way that the informant gives what the interviewer wants to hear [21]. We sought to mitigate the shortcomings by collaboratively creating non-leading questions in the interview guide. Also, being semi-structured, we sought to follow up on the directions where the interviewee wanted to go. We also were, in most of the cases, two researchers doing the interviews, so we could adjust to each other, and in one of the companies the interviews were longitudinal, so we could check the same facts at two different points of time.

To further strengthen the validity of our findings, we performed triangulation by using data collected from different sources and by different methods. Triangulation is the core principle of case study research, which helps ensuring the consistency of the findings [21]. Besides, we presented our findings back to the companies, and sent the final version to all the interviewees to verify our analysis and interpretations.

There is also a limitation in terms of generalizing based on case studies. The main lesson learned in our work is the variety of experiences with RPP and the journey that individual engineers made, which can be viewed as a working hypothesis rather than strong theoretical claims [21]. What strengthens our findings is that we have two cases, spanning several locations. Finally, our findings are indicative as we shed empirical light on a relevant and emerging phenomenon, which could be relevant and interesting for individual engineers as well as software companies working with agile methods.

4 Findings

4.1 Do Engineers Pair Program When Working from Home?

To understand the RPP as a practice, we asked the engineers whether or not they did PP when working from home. We grouped their responses into four categories; "Not all all", "Occasionally", "Regularly, but less frequently than in the office", and "Regularly and more frequently than in the office" (see Fig. 2).

Eight respondents state that they do not do RPP. Of these, two respondents state that it is because it was not done before either, and it is not something they have begun doing now. A third respondent comments that they became more separated during working from home, and that this makes it more challenging to do pair programming. An engineer that states that they do not do pair programming comments: *"We do little real pair programming. However, we try to make a habit out of discussing with the team when you start a task and discuss solutions. This is effective."* (Oskar, Sep 2020).

Nine respondents state they are doing RPP, however very infrequent/occasionally, e.g., once a month. One respondent in this category is an engineer and a tech lead in a team. He describes doing a little bit of pair programming, but that he wants to do more. The challenges are related to the working situation at home and a lot of meetings: *"I have a home office together with my partner, and we switch between sitting in the kitchen and the bedroom when we have meetings at the same time. That makes it difficult to do it ad hoc. Additionally, I am one of those that has too many other meetings already, so it is hard to reserve time"* (Oliver, Sep 2020).

Another engineer, who used to do PP three times a week, notes how it is different doing PP while working from home *"That's not easy. There are a few tools to do it, like we have this Visual Code plugin – but it's just not the same thing, it's not as natural as it was in the office"* (Maya, Sep 2020). This echoes many others who said, that particularly in the beginning of working from home, using digital tools, like screen sharing or more customized tools like Tuple, was radically different from just walking over to the person next to you and sharing the keyboard and screen. Pair programming was more popular then, because it was easier, as one engineer comments: *"It was easier when you sat in the same location, [...] to take that little talk. If I was stuck, and knew that some other had solved the same problem last week, then it was much easier to just pop by and [ask] 'Can you quickly show me how you did it on your PC?', instead of starting to share screens, it is absolutely much better to do it when you are in the same location"* (Trond, Sep 2020).

In the interviews conducted in the early months of the forced WFH situation, many engineers confessed that they either have not done any PP or tried it only a few times. As an interviewee described: *"It's less easy to do [PP] with screen sharing. At least, I've been doing less of that. [...] It's been quite OK, but long term it would be good to have an easier possibility to do pair programming. But for these couple of months, it's OK"* (Ally, May 2020).

One of the reasons why PP failed to take off was that pairs needed to agree on doing PP and finding the time in a way that was not as natural as in the office. As one of the interviewees explained, in the early days of working from home, there were attempts to mimic the "old" way of working, where you could do more ad-hoc PP. But it obviously was not as easy: *"We've tried it once since we started working from home and I think it worked quite well, but I think it's hard, I am not sure why it is harder, but I've tried to say that I want to pair, and then it's Yeah, sure, let's do it after lunch. And then things change after lunch and then you don't do it. Maybe it's because we need to schedule this more explicitly. We have not figured out the solution"* (Sven, May 2020).

As a result, some teams started scheduling RPP sessions, as one explains: *"We started doing some more regular pair programming in our team recently. We booked a daily time slot for this, after our standup, and if during the standup some pairing opportunities come up, we use this dedicated time."* (Robert, Jan 2021).

A clear majority of responses at the end of our study period indicate that engineers pair program regularly. A more detailed analysis of the interviewee responses suggests that about half of those responding positively have increased their interest in pairing remotely over time. As people realised that remote work was not a temporary situation, the need for more collaborative practices increased and new ways of remote pairing were sought in order to address complex problems, like developing something new, or improving a design. The use of PP increased also because engineers became more experienced with remote work.

That both sentiments towards joint, digital collaboration practices, and the very remote practices themselves change is apparent from our data. Consider one engineer, who, when we interviewed him in Sep 2020, was very clear that the new, remote work was far inferior to being collocated. In Feb 2021, he describes how things have improved: *"Since the last time we talked, I think it has been a kind of development*

[...] My impression is that generally everyone became better at answering quickly and calls for handling issues which are difficult to [communicate in text]. I think everyone became better at using Slack and [MS] Teams correctly, and hence complex tasks are not considered that difficult anymore" (Gustav, Feb 2021).

The progression of the interest in RPP over time is also supported by results of the tool support satisfaction survey from InterSoft conducted in Jul 2020 and repeated in Oct 2020 and Jan 2021 (See Fig. 3). The number of positive responses reporting good or great support increased from 54% to 73%.

Finally, two respondents stated that they do more PP than before the pandemic. Because of the need to plan and schedule collaboration, regular pairing sessions became a commodity. The members of the mentioned team do it directly after the standup and in the afternoon, on a daily (or almost daily) basis. One of the respondents explains how pair programming is a new initiative: *"We have in our area/team started focusing on pair programming now after the New year. We did it both with regard to quality, but not the least with regard to people's need for seeing each other and 'feel' that we work together while working from home."* (Albert, Feb 2021).

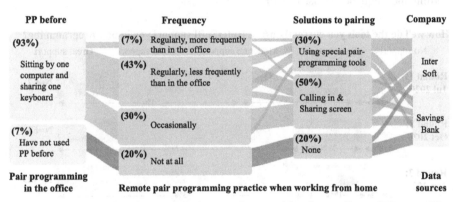

Fig. 2. An overview of PP in the studied companies: transition from collocated PP or no PP to the way RPP is performed with regards to frequency and technical solutions.

4.2   How is Remote Pair Programming Done?

Similar changes as in the adoption of the RPP practice we also found also in the way it is performed. While in the early interviews conducted in April and May many reported to have not done any RPP or to have tried it once or twice, email responses received in January and February 2021 were full of detailed descriptions of tools that were tried, which were working well, and which setups were preferred. In our analysis of the different ways of doing RPP, we have derived two main categories of responses (see Solutions to pairing in Fig. 2).

In the first category, we have gathered experiences of RPP assisted by special tools that allow mimicking the collocated PP practice – looking at a code together and co-editing it and changing the driver and the navigator roles in the pair on a need basis: *"Pairing has gotten a lot better... We've gotten corporate licenses for some software that makes pairing easier. Not just screen sharing, but also controlling each other's computers, and being able to program simultaneously"*. (Conor, Sep 2020).

Among the interviewees, we solicited experiences with Tuple, VSCode extension for PP and "Code with me" extension to IntelliJ. Evidently, the number of interviewees using special tools is not that large. We explain it with the lack of awareness of the tools, the initial skepticism towards the ability of the tools to support "real" PP and the difficulty to pair for a longer period of time.

The lack of awareness of the tools for RPP is also evident in the data collected through the tool satisfaction survey conducted at InterSoft (see Fig. 3). When asked how well the company tools support employees in performing PP tasks we see an increase in employees who are satisfied with the support. At the same time, fewer employees report poor or no support even in early 2021.

Our findings suggest an increasing adoption and support for RPP tools. The few employees discontent with the support suggest that the tools are not working for everyone. However, it is more likely that the respondents are not aware or have not tried out the tools available. The latter is also indirectly supported by our findings from the interviews regarding the frequency of use of RPP.

How well do the tools you currently use at [InterSoft] support you in pair programming?

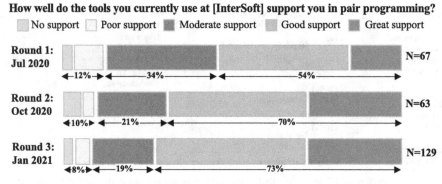

Fig. 3. Survey responses about satisfaction with tool support for pair programming

The next category reflects the adaptation of relatively passive PP practice. In fact, most of the interviewees in our study reported calling in their peers and looking at the code and discussing solutions while sharing their screen. Co-editing the code was not always a part of this practice. This is probably why, admittedly, this practice was not regarded as "real" PP, although still acknowledged to be better than working solo. In practice, one of the developers was said to occupy the driver's role, while the other is restricted to be the navigator, as switching is not technically possible. As one of the interviewees described it, *"[We] do not do it 'by the book', but there is a lot of screen sharing together with one or more [team members]. This is related to debugging (checking logs/config/code), code assessment and implementing new functionality"* (Gustav, Feb 2021). Another interviewee explained, *"[It's] not like pair programming when you sit during four hours in parallel, but usually we do syncing for one hour, going through the code together, and then dividing the tasks, working for two hours in parallel and then syncing again. We call that 'more pair programming'."* (Ally, Sep 2020).

4.3 What Are the Main Challenges in Remote Pair Programming in WFH?

Pair programming "by the book" requires physical collocation, which for obvious reasons is impossible when everyone works from home. In the previous subsections, we described what tools and practices engineers follow to enable RPP, and mentioned that many experience difficulties and said that the fact that you need to do it in separation depending on the tools and internet is an obstacle to practicing PP. In the following we summarize the main challenges of remote setup according to our interviewees.

We learned that one of the key challenges associated with RPP is the very initiation of pairing. Several interviewees mentioned that the threshold to approach the colleagues was higher when working from home because they could not just shout out a question over the shoulder, as in the office, and did not have a good insight into what their colleagues are doing in a particular moment. As someone explained: *"You don't want to disturb people because you don't know what the others are doing right now"* (Ola, Apr 2020). This was even more challenging for the recently onboarded engineers who were not well familiar with other colleagues. As an interviewee explained: *"I prefer to do pair programming when I am at the office, because then it is easier to grab someone. I feel that there is a higher threshold when you are on Slack. The better you know your team, the easier it is."* (Kristine, Feb 2021).

Another important challenge was to find a technical solution that helps to work with the code together. RPP makes engineers depend on tools with varying quality and suitability for the task, for something that you previously did by walking over to the person next to you. Several interviewees said that tool-mediated PP would not feel the same, and therefore had not even tried it. Some tried to "jump on a call" but complained about the connection problems. Finally, some confessed that they wanted to use specific tools but they were not accepted as sufficiently secure in the company. Technical hiccups also contributed to the threshold, as an interviewee explained: *"It takes more time than usual to do [PP]. Difficult if someone gets technical issues with sharing the screen"* (Morten, Feb 2021). And another admitted: *"I do not enjoy PP while working from home, the software can be a bit slow at times, and it's easy to lose control of the cursor if both of us are trying to edit" (Carol, Feb 2021).*

Last but not least, several interviewees admitted that active tool-mediated PP was too intense and tiresome if done for hours, suggesting that a more passive mode was more suitable for the "online" version. As an interviewee explained: *"Proper pair programming is very intense and tiring, and it becomes difficult to hold for a longer time. But a more relaxed variant, where you have video and audio but work mostly separately and share a screen when needed, then you can work for hours"* (Gustav, Feb 2021).

4.4 What Are the Benefits of Remote Pair Programming in WFH?

Despite these challenges, RPP still has a number of benefits. Pair programming is, in essence, a way for engineers to more quickly get a shared understanding of the problem, and then jointly and simultaneously work on solving the problem; means of seeking and receiving feedback and monitoring each other's work. The need for joint problem solving and acquiring a second opinion have not diminished when moving to working remotely, as one engineer notes: *"I feel like I have been an advocate for pairing up and pair programming and doing things together since I started, because I think that's a good way to avoid the buzz factor." (Kristoffer, May 2020).*

This notion is second by another engineer, who also points out how pair programming *"works well for doodling and problem solving" (Andreas, Feb 2021).* In the formerly collocated contexts, engineers were used to working together, and, as a minimum, having a shared understanding of what they are going to do, before they split up and work individually to solve it.

We found that some respondents, despite admitting the difficulties of RPP and preferring to do it in co-location, acknowledge some benefits in tool-mediated pairing that are only available when using tools, such as the ability to control the partner's screen without taking away his or her keyboard. As an interviewee described: *"[Tuple] was the most recent tool that I've tried, and that was very good. [...] I think the big thing that Tuple has is the ability to type on your partner's screen. And I've used it twice recently and it was very quick and very easy, it was very helpful" (Conor, Sep 2020).*

Additionally, there is a clear social component to RPP, which seems to become increasingly important as more time is spent away from the teammates. The following two quotes demonstrate how pairing enhances the work experience not only for the usual purposes, but for the sake of socialization: *"I think PP and writing code together is something we should do more of while working from home, both because two heads work better than one, but in particular because it is something social and it makes what you do feel more important" (Erik, Feb 2021)* and *"We did it both with regard to quality, but not the least with regard to people's need for seeing each other and to get a feel of working together although working from home [...] it adds something positive in terms of more contact with the other team members" (Albert, Sep 2020).*

Another interesting observation relates to few interviewees who perceived RPP as easier because they did not disturb others unlike when working in the office. There was no longer the need to leave your desk and search for a quiet room to pair. As an interviewee explained: *"[Remote] pair programming works well and perhaps better than in the office where you would disturb the neighbour with the talking" (Arvid, Feb 2021).*

Finally, we also associate RPP with more structured or disciplined daily routines. As one interviewee, who have admitted struggling with working from home in the beginning of the pandemic, described that frequent pairing helped him become more disciplined and keep the focus: *"While you are pairing, you don't get distracted, you don't want to get distracted. [...] The difference is, when I am soloing I usually sit in my living room, in a more casual setting, so I can relax, enjoy and have fun. But when I am pairing I feel like I should not be wasting their time, it should be more serious work. So I go to my home office with the chair and monitor to do it properly" (Ola, Sep 2020).*

5   Discussion and Concluding Remarks

In this paper, we presented our findings from studying the changes in PP practices in two companies that sent their employees to work from home as a result of the COVID-19 outbreak. In the following, we summarize and discuss our findings.

In response to our RQ: *"What happened to PP practice in the forced WFH regime?"*, we conclude that the overall use of PP has decreased and some interviewees in our study report not pairing at all for almost a full year. However, we also found that the interest in and the use of RPP over time, since the first months of the forced WFH to the early 2021, has admittedly increased, which is confirmed both by the interviewees and the results of the tool satisfaction survey in one of the companies. The experiences with RPP vary from actively co-editing the code by using special RPP tools (referred to as practicing PP "by the book") to co-reading and discussing the code and solutions by sharing screen (which supports the acceptance of alternative ways of pairing [13]). When it comes to the frequency of PP, we found that most do it less frequently than in the office. The sudden transition to the WFH led engineers to focus on individual tasks, temporarily reversing the social trend in software engineering [1, 2]. Our findings also illustrate how RPP is more intense and tiring than pairing in the office, which supports existing research on RPP being exhausting if performed for a long time [2]. Among the challenges, we found the difficulty of initiating RPP when trying to merely mimic the collocated practices. We can speculate that one reason for this is a lack of tools showing availability [5, 18], or initial failure to create new practices utilizing such tools. We also found how this changed over time. Our findings support the earlier research emphasizing the importance of and consensus over good tools for RPP [19, 20]. With respect to RPP benefits, our study confirms that engineers pair program because they enjoy it [3], especially as an important mean for socialization while WFH, which goes beyond RPP for quality and efficacy [11] and is not much discussed in existing literature.

When reflecting on the individual journeys of engineers in our study made, we notice a few commonalities. We depict them in a conceptual representation of the acceptance of the work from home setup represented by an inverted Hype Curve[1] (see Fig. 4).

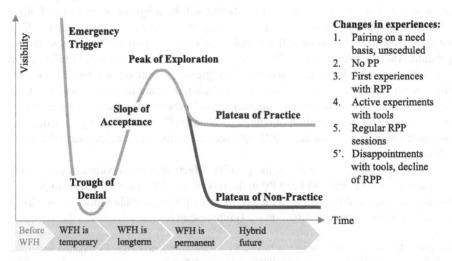

Fig. 4. Trends in acceptance of the WFH setup and respective changes in RPP experiences.

---

[1] Hype curve or cycle is a graphical representation of the maturity, adoption, and social application of technologies, which is developed, used and branded by the American research, advisory and information technology firm Gartner.

The traditional Hype Curve depicts the changes in the adoption of new technologies, starting with a technology breakthrough, the early publicity of which often inflates the expectations, shortly followed by the disillusionment, then continues with the work on advancing the technology, reflected in the enlightenment and increased popularity, finally leading to mainstream adoption. Unlike technology adoption, we believe that the transition to RPP resembles a vertically inverted curve. In the beginning, many of the interviewees did not do any RPP, because it was assumed to fail to provide the experience of the actual collocated PP as experienced in the office. As time went on and the perceiving temporary mode of working from home turned into a new way of living, engineers started to experiment with different ways of pairing. At the end of the first WFH year, RPP became more and more popular, not only as a way to solve complex problems or teach juniors, but also as a way to facilitate collaboration and interaction and satisfy the socialization needs. We evidence the rise of experimentation with the tools and ways of approaching RPP (e.g., changes in the scheduling of regular pairing sessions). Evidently, not all interviewees have gone through the curve, indicating that the speed with the RPP adoption varies.

We can expect those who at the moment of our study, have followed remote pairing occasionally, or who have not yet found the right tool support, will do so in the near future. This is supported by stories we have collected from those who indicate an increasing interest in remote pairing over time.

Yet, we also found that several engineers who used to pair program in the office, have not done it at all, since they were forced to work from home. Besides, our results suggest that remote collaboration is not as natural as the collaboration in the office, and that the success of remote collaboration reported by the interviewees in our study highly depends on the existing social connections. If the future will be a hybrid of remote and office work, and companies will more willingly hire experts from remote locations, we will no longer be able to rely or assume that people will know each other well. This leads to a question, whether future teams will find ways to overcome the threshold of initiating and maintaining the high level of collaboration or regress to a more transaction-relationship. From one hand, PP can become a practice to familiarize the team members and keep the collaboration high even when team members choose to continue working remotely. On the other hand, if perception of being an "unnatural" or "challenging" practice will dominate the mainstream opinion, PP might become extinct in the repertoire of the future software teams.

We believe that given many of the positive effects that are reported from working from home, findings ways to keep PP in the repertoire of the future teams is important. The understanding of the RPP and the very nature of future collaborations at the virtual workplace is one important direction for future research.

Acknowledgements. This research is funded by the Swedish Knowledge Foundation within the ScaleWise project (KK-Hög grant 2019/0087) and the S.E.R.T. research profile project, and the Research Council of Norway through the 10xTeams project (grant 309344).

References

1. Mens, T., Cataldo, M., Damian, D.: The social developer: the future of software development [Guest Editors' Introduction]. IEEE Softw. **36**(1), 11–14 (2019)
2. Dybå, T., Dingsøyr, T.: Empirical studies of agile software development: a systematic review. Inf. Softw. Technol. **50**(9–10), 833–859 (2008)
3. Williams, L., Kessler, R.R., Cunningham, W., Jeffries, R.: Strengthening the case for pair programming. IEEE Softw. **17**(4), 19–25 (2000)
4. Robinson, H., Sharp, H.: Organisational culture and XP: three case studies. In Proceedings of Agile Development Conference (ADC 2005), pp. 49–58. IEEE (2005)
5. Tell, P., Babar, M.A.: Requirements for an infrastructure to support activity-based computing in global software development. In: Proceedings of IEEE Sixth International Conference on Global Software Engineering Workshop, pp. 62–69 (2011)
6. Rizvi, B., Bagheri, E., Gasevic, D.: A systematic review of distributed Agile software engineering. J. Softw. Evol. Process **27**(10), 723–762 (2015)
7. Estácio, B.J., Prikladnicki, R.: Distributed pair programming: a systematic literature review. Inf. Softw. Technol. **63**, 1–10 (2015)
8. Baheti, P., Gehringer, E., Stotts, D.: Exploring the efficacy of distributed pair programming. In: Extreme Programming and Agile Methods—XP Agile Universe, pp. 387–410 (2002)
9. Moe, N.B., Dingsøyr, T., Dybå, T.: A teamwork model for understanding an agile team: a case study of a Scrum project. J. IST **52**(5), 480–491 (2010)
10. Williams, L., Kessler, R.R.: Pair Programming Illuminated. Addison-Wesley Professional, Boston (2003)
11. Williams, L.: Pair Programming. Encyclopedia of Software Engineering, vol. 2 (2010)
12. Chong, J., Hurlbutt, T.: The social dynamics of pair programming. In: 29th International Conference on Software Engineering (ICSE 2007), pp. 354–363 (2007)
13. Wray, S.: How pair programming really works. IEEE Softw. **27**(1), 50–55 (2009)
14. Brannick, M.T., Salas, E., Prince, C.W.: Team performance assessment and measurement: Theory, Methods, and Applications. Psychology Press, Taylor & Francis Group, New York London (1997)
15. Kude, T.: Agile Software Development Teams during and after COVID-19. http://knowledge.essec.edu/en/innovation/agile-software-development-during-after-COVID19.html (2020). Accessed 5 Mar 2021
16. Demir, Ö., Seferoglu, S.S.: A Comparison of solo and pair programming in terms of flow experience, coding quality, and coding achievement. J. Educ. Comput. Res. **58**(8), 1448–1466 (2021)
17. Moe, N.B., Aurum, A., Dybå, T.: Challenges of shared decision-making: a multiple case study of agile software development. J. IST **54**(8), 853–865 (2012)
18. Giuffrida, R., Dittrich, Y.: Empirical studies on the use of social software in global software development–a systematic mapping study. J. IST **55**(7), 1143–1164 (2013)
19. Tsompanoudi, D., Satratzemi, M., Xinogalos, S., Karamitopoulos, L.: An empirical study on factors related to distributed pair programming (2019)
20. Dominic, J., Tubre, B., Ritter, C., Houser, J., Smith, C., Rodeghero, P.: Remote pair programming in virtual reality. In: 2020 IEEE International Conference on Software Maintenance and Evolution (ICSME), pp. 406–417 (2020)
21. Yin, R.K.: Case study research and Applications: Design and Methods, 6th ed. SAGE Publications, Thousand Oaks, California (2018)
22. Robson, C.: Real World Research: A Resource for Social Scientists and Practitioner Researchers, 2nd edn. Blackwell Publishing, Oxford (2002)

Open Access This chapter is licensed under the terms of the Creative Commons Attribution 4.0 International License (http://creativecommons.org/licenses/by/4.0/), which permits use, sharing, adaptation, distribution and reproduction in any medium or format, as long as you give appropriate credit to the original author(s) and the source, provide a link to the Creative Commons license and indicate if changes were made.

The images or other third party material in this chapter are included in the chapter's Creative Commons license, unless indicated otherwise in a credit line to the material. If material is not included in the chapter's Creative Commons license and your intended use is not permitted by statutory regulation or exceeds the permitted use, you will need to obtain permission directly from the copyright holder.

UX Work in Software Start-Ups: Challenges from the Current State of Practice

Sofia A. M. Silveira[1], Joelma Choma[1(✉)], Roberto Pereira[2],
Eduardo M. Guerra[3], and Luciana A. M. Zaina[1]

[1] Federal University of São Carlos (UFSCar), Sorocaba, Brazil
`{sofia,jchoma,lzaina}@ufscar.br`
[2] Federal University of Paraná (UFPR), Curitiba, Brazil
`rpereira@inf.ufpr.br`
[3] Free University of Bozen-Bolzano, Bolzano, Italy
`eduardo.guerra@unibz.it`

Abstract. Software start-ups develop innovative software products working with disruptive technologies in time pressure and market-driven environment. Recently, User eXperience (UX) has become a hot topic that interests software teams of start-ups. However, software and UX professionals have struggled to match UX practices into the development activities, partially because of the lack of resources in the start-ups. This paper investigates how software start-ups handle UX activities during software development and how relevant UX is to these companies' professionals. To achieve our aim, we surveyed 88 professionals who take part in software teams in star-ups, analyzing the responses using descriptive and statistical methods. Our results reveal that regardless of having or not a UX position in the start-up, UX practices are spread in different software development phases and not fitting into them. Results also show although professionals consider UX relevant and recognize important skills to perform UX activities, some obstacles hinder the effective use of UX in software start-ups. From the survey results, we identified a set of challenges to be overcome in consolidating the UX work in software start-ups. By diagnosing the UX state-of-practice in start-up scenarios and identifying such challenges, our work contributes to provides relevant insights to further academic and practical studies in this field.

Keywords: Software start-ups · Agile practices · User eXperience · UX practices · UX challenges · Survey

1 Introduction

Software start-ups focus on developing innovative products or services, often disruptive and in challenging contexts [20]. A start-up is a human institution designed to deliver a new product or service under conditions of extreme uncertainty [21]. To be a start-up, it is not require the company to be small or new.

© The Author(s) 2021
P. Gregory et al. (Eds.): XP 2021, LNBIP 419, pp. 19–35, 2021.
https://doi.org/10.1007/978-3-030-78098-2_2

Start-ups differ from established companies by searching for a scalable, repeatable, and profitable business model with the aim of growing in the market [22]. The continuous seeking for a scalable business model pushes the start-ups to have changes in their process and operations constantly. Start-ups usually work with a small team of professionals, exploring new technologies, being marked by rapid evolution, high uncertainty about customers and market conditions, and high failure rate [1,20]. The literature has emphasized the need for studies on Software Engineering practices that are specific and appropriate to the characteristics of start-ups [20,22].

The combination of innovation and a market-driven context leads to a situation where a specific (and restrict) set of software development practices may be useful for start-ups [19]. Besides, some studies point out user experience (UX) as a critical factor for software start-ups, generating value for users, and creating competitive advantage [8,12,20,22]. Although different UX definitions are found in the literature, it is a consensus that UX work can affect a product acceptance [14]. The ISO-9241 norm [2] defines UX as "*user's perceptions and responses that result from the use and/or anticipated use of a system, product or service.*" This norm emphasizes human-centred design, highlighting the adoption of different software development practices, such as user research, interactive design, user involvement, and cross-functional design teams.

For the Software Start-ups Global Research Network group[1], good UX can help start-ups to move towards successful and sustainable business creation, promoting genuine interest from users and opportunities for meaningful feedback [22]. UX can be crucial to test a value proposition early on [6]. At the beginning of product development, a good understanding of the problem the software will solve can helps to find a suitable market and drive the UX work. To assess market interest and to establish a customer base, studies indicate that many start-ups attempt a balance between customer value by focusing on functionality and UX while keeping engineering effort minimal [12]. In this sense, a trade-off between features, quality, time, and cost can determine the scope of the minimum viable product [21]. However, there is a gap in knowledge about UX practical actions more compatible with reality in start-ups. To accomplish this gap, we carried out a survey in Brazil's start-up ecosystem to identify how UX work has been applied in these fast-growing innovative environments. In this paper, we present our findings on UX relevance from a software professionals' standpoint and identified a set of challenges faced for the adoption of UX practices taking into account the reasons, obstacles, and skills needed for UX work.

Our survey's target audience was professionals working with software development in start-ups, covering start-ups of any size, lifetime, and market segment. Based on 88 valid answers from professionals who work on software development positions in start-ups, our results offer a diagnosis about UX, revealing that although it is considered relevant and present, it remains often in the frontiers of the software development process and not integrated into it. Our work contributes to research and practice of UX in start-ups, both by bringing more

---

[1] https://softwarestart-ups.org/.

discussions about the critical role of UX in the different phases of software development, as well as by showing that how much have or not have UX positions allocated in software start-ups can influence the use of UX in the practice. Additionally, six challenges related to UX adoption were identified, providing important insights to further academic and practical studies in the software start-ups context.

This paper is organized as follows. Section 2 introduces the related works to UX in start-ups. Section 3 outlines the research method adopted. Section 4 presents the main findings and discusses the study limitations and threats to validity. Section 5 highlights the challenges that start-ups face on UX work. Finally, Sect. 6 concludes the paper and presents directions for further work.

2 Related Work

UX's importance in software development in start-ups was raised in the literature in 2012 [17]. Five recommendations about software engineering practices for developing start-up products are reported, and *Good UX is essential* recommendation warns on risks of skipping UX validation in the early stages of the product conception. In 2016, a global research agenda on software development in start-ups restated the importance of put UX in practice from the early stages of software development [22]. However, this work pointed out that it is still an open question which UX practices are in fact useful for these organizations.

Although software practitioners in start-ups recognize UX's relevance to product development, start-ups have faced difficulties in setting the UX methods and practices to the fast-paced environment [6,7]. The software teams' mindset and organizations' culture can often be an obstacle to UX work [16]. There is also an influence of the limitations in human resources, common in most start-ups, which can make it difficult to hire experienced UX professionals [9,12,13].

Collecting users' feedback about the product appears as the main concern of start-ups [7,8,12]. User interface prototypes (i.e. mockups and wireframes) [9,12,17], user testings [9], questionnaires [13] and analysis of data log [7,8] are mentioned as the UX practices frequently used by software practitioners in that context. However, start-ups also struggle with the effective use of information collected about their users [5,8,9]. Moreover, UX methods and practices have different aims depending on the software development stage [12], requiring UX-skilled professionals to know which one to use and how to get the best benefit from their application. Some studies stand out that the relation between UX and business models could support decision-making about product development and contribute to a positive image of the organization [9,12,22].

From the literature review, we identified only two surveys focused on exploring the topic of UX in start-ups [9,15]. In the survey conducted from interviews with 21 professionals of 20 software start-ups from different countries, Hokkanen et al. [9] identified three main categories of factors that affect UX work in start-ups were identified: (1) *Strategy*, as strategic choices on resource allocation and Product qualities that affect actions for creating good UX; (2) *Team*

Qualities, as they can be improved by having UX expertise, domain knowledge, and UX mindset; and, (3) *Interaction with Users* that focus on how actively involving users in their process of creating UX. Salgado et al. [15] conducted a survey involving 26 small Brazilian software companies of which 17 were software start-ups. Their survey results pointed out (1) the need of improving the professional awareness of the importance of usability and UX, (2) a demand for more appropriate usability and UX practices to fulfill the context of small businesses.

3   Research Method

Our research method followed the guidelines recommended by Kitchenham and Pfleeger [11]. This survey addressed two research questions. First, *what is the role of UX in the different software development activities?* Second, *how do professionals consider UX in start-ups that have UX-related roles and those that do not?* By answering the first question (RQ1), we intend to explore how often UX activities have been carried out in the start-ups throughout software development, and what UX practices have been employed to support the professionals' tasks. To address the second question (RQ2), we intend to investigate how professionals perceive UX work in the start-ups by exploring the reasons that drive and factors that hinder the use of UX practices in the start-up. Furthermore, we look at UX work relevance and essential related skills in software start-ups from the point of view of professionals who work in the UX area in comparison with those professionals with positions only in the software engineering area.

The survey's target audience was professionals working in software development areas at start-ups in Brazil, including software engineers, software developers, UX designers, testers, project managers, product managers, and software architects. In this survey, we do not impose any restrictions on the start-up size. As the data collection method, we prepared an online survey with 26 questions, including an informed consent describing study objectives and a statement about the guarantee of participants' confidentiality and anonymity.

The questionnaire was evaluated in two steps. First, three researchers of UX, software engineering (SE), and start-up areas reviewed the survey design. Second, we conducted a pilot test with six graduate students from UX and SE areas to verify the questionnaire clarity and easiness of understanding. Our instrument was refined based on that feedback by: (a) rewriting questions; (b) modifying answers' format; (c) reordering questions to a more logical sequence; or (d) splitting questions to improve readability. Despite the survey's broader scope, we used a subset of questions related to this paper's aim, presented in Table 1. The online survey was open from June until the middle of September 2020. An invitation email was sent directly to start-ups and researchers' contact networks, asking to forward it to other potential participants. The respondents were guided to answer considering the start-up where they currently work.

In our analysis, we first verified responses' consistency and integrity, eliminating inconsistent, incomplete, and duplicate questionnaires. In the next step, we did the partitioning of the responses (see Table 1). To analyze the responses

Table 1. Survey questions

No.	Question (simplified version)	Type	RQ
Q1	How many years of experience do you have?	Multiple-choice	–
Q2	What roles do you play in the start-up?	Multiple-choice	–
Q3	What year was the start-up founded?	Free text	–
Q4	What market-segment does the start-up operate in?	Multiple-choice	–
Q5	How many employees does the start-up have?	Multiple-choice	–
Q6	What frameworks and methodologies are applied?	Multiple-choice	–
Q7	How long has the start-up been using UX practices?	Multiple-choice	RQ1
Q8	How often is UX applied in the following software development activities: (i) software ideation, (ii) product specification, (iii) requirements analysis, (iv) design and prototyping, (v) development, (vi) testing and integration, (vii) deployment, and (viii) maintenance	Likert scale	RQ1
Q9	For the start-up's development team, how often do the following activities occur: (a) user involvement in the requirements elicitation, and (b) user involvement in prioritizing requirements	Multiple-choice	RQ1
Q10	What UX practices has the start-up used?	Multiple-choice	RQ1
Q11	Does the start-up have specific UX-related positions? *options with different team configuration	Multiple-choice	RQ2
Q12	What are the reasons that do the start-up use UX practices?	Multiple-choice	RQ2
Q13	Which factors hinder the use of UX practices in the start-up?	Multiple-choice	RQ2
Q14	How much the skills are needed for collecting, interpreting and analyzing UX data: (a) know-how to collect feedback, (b) know-how to interpret feedback, (c) know-how to collect user information, (d) know-how to interpret user information, (e) ability to analyze a large amount of data	Likert scale	RQ2
Q15	How much the skills are needed to perform UX work: (a) experience in graphic design, (b) know-how to perform activities with the user, (c) knowledge in usability theories, (d) knowledge of heuristics	Likert scale	RQ2
Q16	How important the items are to the software team: (a) UX practices in product development e (b) having a mindset focused on programming	Likert scale	RQ2

related to RQ1, we did a first division based on the respondent's information on how long the start-up has been using UX practices (Q7). Regarding responses related to RQ2, we did a second division based on the respondent's information about whether the start-up had UX positions (Q11) to analyze the responses from Q12 and Q13. To analyze how much certain skills were necessary to perform UX activities (Q14 and Q15), we did a third division, considering whether the respondent plays a UX-related role or not (Q2). Finally, we considered the last two divisions to analyze how relevant is UX to the development team evaluating the influence of having a mindset focused on programming (Q16).

We analyzed the data using descriptive and statistical methods. A nonparametric test Kruskal–Wallis (KW) was applied to verify statistically significant differences between observed groups [18]. For cases where the KW test showed a significant difference, we ran a *post hoc* analysis using the Dunnett' method [3] to identify the differences.

4   Results

A total of 99 responses have been collected, out of which 88 have been used in our analysis as valid responses. Invalid responses refer to 9 duplicate answers, 1 with incomplete answers, and 1 with inconsistent answers. Of the 88 respondents, about 80% of them have more than 3 years of professional experience, and out of these, 29 respondents have more than 10 years. About 51% of respondents (45 of 88) play roles only in the software engineering area, 23% of respondents (20 of 88) play roles only in the UX area, and 26% of respondents (23 of 88) accumulate positions in both areas.

Of the 43 respondents who informed work on UX-related roles, the main reported roles were UX Designer (38–88%), and UX Researcher (21–49%). Regarding SE-related roles, we mainly found Software Developer (33 of 88) and Software Architect (16 of 88). About 40% of respondents played the role of product manager (35 of 88) and 23% product owner (20 of 88). The respondents' start-ups develop products for different market segments, and some of them for more than one segment. The three most cited start-ups segments are Information Technology, Finance, and Education.

Figure 1 introduces a heat map chart presenting the number of start-ups that fit into each category related to some characteristics, such as size (in terms of employees), foundation year, and the amount of time start-ups have been applying UX practices. Lighter colors represent that few start-ups fit into those categories, whereas darker colors represent that plenty of start-ups fit into those categories.

Size (employees)	<1 year	1–2 years	>3 years	<1 year	1–2 years	>3 years	<1 year	1–2 years	>3 years
More than 1001	0	0	0	0	0	0	0	0	6
501 – 1000	0	0	0	0	0	0	0	0	0
101 – 500	0	2	0	0	3	1	0	2	3
71 – 100	0	0	0	2	1	3	0	0	1
31 – 70	0	2	0	0	6	1	1	0	3
11 – 30	1	1	0	2	1	2	3	6	0
Up to 10	8	6	2	0	2	3	1	0	3
Time applying UX practices	<1 year	1–2 years	>3 years	<1 year	1–2 years	>3 years	<1 year	1–2 years	>3 years
Start-up foundation		< 3 years			3 - 6 years			> 6 years	

Fig. 1. Start-up time applying UX practices by size and foundation year.

Regarding the frameworks and methodologies applied in start-ups (Q6), the participants were allowed to select more than one option. SCRUM (55–63%) and Kanban (54–61%) are the most recurrent among respondents. Only respondents who work at start-ups that apply UX practices (78 of 88 respondents) mentioned

Design Thinking (41–53%), Design Sprint (31–40%), and Lean UX (25–32%). The least applied methodology is Hypothesis-driven development (5–6%).

4.1 UX in the Software Development Activities

We asked the participants how often UX is applied throughout software development (Q8), how often activities involving users occur (Q9), and which UX practices were commonly used in the start-ups (Q10). Of the 88 valid responses, 78 respondents answered these questions, while the other 10 respondents reported that their start-ups did not use UX practices. To analyze these questions, we split the 78 participants' responses according to information about how long the start-up has been using UX practices (Q7). We found that 18 respondents were from start-ups that have applied UX for *up to 1 year*, 32 respondents from start-ups that have applied UX *from 1 to 2 years*, and 28 respondents from start-ups that have applied UX for *over 3 years*.

Table 2. UX in the software development

Software ideation

	Always	Often	Rarely	Never
Up to 1 year	33%	33%	28%	6%
From 1 to 2 years	38%	41%	19%	3%
Over 3 Years	64%	25%	11%	0%
			p-value:	0.041*

Product specification

	Always	Often	Rarely	Never
Up to 1 year	28%	44%	28%	0%
From 1 to 2 years	28%	59%	13%	0%
Over 3 Years	71%	29%	0%	0%
			p-value:	0.001*

Requirements analysis

	Always	Often	Rarely	Never
Up to 1 year	22%	33%	33%	11%
From 1 to 2 years	28%	47%	22%	3%
Over 3 Years	43%	36%	11%	0%
			p-value:	0.038*

Design and prototyping

	Always	Often	Rarely	Never
Up to 1 year	44%	44%	11%	0%
From 1 to 2 years	53%	34%	13%	0%
Over 3 Years	75%	18%	7%	0%
			p-value:	0.112

Development

	Always	Often	Rarely	Never
Up to 1 year	22%	44%	28%	6%
From 1 to 2 years	38%	28%	25%	9%
Over 3 Years	43%	43%	14%	0%
			p-value:	0.206

Testing and integration

	Always	Often	Rarely	Never
Up to 1 year	22%	44%	22%	11%
From 1 to 2 years	22%	41%	25%	13%
Over 3 Years	39%	43%	14%	0%
			p-value:	0.067*

Deployment

	Always	Often	Rarely	Never
Up to 1 year	28%	33%	28%	11%
From 1 to 2 years	16%	47%	25%	13%
Over 3 Years	43%	32%	14%	11%
			p-value:	0.178

Maintenance

	Always	Often	Rarely	Never
Up to 1 year	39%	33%	17%	11%
From 1 to 2 years	19%	28%	47%	6%
Over 3 Years	29%	57%	14%	0%
			p-value:	0.033*

Users in requirements elicitation

	Always	Often	Rarely	Never
Up to 1 year	44%	22%	33%	0%
From 1 to 2 years	13%	50%	25%	13%
Over 3 Years	43%	39%	18%	0%
			p-value:	0.022*

Users in requirements prioritizing

	Always	Often	Rarely	Never
Up to 1 year	33%	33%	33%	0%
From 1 to 2 years	13%	56%	22%	9%
Over 3 Years	36%	46%	18%	0%
			p-value:	0.115

Start-ups applying UX: up to 1 year (N = 18) | from 1 to 2 years (N = 32) | over 3 years (N = 28)

UX in the Software Development. In Table 2, we see the respondent's perception of how often the start-ups are concerned with applying UX in the software development. Overall, almost 90% of respondents stated to use UX practices more often during product specification, design, and prototyping activities, while more than 40% of them rarely apply it in the software maintenance. We found that more than 80% of start-ups working with UX for more than 3 years are significantly more concerned with it during the software ideation (p-value 0.041) and requirements analysis (p-value 0.038) activities than the start-ups that started using UX less than a year. Besides, more than 80% of start-ups that have applied UX for more than 3 years are significantly more concerned with involving users in eliciting requirements (p-value 0.022), applying UX in testing and integration (p-value 0.067), and maintenance (p-value 0.033) than the group of start-ups using UX from 1 to 2 years. In the product specification phase, we found that both groups with applied UX for less than 1 and 2 years differ significantly from the group that has applied UX for longer.

UX Practices Applied in the Start-Ups. Table 3 presents the respondents' information about which UX practices are used in their start-ups, as well as their frequency. Overall, the most commonly applied practices are prototyping (66 of 78), user interview (63 of 78), and usability testing (51 of 78). Heuristic evaluation (28 of 78), storyboard (26 of 78), and card sorting (19 of 78) are the least used practices in start-ups. KW test revealed a statistically significant difference in four practices: user interview (p-value = 0.05), usability testing (p-value = 0.006), personas (p-value = 0.007), and storyboard (p-value = 0.004). The *post hoc* test indicated that start-ups from Up to 1 year group use significantly less of these practices than the star-ups from over 3 years group.

Table 3. UX practices applied in the start-ups

UX Practices	F	Up to 1 year (N = 18)*			1 to 2 years (N = 32)*			Over 3 Years (N = 28)*			p-value
		Always	Often	Rarely	Always	Often	Rarely	Always	Often	Rarely	
Prototypes	66	11%	28%	22%	31%	38%	25%	43%	39%	7%	0.076
User Interview	63	11%	28%	33%	31%	34%	16%	39%	36%	11%	**0.049***
Usability Test	51	6%	17%	33%	31%	16%	6%	43%	32%	11%	**0.006***
Personas	48	6%	22%	28%	25%	28%	9%	39%	21%	4%	**0.007***
User Flow	40	11%	11%	0%	19%	28%	13%	32%	25%	4%	0.263
Heurisctic	28	11%	6%	11%	22%	16%	0%	32%	4%	4%	0.196
Storyboard	26	0%	6%	22%	19%	13%	0%	29%	7%	4%	**0.004***
Card Sorting	19	0%	6%	0%	9%	6%	0%	25%	18%	4%	0.612

* Time period that the start-ups have applied UX practices

Figure 2 shows the UX practices used according to the foundation year of the start-ups. From the heat map chart, we can see that the newer companies (i.e. <3 years) use more personas technique than user testing. This result shows that these organizations need to have more details on the users' characteristics. These organizations are in the early stage of product exploration, and, consequently,

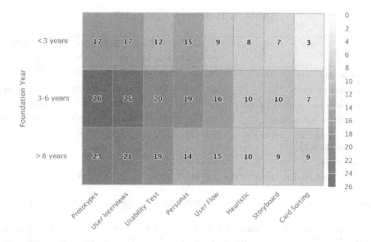

Fig. 2. UX practices applied in the start-ups.

the users are not well defined, the product is not stable, and they are subject to pivot more. In older start-ups (i.e. >3 years), the testings are running more frequently than in newer ones, which can be a consequence of their product has already achieved a degree of maturity and been considered stable.

4.2 UX Work from the Perspective of Start-Ups Professionals

To explore perceptions about the main reasons why the start-up uses UX practices (Q12) and the main factors that hinder their usage (Q13), we divided the participants' responses considering whether or not respondents' start-ups had UX-related professionals (Q11). Of the 78 respondents who answered these questions, we found that 33 respondents were from start-ups that have a fully or partially dedicated UX team (*UX-Team*), 25 respondents were from start-ups that have at least one fully or partially dedicated UX professional (*UX-Pro*), 12 respondents from start-ups that do not have a UX professional (*No-UX*), and 8 respondents from start-ups that train employees from other areas to do UX work (*Train-E*).

Reasons for Using UX. Table 4 summarizes the results on the reasons that lead start-ups to apply UX practices in the development of their products. From the respondents' point of view, the three main reasons for the start-up to use UX practices are to *create value for the user* (70 of 78), *create successful products* (66 of 78), and *create value for business development* (56 of 78). KW test reveled a statistically significant difference in respondents' opinions on *obtaining competitive advantages* (p-value = 0.020). This reason was highlighted by 67% (39 of 58) of respondents from *UX-Pro* group. In the opinion of respondents from *Train-E* group, the two main reasons to apply UX are the *successful product*

Table 4. Reasons for using UX

Reasons	Overall (N = 78)	UX-Team (N = 33)	UX-Pro (N = 25)	No-UX (N = 12)	Train-E (N = 8)	p-value
Create value for the user	70 (90%)	94%	88%	92%	75%	0.454
Create successful products	66 (85%)	91%	84%	67%	88%	0.264
Create value for business development	56 (72%)	79%	72%	67%	50%	0.425
Obtain competitive advantages	46 (59%)	76%	56%	25%	50%	**0.020***
Reduce risk of injury inherent in the creation of new features	37 (47%)	55%	36%	58%	38%	0.418
Acquire more users	34 (44%)	55%	32%	33%	50%	0.311
Present a more professional image of the product	32 (41%)	39%	32%	58%	50%	0.458
Understand how to sustain the long-term business model	26 (33%)	36%	28%	50%	13%	0.324

UX-Team = fully or partially dedicated UX team | UX-Pro = fully or partially dedicated UX professional | No-UX = No UX professional | Train-E = the start-up trains employees when necessary.

creation (7 of 8) and the *value for the user* (6 of 8), and the least cited reason is about *understanding how to sustain the long-term business model* (1 of 8).

Factors that Hinder the Application of UX. Table 5 presents respondents' opinions about factors that make it difficult to apply UX practices. Overall, more than 40% of respondents pointed out that the main difficulties are the *short time available* (36 of 78) and the *scarce financial resources* (31 of 78). Unsurprisingly, *lack of a designated professional to work with UX* is a difficulty most often

Table 5. Factors that hinder the application of UX

Factors	Overall (N = 78)	UX-Team (N = 33)	UX-Pro (N = 25)	No-UX (N = 12)	Train-E (N = 8)	p-value
Short time available	36 (46%)	48%	36%	42%	75%	0.280
Few financial resources	31 (40%)	30%	36%	50%	75%	0.113
Lack of consensus on UX relevance,skills, and responsibilities	28 (36%)	42%	36%	25%	25%	0.654
Dispersion of UX information	28 (36%)	36%	32%	50%	25%	0.660
Lack of a professional designated to work with UX	25 (32%)	9%	24%	92%	63%	**0.001***
Difficulty fitting UX work using agile practices	23 (29%)	33%	32%	17%	25%	0.724
Communication and collaboration gap between UX and other professionals	25 (32%)	48%	20%	25%	13%	**0.031***
Late start of UX activities	20 (26%)	27%	32%	17%	13%	0.618
Difficulty transforming UX needs into design solutions	13 (17%)	12%	16%	17%	38%	0.398
Difficulty knowing how to get infor-mation from users	9 (12%)	12%	12%	0%	25%	0.397
Few start-up-specific UX practices	7 (9%)	6%	16%	8%	0%	0.455

UX-Team = fully or partially dedicated UX team | UX-pro = fully or partially dedicated UX professional | No-UX = No UX professional | Train-E = the start-up trains employees when necessary.

pointed out by respondents from start-ups that do not have UX professionals, while the difficulty related to *communication and collaboration gap between UX and other professionals* is a difficulty most often pointed out by respondents from start-ups that have UX teams.

Skills to Perform UX Activities. To explore how much certain skills were necessary to carry out UX activities from respondents' viewpoints (Q14 and Q15), we analyzed 78 responses considering whether or not the respondents played the role of UX in the start-up (Q2). We found 43 respondents who play some UX-related role in their start-ups and 45 respondents who play roles only in the area of software engineering. See the results in Table 6. Overall, skills *know-how to collect and interpret feedback* and *Know-how to collect and interpret user information* were considered much-needed for the group of professionals who play the UX-related role (an average of 72% of them), and to a lesser proportion for SE professionals (an average of 54% of them). When running the KW test, we found no significant differences between groups.

Table 6. Skills to perform UX activities

Skills	Play UX role				No-play UX role				
	MN	NE	LN	NN	MN	NE	LN	NN	p-value
Know-how to interpret feedback	79%	19%	2%	0%	69%	31%	0%	0%	0.330
Know-how to collect feedback	72%	26%	2%	0%	51%	49%	0%	0%	0.079
Know-how to interpret user information	72%	23%	5%	0%	54%	43%	3%	0%	0.138
Know-how to collect user information	67%	23%	9%	0%	46%	46%	9%	0%	0.094
Knowledge in usability theories	47%	35%	19%	0%	40%	49%	6%	3%	0.978
Ability to analyze a large amount of data	37%	40%	16%	5%	31%	20%	31%	17%	0.066
Knowledge of usability heuristics	35%	47%	16%	2%	23%	46%	17%	6%	0.308
Know-how to perform activities with the user	33%	49%	14%	5%	40%	37%	20%	0%	0.592
Experience in graphic design	19%	47%	26%	9%	17%	54%	23%	3%	0.533

MN much-needed | NE needed | LN a bit needed | NN unnecessary

UX Relevance and Focus on Programming. The question about the importance of UX practices for the development team considering a mindset focused on programming from the respondents' perspective (Q16) was analyzed in two ways. Table 7 shows on the left side, the results considering the relation of UX relevance and the UX positions in the start-ups (i.e., UX-Team, UX-Pro, No-UX, Train-E). On the right side, the table shows the results considering a mindset focused on programming. We found out that there are no significant differences between groups in both questions, according to the KW test. Regarding the importance of UX, only 13% (10 of 78) of the respondents responded that UX is rarely important for the development team. Development teams are always concerned with UX in the opinion of 46% (19 of 41) of respondents within *UX-Team* and *Train-E* groups. Table 7 also shows an overall perspective of the results by dividing the data into UX and SE professional groups. As in the previous analysis, we did not find significant differences between these groups for both questions.

4.3   Threats to Validity

The respondents' perception and their inadequate knowledge of the domain are potential threats to the internal validity of surveys [4]. We conducted a pilot test with researchers in the UX domain and start-ups to check possible problems with the survey questions, and then, we refined the instrument to mitigate misinterpretations by respondents. The survey participants were recruited using a convenience sampling [4]. Regarding external threats referring to sample representativeness and heterogeneity within the target population [23], we use a network of start-up professionals and researchers distributed in different states of Brazil to engage professionals working for software start-ups and playing different roles.

Table 7. UX relevance and focus on programming

Groups	N	UX relevance				Focus on programmingp			
		Always	Often	Rarely	Never	Always	Often	Rarely	Never
UX Team	33	45%	36%	15%	0%	30%	36%	27%	3%
UX Pro	25	36%	48%	12%	4%	32%	56%	12%	0%
No-UX	12	33%	58%	8%	0%	25%	33%	25%	17%
Train-E	8	50%	38%	13%	0%	38%	38%	25%	0%
		p-value = 0.859				p-value = 0.476			
Plays UX role	43	44%	42%	12%	0%	40%	33%	23%	2%
Does not play UX role	45	38%	38%	20%	2%	18%	58%	18%	7%
		p-value = 0.300				p-value = 0.146			

UX Team = fully or partially dedicated UX team | UX-pro = fully or partially dedicated UX professional | No-UX = No UX professional | Train-E = the start-up trains employees when necessary.

We refined our questionnaire by changing some types of questions, such as adopting the multi-point Likert scale to mitigate possible construct threats referring to measurement fails. In multiple-choice questions, we add the option "other" to avoid an exhaustive list of possible answers. And, for all multiple-choice and Likert scale questions, we include the "I do not know" option to avoid inconsistent responses. Due to space limitations, however, we did not add the answers to these options in the tables of this paper. Specifically, the list of UX practices and the reasons and obstacles statements for using UX in the start-up were derived from existing studies [8,9,15]. To mitigate the evaluation apprehension effect, we have guaranteed the respondents anonymity and made the survey results available through a technical report. Regarding conclusion threats, we used the Kruskal-Wallis non-parametric tests and the Dunnett' method that are appropriate to perform multiple comparisons from multiple choice answers or the Likert scale [18].

5   Challenges for UX in Software Start-Ups

Regarding RQ1, our findings revealed that in start-ups applying UX for over 3 years, UX is more present in the different software development activities, and the adoption of UX practices is less frequent for start-ups that apply UX for less than 3 years. This result suggests these start-ups become more mature in understanding the importance of UX and using UX practices in their work.

Regarding RQ2, our results revealed that independently of the start-up having UX-related roles, respondents considered the creation of value for the user and the business reasons for using UX. The respondents also pointed out the lack of resources and time as the main impediments that blocked UX adoption. Our findings showed that UX is considered relevant even in start-ups where there were no UX professionals. The ability to handle user information from different perspectives was seen as the primary skill to conduct UX work in start-ups. Taking into account our findings, we outline some challenges on UX work in start-ups as the following:

Challenge 1 - Matching UX Work into Agile Practices to Running at Different Stages of Product Development. Frequently, start-ups guide their software development by agile practices [20]. Nevertheless, we found that although the professionals see the UX relevance, they face difficulties of fitting UX work into agile practices, as shown in Table 5. Furthermore, our results showed that UX's concerns are spread throughout the different frequency of application for start-ups that applied UX for up to 1 year (see details in Sect. 4.1). These results can indicate these start-ups are struggling to add the UX work to their software development activities. However, providing a good user experience (UX) from the beginning of product development can have a meaningful positive impact on product acceptance [5].

Challenge 2 - Making Practices Leaner for UX Work. When adopting UX practices, start-ups are often concerned with the cost their application can bring, requiring them to find a balance between the UX work application and the less resource-consuming [22]. The pressure to put the product on the market and the lack of UX professionals can be among the causes for a low frequency on the application of UX practices. A report on design maturity points that organizations with less expertise in UX have difficulty accommodating practices throughout the software development process [10]. From a similar perspective, the report results can explain why start-ups that have been applying UX for less than 1 year do not frequently use UX practices (see Table 3). Especially for early-stage start-ups, UX practices need to be adopted to do just enough to validate the product ideas without waste resources [5]. Nonetheless, a key question continues unanswered: "how to make UX practices more lightweight in order to be incorporated into the start-ups daily work?".

Challenge 3 - Adjusting the Pace of UX Work in a Highly Reactive Environment. Our findings pointed out that *creating successful products* is a trigger for UX's work (see Table 4). However, it may be harder for start-ups to add UX practices into their software development process by being highly reactive to market demands. When the start-up decides to change its product drastically, UX work may need to be started from scratch, e.g., conducting research with a new group of users [5]. In addition, UX professionals may have to deal with the frustration of discontinuing a project if they are not prepared to work at the pace of these innovation-driven environments. Start-ups do not always have UX specialists who may be involved in assessing the business model from the early stages.

Challenge 4 - Aligning UX Work with the Business Model and User Needs. In our survey, the most cited reasons for applying UX in start-ups are *create value for the user* and *create value for business development*, as shown in Table 4. However, the lack of resources and time to conduct UX activities appeared as factors that harm UX activities (see Table 5), while the *understanding how to sustain the long-term business model* is not seen as an important factor by professionals in start-ups that have UX-related roles (i.e., UX-Pro, see Table 4). This result could be a consequence of UX not being seen as a cross-cutting attribute. Our results have similarities with others from the literature which also point out that UX impacts on the business model and is important to create a user-product linked [9,12,22].

Challenge 5 - Training and Skills Development to Perform UX Activities. Our results showed that professionals from start-ups that do not have a designated UX professional recognize the importance of this professional for carrying out UX work (see Table 5). Also, our results show that both professionals from start-ups with and without UX-related roles have similar perspectives about the skills needed to perform UX activities (see Table 6). In addition to expertise in UX, Hokkanen et al. [9] highlighted the expertise of domain as an associated factor that should drive how and what type of UX can be created and tailored to the start-ups' business niche. In the same work, the participants reported that two key factors to UX work are the development of the abilities to get user feedback and to promote user involvement. Our results restate the concerns on collecting and handling user feedback and information (Table 6), as discussed in [5,7,9,13]. However, we add a new detail by showing that these concerns are seen as important skills by professionals independently if they have or not UX-related roles. These findings lead us to the idea that there is a common consciousness about what skills should be developed or improved by start-ups professionals. We have not found out in the literature the best practices or lessons learned about how to introduce these skills in start-ups' teams.

Challenge 6 - Conducting Research with Real Users. Although usability testing appeared as an often approach used by start-ups, the literature shows that professionals face difficulties in conducting user testing with real end-users [7]. In many situations, user testing is carried out with friends and with other internal members of the start-up. Differently of the literature, *know-how to get information from users* did not appear in the top as an obstacle to applying UX (Table 6). Hokkanen et al. [8], however, point that start-ups had challenges in collecting meaningful information from users and need of a systematically way to handle user information. Our sample did not provide us inputs to get an explanation of our different result. However, we consider this issue deserves a better further investigation.

6   Conclusions

This paper presented an investigation on the UX state-of-practice in software start-ups from a survey conducted with 88 professionals who work in software start-ups in Brazil. The respondents were in UX and SE positions. In our analysis, we addressed the role of UX in software development and the main practices used in the fast-paced environment of start-ups. We also looked at the reasons that influence or hinder UX work, the essential UX-related skills, and UX relevance from professionals' point of view. In summary, our findings showed that even considering UX relevant, professionals have faced problems to fit UX in the software development work, regardless of having UX-related positions allocated. We concluded that more than developing professionals' mindset about UX relevance, software start-ups need a set of practices to support decision-making about how and when UX work can be effectively embedded into their software development activities.

By analyzing these issues in a critical way, we have identified a set of challenges faced by software start-ups in the adoption of UX practices. The identification of these challenges is a significant contribution achieved by this work since these can be used to drive actions on start-ups and to guide future studies on the field. Besides, our discussion provides insights to encourage researchers and software practitioners to carry out more in-depth investigations on topics, such as the UX value for users and business, and UX in the volatile scenario of early-stage start-ups. Future work includes examining the remaining survey questions and the replication of our survey to other start-up ecosystems.

Acknowledgments. We thank the support of grant #2020/00615-9 and grant #2020/10429-8, São Paulo Research Foundation (FAPESP), and grant 313312/2019-2, Conselho Nacional de Desenvolvimento Científico e Tecnológico (CNPq - Brazil).

References

1. Berg, V., Birkeland, J., Nguyen-Duc, A., Pappas, I.O., Jaccheri, L.: Software startup engineering: a systematic mapping study. J. Syst. Softw. **144**, 255–274 (2018)

2. DIS, I.: 9241-210: 2010. ergonomics of human system interaction-part 210: Human-centred design for interactive systems (formerly known as 13407). International Standardization Organization (ISO). Switzerland (2010)
3. Dunnett, C.W.: A multiple comparison procedure for comparing several treatments with a control. J. Am. Stat. Assoc. **50**(272), 1096–1121 (1955)
4. Ghazi, A.N., Petersen, K., Reddy, S.S.V.R., Nekkanti, H.: Survey research in software engineering: problems and mitigation strategies. IEEE Access **7**, 24703–24718 (2018)
5. Hokkanen, L., Kuusinen, K., Väänänen, K.: Early product design in startups: towards a UX strategy. In: Abrahamsson, P., Corral, L., Oivo, M., Russo, B. (eds.) PROFES 2015. LNCS, vol. 9459, pp. 217–224. Springer, Cham (2015). https://doi.org/10.1007/978-3-319-26844-6_16
6. Hokkanen, L., Kuusinen, K., Väänänen, K.: Minimum viable user experience: a framework for supporting product design in startups. In: Sharp, H., Hall, T. (eds.) XP 2016. LNBIP, vol. 251, pp. 66–78. Springer, Cham (2016). https://doi.org/10.1007/978-3-319-33515-5_6
7. Hokkanen, L., Leppänen, M.: Three patterns for user involvement in startups. In: Proceedings of the 20th European Conference on Pattern Languages of Programs, pp. 1–8 (2015)
8. Hokkanen, L., Väänänen-Vainio-Mattila, K.: UX work in startups: current practices and future needs. In: Lassenius, C., Dingsøyr, T., Paasivaara, M. (eds.) XP 2015. LNBIP, vol. 212, pp. 81–92. Springer, Cham (2015). https://doi.org/10.1007/978-3-319-18612-2_7
9. Hokkanen, L., Xu, Y., Väänänen, K.: Focusing on user experience and business models in startups: Investigation of two-dimensional value creation. In: Proceedings of the 20th International Academic Mindtrek Conference, AcademicMindtrek 2016, pp. 59–67. ACM, New York (2016)
10. InVision: The new design frontier (2018). https://www.invisionapp.com/design-better/design-maturity-model/
11. Kitchenham, B.A., Pfleeger, S.L.: Personal opinion surveys. In: Guide to Advanced Empirical Software Engineering, pp. 63–92. Springer, Heidelberg (2008). https://doi.org/10.1007/978-1-84800-044-5_3
12. Klotins, E., Unterkalmsteiner, M., Gorschek, T.: Software engineering in start-up companies: an analysis of 88 experience reports. Empir. Softw. Eng. **24**(1), 68–102 (2019)
13. Kuusinen, K., Sørensen, M.K., Frederiksen, N.M., Laugesen, N.K., Juul, S.H.: From startup to scaleup: an interview study of the development of user experience work in a data-intensive company. In: Bogdan, C., Kuusinen, K., Lárusdóttir, M.K., Palanque, P., Winckler, M. (eds.) HCSE 2018. LNCS, vol. 11262, pp. 3–14. Springer, Cham (2019). https://doi.org/10.1007/978-3-030-05909-5_1
14. Law, E.L.C., Roto, V., Hassenzahl, M., Vermeeren, A.P., Kort, J.: Understanding, scoping and defining user experience: A survey approach. In: Proceedings of the SIGCHI Conference on Human Factors in Computing Systems, CHI 2009, pp. 719–728. Association for Computing Machinery, New York (2009)
15. de Lima Salgado, A., Amaral, L.A., Freire, A.P., Fortes, R.P.M.: Usability and UX practices in small enterprises: Lessons from a survey of the Brazilian context. In: Proceedings of the 34th ACM International Conference on the Design of Communication, SIGDOC 2016, pp. 18:1–18:9. ACM, New York (2016)
16. Lindgren, E., Münch, J.: Raising the odds of success: the current state of experimentation in product development. Inf. Softw. Technol. **77**, 80–91 (2016)

17. May, B.: Applying lean startup: an experience report - lean & lean UX by a UX veteran: lessons learned in creating & launching a complex consumer app. In: Proceedings - 2012 Agile Conference, Agile 2012, pp. 141–147 (2012)
18. McCrum-Gardner, E.: Which is the correct statistical test to use? Brit. J. Oral Maxillofacial Surg. **46**(1), 38–41 (2008)
19. Melegati, J., Chanin, R., Sales, A., Prikladnicki, R.: Towards specific software engineering practices for early-stage startups. In: Paasivaara, M., Kruchten, P. (eds.) XP 2020. LNBIP, vol. 396, pp. 18–22. Springer, Cham (2020). https://doi.org/10.1007/978-3-030-58858-8_2
20. Paternoster, N., Giardino, C., Unterkalmsteiner, M., Gorschek, T., Abrahamsson, P.: Software development in startup companies: a systematic mapping study. Inf. Softw. Technol. **56**(10), 1200–1218 (2014)
21. Ries, E.: The Lean Startup: How Today's Entrepreneurs Use Continuous Innovation to Create Radicall Successful Businesses. Crown Publishing Group, New York (2011)
22. Unterkalmsteiner, M., et al.: Software startups - a research agenda. e-Informatica Softw. Eng. J. **10**(1), 89–123 (2016)
23. Wohlin, C., Runeson, P., Höst, M., Ohlsson, M.C., Regnell, B., Wesslén, A.: Experimentation in Software Engineering. Springer, New York (2012). https://doi.org/10.1007/978-3-642-29044-2

Open Access This chapter is licensed under the terms of the Creative Commons Attribution 4.0 International License (http://creativecommons.org/licenses/by/4.0/), which permits use, sharing, adaptation, distribution and reproduction in any medium or format, as long as you give appropriate credit to the original author(s) and the source, provide a link to the Creative Commons license and indicate if changes were made.

The images or other third party material in this chapter are included in the chapter's Creative Commons license, unless indicated otherwise in a credit line to the material. If material is not included in the chapter's Creative Commons license and your intended use is not permitted by statutory regulation or exceeds the permitted use, you will need to obtain permission directly from the copyright holder.

How to Write Ethical User Stories?
Impacts of the ECCOLA Method

Erika Halme$^{(\boxtimes)}$ (ID), Ville Vakkuri (ID), Joni Kultanen (ID), Marianna Jantunen (ID),
Kai-Kristian Kemell (ID), Rebekah Rousi (ID), and Pekka Abrahamsson (ID)

University of Jyvaskyla, PL35 Jyvaskylä, Finland
{erika.a.halme,ville.vakkuri,joni.m.kultanen,marianna.s.p.jantunen,
kai-kristian.o.kemell,rebekah.rousi,pekka.abrahamsson}@jyu.fi

Abstract. Artificial Intelligence (AI) systems are increasing in significance within software services. Unfortunately, these systems are not flawless. Their faults, failures and other systemic issues have emphasized the urgency for consideration of ethical standards and practices in AI engineering. Despite the growing number of studies in AI ethics, comparatively little attention has been placed on how ethical issues can be mitigated in software engineering (SE) practice. Currently understanding is lacking regarding the provision of useful tools that can help companies transform high-level ethical guidelines for AI ethics into the actual workflow of developers. In this paper, we explore the idea of using user stories to transform abstract ethical requirements into tangible outcomes in Agile software development. We tested this idea by studying master's level student projects (15 teams) developing web applications for a real industrial client over the course of five iterations. These projects resulted in 250+ user stories that were analyzed for the purposes of this paper. The teams were divided into two groups: half of the teams worked using the ECCOLA method for AI ethics in SE, while the other half, a control group, was used to compare the effectiveness of ECCOLA. Both teams were tasked with writing user stories to formulate customer needs into system requirements. Based on the data, we discuss the effectiveness of ECCOLA, and Primary Empirical Contributions (PECs) from formulating ethical user stories in Agile development.

Keywords: User story · Agile development · Ethics · Artificial Intelligence

1 Introduction

During recent years, the role of ethics has been emphasized in the context of Artificial Intelligence (AI) and Autonomous Systems (AS). In the field of Software Engineering (SE) however, few tools or methods are available for systematically incorporating ethics into development. Furthermore, AI ethics has seldom been studied from the perspective of practical application in SE. Ethically aligned AI/AS development principles and guidelines exist [1], yet as recent research demonstrates [2], there are still major challenges in translating these to practice.

© The Author(s) 2021
P. Gregory et al. (Eds.): XP 2021, LNBIP 419, pp. 36–52, 2021.
https://doi.org/10.1007/978-3-030-78098-2_3

Overall, AI ethics currently seems to be an area with a prominent gap between research and practice [2]. While we now have some degree of consensus on what AI ethics is and what ethical principles and issues are important to consider in AI development [1], translating these principles into concrete action is challenging [2,3]. Organizations and developers seem to struggle with turning ethical guidelines into tangible requirements.

We have attempted to tackle this issue by proposing a method for implementing AI ethics in SE. The method is called ECCOLA.

The ECCOLA method has been iteratively developed and validated. This current paper reports on one of these iterative validations. Additionally, we wish to better understand how AI ethics should be practically applied to design and development. Another goal of the paper in the context of ethics, is to examine *user stories* and further knowledge of how to write ethical user stories in terms of translating ethical principles into tangible engineering requirements. ECCOLA will be discussed in greater detail in the next section.

Writing user stories is a practice commonly used to help define requirements during development, especially in Agile software development. Thus, we felt that ethical user stories could be one way of making (AI) ethics a part of the workflow of developers. To study user stories in the context of (AI) ethics, we conducted an empirical study of 15 projects. These projects were split into two, with half of the project groups using the ECCOLA method to guide the user story writing process, and the other, the control group, writing user stories without ECCOLA yet with another set of non-ethically oriented cards ('placebos'). The main research question of the current study is: "How can Non-Functional ethically-oriented User Stories be written with the assistance of the ECCOLA method?"

2 Background

2.1 Implementing Ethics into Software Development

Research seems to point to both challenges and benefits in applying ethics within Agile methods. Miller and Larson [4], on human values in Agile software development, highlighted the importance of developers acquiring an awareness of and skill in performing ethical analysis. This was in order to be able to evaluate development methods on a more sophisticated level. Yet, developers may experience difficulties in articulating ideas about human values, due to their technical language orientation [4]. While comparing Agile Principles with software ethics, Judy [5] concluded that the conversation of ethical dilemmas is largely absent from the Agile context. Particularly in instances where ethical issues do not directly affect business value or teams. Miller and Larson [4] call for tools of ethical analysis; they propose that parties involved in software development need intellectual skills and a vocabulary that will help them understand and communicate competing human duties, values and consequences.

Agile practices are "designed to navigate essential complexity" [5]. Their growing rate of adoption is based on an inclination towards harnessing values and culture in development processes and practices [5]. At the same time, Miller and Larson [4] propose that through deontological analysis, the Agile Manifesto itself can be seen to place emphasis on human values. According to Judy [5], the Agile community serves as a "vital resource" for peers with shared values.

It would seem that ethical building blocks exist in the Agile methodology itself, but applying ethical analysis tools could further improve the situation through clarifying ethical targets and what they mean in action, even in the absence of "standard" methods.

To address the unique challenges posed by information technology (IT), concepts such as Information Ethics, and further, Computer Ethics, have emerged. The discussion around guidelines and codes of conduct for ethical considerations, as well as initiatives to promote ethical software development, progress as technology evolves. For example, the *ACM Code of Ethics and Professional Conduct* for ethical software development dates back to 1992. It was subsequently updated to better suit the advancement of technology in 2018[1]. This ACM Code of Ethics, as an example of an acknowledged resource of computer ethics, presents principles of responsibility for all who "use computing technology in an impactful way". It considers ethical principles such as prioritizing human well-being, trustworthiness, fairness and privacy.

The ethical principles of computer ethics proceeded into the evolving discussion of autonomous, intelligent technologies. Debates and discussion regarding AI ethics has produced a widely recognized understanding of AI ethics guidelines, that consist of partially the same principles as those in computer ethics. For example, a study of the guidelines [1] identified a "global convergence emerging around five ethical principles", namely: transparency, justice and fairness, non-maleficence, responsibility and privacy.

When discussing ethics in IT, Value-Sensitive Design (VSD) is also worthy to mention. Having emerged from the Human-Computer Interaction (HCI) community in the 1990s, it is "a theoretically grounded approach to the design of technology that accounts for human values in a principled and comprehensive manner throughout the design process" [6]. It has been utilized in various domains and tools including a ToolKit (for envisioning practices), consisting of 32 cards for envisioning the use case scenario themed in stakeholders, time, values, and pervasiveness [7].

While codes for ethical conduct in SE exist, an issue across domains of software development is in that these codes do not carry over into practice. As suggested by [8], any number of guidelines, policies, and procedures to encourage ethical behavior cannot guarantee their implementation. They state that, "credible results and a strong discipline of empirical software engineering are based on mutual trust that everyone will behave ethically" [8]. However, this trust has not proven to be sufficient in facilitating ethical thinking. For example, McNamara et al. [9] replicated a prior behavior ethics study, and found out that explicitly instructing participants to consider the ACM Code of Ethics in relation to the impacts of their software development decision-making had no influence on actual ethical decision-making itself. In the field of AI ethics, [2]

---

[1] https://www.acm.org/articles/bulletins/2018/july/new-code-of-ethics-released.

discovered a gap between research and practice regarding the ways in which AI ethics are implemented. While on the one hand, AI ethics are discussed in academic circles, on the other hand, discussions had not carried over to industrial application.

2.2   ECCOLA Method and It's Application

Inspired by the challenges of implementing ethics in AI development, the ECCOLA method [10] used in the current study, was developed with the intention to provide developers with "an actionable tool for implementing [AI] ethics". The method considers topics of AI ethics created in reflection of AI ethics principles from relevant literature while aiming to make them more practical and applicable for development. The ECCOLA method is a deck of 21 cards, with eight (8) themes and one to six (1–6) topics in each theme (see Table 1). Developers can utilize the ECCOLA cards to implement the various ethical consideration prompts in software development by using the questions provided on the cards. Each card consists of one topic like the theme transparency considers topics under Communication and Explainability, while Accountability considers topics such as Auditability and Ability to Redress. One additional card, called the Game sheet, explains how the method is used in practice. The cards are split into three sections to motivate what to do while providing a practical example. The cards also contain a note-making space to make it even more practical in real life development work.

Table 1. ECCOLA card themes

Card themes (8)	Card number (0–20)	Card amount (total 21)
Analyze	#0	1
Transparency	#1–6	6
Safety & Security	#7–9	3
Fairness	#10–11	2
Data	#12–13	2
Agency & Oversight	#14–15	2
Wellbeing	#16–17	2
Accountability	#18–20	3

ECCOLA is a modular, sprint-by-spint process, where relevant cards are chosen in advance in order to make the method manageable and focused in the proceeding development work. This process results in a paper trail of ethical choices to be made during the development of software product.

In short, the three (3) phases of prepare, review and evaluate are repeated in every iteration during the development process. Decisions and card selection processes become easier and more productive when developers/users familiarize themselves with the card themes and contents. The cards are to be sorted into three (3) piles before development. The first pile is for the planning stages of the project. The second one is for different parts of the development and the third pile, if needed during the project's final phase. The project or product defines what cards are selected and utilized at different development stages. Tutorial sessions are held before the interested parties start to deploy the method. The sessions contain some exercises and an introduction to the method and AI ethics, if needed. In this sense, ECCOLA is, in Agile methodology, a continuum for ethical building blocks in the form of an analysis tool and this we will elaborate upon more in the coming paragraphs.

2.3   User Stories in Ethically Aligned Software Design

User stories in the field of SE and Agile software development connect the two sides of software project parties - business and development - in relation to information about customer requirements [11]. User stories are highly apt for Agile environments (as originated from the XP method) due to the fact that they can be utilized for planning iterations and within iterative development processes [11]. From the outset, Agile practices "focus on the development and delivery of only those features that are really useful to customer" [12]. These methods are applied in development projects with fast moving targets, where development teams and applied tools should adapt easily to changes [13]. As the name suggests, this provides software projects with manageable agility, particularly in terms of bringing value to customer needs. This value delivery is enabled through requirements engineering (RE) practices such as user stories [12].

User stories serve as mediators or boundary objects between users and the development team. In the user story process, the decision-making and idea of the software outcome is spread along the development project duration [11]. This simple yet unifying function offers the development team an effective tool to handle information just-in-time. In practice, user stories are handwritten cards or paper notes generated by the customer team. If the customer is not involved in the process the product owner - part of the development team - answers for the customer software requirement needs.

The user story card or template generally contains two sections that describe the requirements at a high level. This is formulated into three leading sentences: "As a <role>, I can <action>, so that <goal>." This progresses with acceptance criteria that are utilized to evaluate the user story execution [14]. Based on Cohn's [14] original developments, Dimitrijevic et al. [12] capsulize the user story process into seven steps: user stories gathering, user role modeling, acceptance testing, estimating and planning releases and iterations, as well as tracking and communicating. These seven areas of user story processing emphasize the unpretentious nature of what the process components should entail.

The user stories are classified according to functional and non-functional requirements. The functional requirements represent stories that are "comprehensible by both the developer as well as the customer team... and it's a discrete piece of functionality; that is, something a user would be likely to do in a single setting" [11]. The goal for requirements that are classified as non-functional requirements address the system needs, e.g. performance, availability, usability, security and capacity [11], which represent the system quality in general. Ethical requirements can be classified as non-functional requirements as they share similarities with quality requirements, for instance in terms of qualities such as security.

3 Research Framework

Sketching and prototype generation have been described as extensions of designer and developer cognition (see e.g., [15]). Likewise, for decades cards have been used as highly practical and effective tools for not only materializing thoughts but also representing how we mentally structure, categorise, and prioritise information [16].

Through utilizing cards in combination with light weight methods such as user stories in Agile processes, we may observe benefits from several perspectives: 1) concretizing the mental arrangements of information through arranging the cards; 2) physically re-ordering these cards to find better alternatives and smoother streams of logic; 3) direct information and guides for development; and 4) the ability to test user logic – in and of itself, and/or in light of the system and its re-design/re-development or improvement, and/or in relation to software developer logic while translating ideas generated form the cards into coherent and actionable stories (from scenario to program) [17].

In this study, we empirically evaluated the ECCOLA method. ECCOLA is a method for implementing AI ethics, which we have presented in an existing paper [10] and briefly above. The advantage of thinking tools such as cards and user stories – the types of tools utilised within this current study – for instance, are that they can be used repeatedly and iteratively throughout the design and development process. As their forms and functions also suggest, not only are these tools instruments for extending and validating thought, but they are also a means of engaging multiple minds – the input of several or many people – within the thought structuring, or cognitive development-action process. This facilitates and enables collective cognition through teams and developer-stakeholder (end-user) interactive and iterative processes [18]. In terms of designing for immaterial qualities, or non-functional requirements such as ethics, values and emotional experience for instance, these forms of tools are highly valuable as they serve to connect immaterial qualities to tangible and concrete design and development decisions.

For this study, we selected four cards for the teams to apply to their processes in order to see how using ECCOLA would affect how the teams take ethical issues into account while writing user stories. These cards were predetermined and were the same for each team, i.e., in this case the development teams did not pick the cards themselves. Due to research technical reasons, only four cards were chosen to conduct this study. We discuss the role of ECCOLA in this study in detail in the next section.

4   Study Design

In this section, we discuss the methodology used in the study. The purpose of the study was to understand how user stories could be written in terms of integrating ethical considerations (principles) into the actionable logic of the interaction design and SE process. The study was conducted as an experiment in a controlled research setting via the university's distance learning tools. According to Wohlin et al. "experiments involve more than one treatment to compare the outcomes. For example, if it is possible to control who is using one method and who is using another method, and when and where they are used, it is possible to perform an experiment" [19]. Our main interest was to compare the output of two types of user story generating student groups - the test groups utilising ECCOLA and a control group utilising a card set without explicitly concentrating on ethics. ECCOLA was used as a framework to guide the user story creation in the student groups who were assigned the test group role. The main goal of ECCOLA as a development tool and artefact is to aid the translation of seemingly non-functional requirements such as ethics, into operational SE actions. This experimental setting was considered apt for determining ECCOLA's effectiveness from this perspective.

4.1   Data Collection Methodology and Study Context

In the current study, focus was placed on the production of ethical user stories through utilising ECCOLA cards. ECCOLA had a two-fold function in this exercise: 1) as a guide for deliberating ethics in SE based on ethical AI principles; and 2) as a subject of appraisal - we sought to validate ECCOLA's effectiveness through its operationalization in user stories. In order to achieve this, data was collected in the form of user stories (n = 298) from 15 project teams. Out of these 15 teams, nine teams utilized ECCOLA to aid the user story writing process, while six did not. Originally there was a more equal delegation of the two groups (ECCOLA and non-ECCOLA/control), but some groups were merged to avoid undermanned teams as some students opted to not complete the course.

The data for this study were collected from a Master's level Information Systems (IS) course at the University of Jyväskylä, Finland. In the course, students worked in teams of 3–5 students to carry out a project for a real case company.

The duration of the software project was six weeks. During this time, the students received five assignments, one each week after the first week's introductory lecture. These assignments comprised two parts: non-technical and technical. The non-technical part was the focus of this study and formed the basis of data collection. User stories were discussed during the lectures to familiarize the teams with the practice of producing them.

The students were split into teams based on self-evaluations of their software development skills. In a pre-course questionnaire, students were asked to evaluate their confidence in programming abilities in any programming language on a scale of 0 to 100. Students were organised in an ascending order based on their level of programming confidence, and divided incrementally into teams (i.e., the most confident students into one group, the least confident into another, and the rest in between). Division was made in this manner in order to avoid imbalance of technical skills, and thus, workload distribution within each team.

For demographic data, students were also required to report their previous work experience in software engineering/development, in Agile development, and their experience in utilizing Scrum (see Table 2). While 61 percent of the students reported to have at least some experience in SW development (the distribution of experience levels between students in both ECCOLA and non-ECCOLA groups were similar) some difference in experience related to Agile development and Scrum can be seen between the two groups - to the benefit of the ECCOLA group. Students' experience in Agile development can be seen to relate to their prior knowledge about user stories as user stories are used as a RE tool in agile development work.

Table 2. Demographic data of working experience

Work experience:	How much work experience in the field of software engineering/development do you have?	How much experience in Agile development do you have?	How much experience of Scrum do you have?
	ECCOLA —— Control	ECCOLA-Control	ECCOLA-Control
None	38% ————41%	49%————-64%	51%————-64%
Less than 1 year	28% ————-23%	26%————-27%	28%————-23%
1–5 years	28% ————-36%	21%————-9%	15%————-14%
6–10 years	0% ————-0%	3%————0%	3%————0%
More than 10 years	3% ————-0%	0%————-0%	0%————-0%
N/A	3% ————-0%	3%————-0%	3%————-0%
TOTAL	100%————-100%	100%————-100%	100%————-100%

These teams were then split into two groups (X for odd numbers and Y for even numbers). Teams in group X used ECCOLA to help devise user stories, while group Y did not. Group Y, however, also received a set of cards. The cards issued were created for the present study setting. These cards contained instructions on writing user stories but did not discuss ethical issues. The purpose of the second set of cards was to encourage a sense of equal treatment between groups. Furthermore, the equality in issuing all groups with card sets was to ensure that learning outcomes were not compromised by perceived varying conditions and resources (i.e., tools at each group's disposal). Materials such as Card decks X & Y, the User Story Template, instructions and weekly assignments can be found at external repository at Figshare[2].

As the course progressed, so too did the user story development process. During the first week of the project, after gaining a firm understanding of user stories, the groups were to write 4–6 user stories that featured functional requirements. Each user story was written on a template provided to the teams.

---

[2] https://doi.org/10.6084/m9.figshare.14210753.

The first week's assignment required the students to utilize one card from their given set that comprised a Stakeholder Analysis theme. The second week's assignment focused on examining the customer need/desired product description and writing 4–6 user stories through the lens of non-functional requirements (NFR). Students were informed about the differences of functional and non-functional requirements including examples of both types of requirements. For the rest of the project timeline the groups with X deck were allocated three additional cards to reference (four cards in total): Stakeholder Analysis, System Reliability, Privacy and Data, and System Security. The groups with Y deck were provided with two new cards in addition to Stakeholder Analysis (three in total): Non-Functional Requirements and Functional Requirements.

After the second week, each week featured user story revision, creation of new user stories if applicable, and a check to see if user stories were implemented into the product. At the end of the course, the groups were to review and return all their user stories with concluding remarks about the implementation process.

4.2   Data Analysis

The data was analyzed with coding techniques according to Grounded Theory Method (GTM) and the INVEST model. The use of GTM in IS studies varies in application rigour (degree of adoption) and type of research contribution [20].

There is no "unique, generally accepted set" of GTM procedures to guide the coding process [20], and the use of the method has evolved since its development. Regardless of the type of application, a key concept in GTM includes *coding* as a way to classify themes that arise in the data.

Before commencing analysis, the user stories were submitted by the student teams, categorized by assignment/week, and finally summarized in a table. The data were then analyzed in three phases. First, we looked at the data quantitatively in order to gain an overview and to look at any quantitative differences between the data from the two groups of teams. This was done due to the high volume of otherwise qualitative data.

In the second phase, we utilized a GTM approach to code the user stories one at a time. This process was carried out iteratively, with the list of codes updated during the process as new codes emerged. We chose this approach due to the fact that this is a novel area of research: we were not able to identify any existing studies on writing ethical user stories. Moreover, we chose a GTM approach as it is well-suited for discovering phenomena inductively [20]. We wanted to study the data by limiting possibilities for bias as much as possible. We also did not know which aspects of user story creation the use of ECCOLA might affect and how. Thus, we saw the need to examine the findings against a blank slate, making GTM ideal. In analyzing the user stories, we applied the GTM coding methodology of *open coding*, a coding where initial labels are attached to data [20]. The codes were not pre-determined, as we wanted to first apply themes to the data, and later categorize them in terms of their relevance to the research. It is possible, however, that a researcher bias from previous AI ethics research may have contributed to the themes that arose from the data.

In the third and final phase, we utilized the INVEST model. According to the INVEST model, the quality of the user stories can be evaluated with six attribute lists, in a method called INVEST [11,12]. The acronym, introduced by William Wake (2003) stands[3], for: I as an Independent, N as a Negotiable, V as Valuable to Purchasers or Users, E as an Estimatable, S as Small and T as Testable. A good user story can be composed through these elements, particularly when: it is not dependent on other user stories; can be negotiated as it does not go into detail; brings value to the customer; can somehow be estimated in terms of resourcing and anticipated amounts of customer support; and is small in size in order to be as accurate as possible for producing estimations. It should also be testable to assure the accuracy of the requirements.

To operationalize INVEST, firstly two teachers from the course evaluated the user stories through the framework. Each teacher analyzed equal number teams producing the user stories. Both teachers evaluated as many control group teams and ECCOLA teams each to reduce any potential bias. Then, one of the researchers scored all the user stories using INVEST, independently of the teachers' evaluations. The evaluation was binary: either a user story fulfilled the requirements of an INVEST attribute or not.

5   Findings

As discussed in the study design section, we collected 298 user stories from 15 student teams. These teams were split into two groups: group Y (the control group, i.e. the teams that did not use ECCOLA) and group X (the teams that used ECCOLA). Group Y had six teams in it, whereas group X had nine. Overall, group Y produced 119 users stories (average 19,8 per team) and group X produced 179 user stories (average 19,9 per team).

In the GTM coding, each story was attributed three high-level themes: (1) stakeholder, (2) requirement, and (3) technical orientation (T) vs human orientation (H). Inside these themes were lower level codes attributed to each theme, as seen in Fig. 1. Not all codes were present in every user story. For example, every user story had some stakeholder(s) present but the stakeholder(s) varied between user stories. Additionally, the human orientation vs. technical orientation codes were mutually exclusive, serving as a way of categorizing the user stories into two groups.

Whether a particular user story was human-focused or technology-focused was considered interesting from the point of view of ethics. This was of interest from the ECCOLA viewpoint, as we wished to understand to what extent ECCOLA might have influenced the user stories in relation to, e.g. consideration for human aspects. While this was a binary split in our analysis, the stories involved both human and technical aspects of the system, and were categorized based on which aspect was more dominant.

---

[3] https://xp123.com/articles/invest-in-good-stories-and-smart-tasks/.

The ECCOLA group produced more human-centric user stories (61%) than technology-centric ones (38%). The control group, on the other hand, produced more technology-centric user stories (65%) than human-centric user stories (31%). Based on these results, it seems that the use of ECCOLA could encourage developers to be produce more human-centric user stories.

PEC1: (Primary Empirical Contribution): Using ECCOLA seems to result in more human-centric user stories.

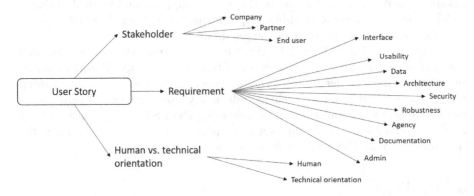

Fig. 1. Grounded theory coding from user stories

Regarding the codes under the other two themes, the codes under the requirement theme were largely similarly represented in the user stories of both groups. For example, *security* codes were found in exactly 15% of the user stories of both groups. Thus, ECCOLA did not seem to result in any significant differences in the requirement codes.

The only notable differences could be seen in the *usability* and *agency* codes. The usability code was present in 29% of the user stories of the ECCOLA group, but only 9% of the user stories of the control group. The agency code was present in 8% of the ECCOLA group's user stories, but only in 2% of the control group's. It could be that the ECCOLA cards, in addition to resulting in more human-centric user stories in general, also served to highlight the user in terms of e.g., ease of use. The agency %'s in both groups were ultimately so low that it is too weak of an indicator of anything based on this data alone. Thus, using ECCOLA did not seem to increase consideration related to the ECCOLA card themes (System Security, Privacy & Data, and System Reliability) that were present in the cards utilized by the ECCOLA groups.

PEC2: Using the ECCOLA cards did not affect how the teams wrote user stories in terms of the themes present in the cards.

In addition to the GTM analysis, we utilized the INVEST framework to analyze the user stories. The results of this analysis are summarized in Table 3. Overall, the ECCOLA teams scored higher in quality according to the INVEST framework. The ECCOLA group had an average INVEST score of 60,68% and the control group had an average score of 53,17%. The ECCOLA teams scored higher in every category of the INVEST framework aside from V(aluable). All the highest individual team scores were also in the ECCOLA group.

PEC3: Teams using ECCOLA produced higher quality user stories when measured using the INVEST framework.

Additionally, one of the largest differences in the INVEST scoring categories could be seen in the I(ndependent) category. Average INVEST scores for I – Independent for ECCOLA teams was 69,92% and for Control teams 46,54%. The user stories of the ECCOLA groups were notably more stand-alone than those of the control groups, i.e. they overlapped less in concepts. This can be beneficial as independent user stories can be produced and tackled before subsequent ones are written (as opposed to e.g., functionality 1 ->functionality 2).

PEC4: Using ECCOLA results in more independent user stories that consider the software from a wider perspective than just that of its functionalities.

Table 3. User store quality

Group	I	N	V	E	S	T	Average
Control	46,54%	8,80%	78,12%	70,53%	52,00%	63,01%	53,17%
ECCOLA	69,92%	12,88%	72,74%	81,25%	62,34%	64,97%	60,68%
Difference	−23,38	−4,08	5,38	−10,72	−10,34	−1,96	−7,52

INVEST analysis is conducted with binary coding. 1=User story fulfilled the requirements of an INVEST attribute 0=User story didn't fill the requirements. Shown on the table is percentage of positive scores.

In addition to the general INVEST analysis of all the user stories produced during the project, we looked at the second week's user stories in detail. During the second week, the teams were tasked with producing non-functional user stories. The scores for each group and how they differed from the average INVEST scores of that group can be found in Table 4. Based on these scores, ECCOLA seemed to improve the quality of the non-functional user stories. More importantly, the overall good INVEST scores of the non-functional user stories of the ECCOLA group seem to support the idea that non-functional user stories can be written with ECCOLA, and particularly user stories of high quality.

In summary, the teams utilizing ECCOLA, while writing more human-centric user stories, considered ethical aspects in their user stories more than the control group. The control group largely focused on traditional SE aspects such as features and other technical design properties (Table 4).

Table 4. Non-functional user story quality

Group	I	N	V	E	S	T
Control group - Week 2 scores	92,61 %	N/A	77,71 %	44,46 %	29,56 %	29,68 %
Control group - difference from avg	46,07	N/A	4,83	−26,07	−22,44	−33,33
ECCOLA group - Week 2 scores	82,24 %	N/A	71,14 %	68,87 %	53,33 %	51,11 %
ECCOLA group - difference from avg	12,32	N/A	−1,60	−12,38	−9,01	−13,86

INVEST analysis is conducted with binary coding. 1=User story fulfilled the requirements of an INVEST attribute 0=User story didn't fill the requirements. Shown on the table is percentage of positive scores.

PEC5: Non-functional user stories can be written with the assistance of the ECCOLA method.

These findings and observations indicate that the team members utilizing the ECCOLA cards consider ethics in user story processing, while the control groups concentrated more on traditional SE development activities such as features and other technical design properties. Even though the chosen ECCOLA cards were the most technically-oriented the end result was then a human-oriented approach to user story production.

5.1 Validity Threats

In discussing ethical user stories, one limitation to consider is related to construct validity. How to measure the level of ethical consideration? This is also a general question related to studying the implementation of AI ethics. In this case, we have utilized a framework based on existing literature (ECCOLA). While there is currently no universally accepted consensus on what AI ethics is and what principles it should comprise, ECCOLA is constructed from some of the most prominent AI ethics principles (many of which e.g. [1] discuss).

Another potential limitation of the study is the empirical setting. To improve the reliability of the results, we chose an A/B testing based study setting and formed standardized procedures for data collection and analysis. We also utilized student data in this study. In this regard, we turn to Höst et al., [21] who argue that the differences between students and professionals are not statistically significant. We also argue that the use of students is justified by the novelty of the topic: we are not aware of any existing study that has looked into ethical user stories.

6　Discussion and Conclusion

In this paper, we have studied ethical user stories through the lens of the ECCOLA [10] method. In an experiment, we had developer teams (n=15) write user stories related to a real-world project. These teams were split into an ECCOLA group that utilized the tool to support them in writing user stories, and a control group that did not use ECCOLA to do so. We analyzed 298 user stories from these teams using two different analysis approaches. In Table 5 below, we summarize the Primary Empirical Contributions (PECs) of this study that we highlighted in the preceding section. Here, we discuss the implications of these findings before concluding the paper.

Table 5. List of primary empirical contributions

PEC	Description
1	Using ECCOLA seems to result in more human-centric user stories
2	Using the ECCOLA cards did not affect how the teams wrote user stories in terms of the themes present in the cards
3	Teams using ECCOLA produced higher quality user stories when measured using the INVEST framework
4	Using ECCOLA results in more independent user stories that consider the software from a wider perspective than just that of its functionalities
5	Non-functional user stories can be written with the assistance of the ECCOLA method

As the summarizing PECs in the above table show, the ECCOLA method [10] seemed to improve user stories in various ways. However, PEC2 also highlights an interesting observation in that ECCOLA did *not* make the user stories notably more focused on the themes of the ECCOLA cards in question. Moreover, the ECCOLA cards used in this study contained typical SE themes such as system security and privacy & data. These themes should be familiar for anyone concerned with SE and thus their lack of an effect in this study needs to be considered when moving forward with developing the method. Even if overall, ECCOLA produced positive results in this study, the contents of the cards may need adjusting based on PEC2.

Aside from evaluating ECCOLA, this study provides an initial look into writing ethical user stories. Bridging the gap between research and practice in AI ethics has been a recurring challenge in the area, with companies struggling to implement abstract ethical guidelines in practice [2,3]. User stories can help us bridge this gap. Ethical issues should be considered as non-functional requirements among other '-ilities,' such as usability and quality, and user stories can help companies formulate them into such. Although the ECCOLA method resulted in more ethical user stories in this study, it is but one option for supporting the creation of user stories that involve ethical consideration.

User stories traditionally place emphasis on Functional Requirements (FR) over Non-Functional Requirements (NFR) [22]. Depicting NFRs as User Stories has been suggested to include certain added challenges compared to FRs, such as that NFRs are not backlog items themselves, but rather constraints on development that are defined in the acceptance criteria for multiple backlog items[4],

---

[4] https://www.scaledagileframework.com/nonfunctional-requirements/.

and being solution-wide, they may conflict with the user story requirement of independence[5]. The use of user stories in defining NFRs is not a novel concept, but the perceived difficulties taken into account, the creation of NFR user stories in this paper can be deemed successful.

Indeed, this study serves as Proof-of-Concept for ethical user stories. Using ECCOLA, developer teams were able to produce non-functional user stories that received high scores in INVEST (a framework for evaluating user stories). To facilitate the implementation of ethics in different context, such as AI ethics, formulating ethical issues into user stories can go a long way in making ethical issues tangible. Industry expert Mike Cohn posited that producing non-functional user stories is challenging but possible[6], and our results seem to support this idea in the case of ethics as well, at least from the point of view of INVEST.

Future studies should look further into how ethics could be more easily transformed into requirements in SE. While user stories provide one possible avenue for doing so, other alternatives are also worth investigating. If the challenge in implementing ethics in practice (AI ethics or otherwise) is that ethical principles are difficult to translate into code and action, we should look into tools that developers are familiar with in order to make this process more accessible for those working hands-on with these systems.

Acknowledgments. The authors would like to thank the students for their active participation in the experiment. The authors also gratefully acknowledge being funded by three Business Finland research projects: Sea4Value Fairway, APPIA, and AMALIA-2020.

References

1. Jobin, A., Ienca, M., Vayena, E.: The global landscape of AI ethics guidelines. Nat. Mach. Intell. **1**(9), 389–399 (2019)
2. Vakkuri, V., Kemell, K.K., Kultanen, J., Abrahamsson, P.: The current state of industrial practice in artificial intelligence ethics. IEEE Softw. **37**, 50–57 (2020)
3. Mittelstadt, B.: Principles alone cannot guarantee ethical AI. Nat. Mach. Intell. **1**, 1–7 (2019)
4. Miller, K.W., Larson, D.K.: Agile software development: human values and culture. IEEE Technol. Soc. Mag. **24**(4), 36–42 (2005)
5. Judy, K.H.: Agile principles and ethical conduct. In: 2009 42nd Hawaii International Conference on System Sciences. IEEE (2009)
6. Friedman, B., Kahn, P.H., Borning, A.: Value sensitive design and information systems. In: The Handbook of Information and Computer Ethics, pp. 69–101 (2008)
7. Nathan, L.P., Friedman, B., Klasnja, P., Kane, S.K., Miller, J.K.: Envisioning systemic effects on persons and society throughout interactive system design. In: Proceedings of the 7th ACM Conference on Designing Interactive Systems (2008)

---

[5] https://www.linkedin.com/pulse/how-can-agile-teams-capture-non-functional-phil-robinson/.

[6] https://www.mountaingoatsoftware.com/blog/non-functional-requirements-as-user-stories.

8. Andrews, A.A., Pradhan, A.S.: Ethical issues in empirical software engineering: the limits of policy. Empir. Softw. Eng. **6**(2), 105–110 (2001). https://doi.org/10.1023/A:1011442319273

9. McNamara, A., Smith, J., Murphy-Hill, E.: Does ACM's code of ethics change ethical decision making in software development? In: Proceedings of the 2018 26th ACM Joint Meeting on European Software Engineering Conference and Symposium on the Foundations of Software Engineering, pp. 729–733 (2018)

10. Vakkuri, V., Kemell, K.K., Abrahamsson, P.: ECCOLA: a method for implementing ethically aligned AI systems. In: Proceedings of the 46th Euromicro Conference on Software Engineering and Advanced Applications, (SEAA2020), pp. 195–204. IEEE (2020)

11. Cohn, M.: User stories applied for agile software development. In: Cohn, M. (ed.) 13th ed. Pearson Education Inc., Indiana (2009)

12. Dimitrijevic, S., Jovanović, J., Devedžić, V.: A comparative study of software tools for user story management. Inf. Softw. Technol. **57**, 352–368 (2015). Mihailo Pupin Institute, Volgina 15, Belgrade, Serbia; FON, School of Business Administration, University of Belgrade, Jove Ilića 154. Belgrade, Serbia

13. Abrahamsson, P., Salo, O., Ronkainen, J., Warsta, J.: Agile software development methods: review and analysis. Proc. Espoo **2002**, 3–107 (2002)

14. Cohn, M.L., Sim, S.E., Lee, C.P.: What counts as software process? Negotiating the boundary of software work through artifacts and conversation. Comput. Support. Cooper. Work (CSCW) **18**(56), 401 (2009). https://doi.org/10.1007/s10606-009-9100-4

15. Suwa, M., Gero, J.S., Purcell, T.: The roles of sketches in early conceptual design processes. In: Proceedings of Twentieth Annual Meeting of the Cognitive Science Society, pp. 1043–1048. Lawrence Erlbaum Hillsdale, New Jersey (1998)

16. Rugg, G., McGeorge, P.: The sorting techniques: a tutorial paper on card sorts, picture sorts and item sorts. Exp. Syst. **14**, 80–93 (1997)

17. Bers, M.U.: Coding as a Playground: Programming and Computational Thinking in the Early Childhood Classroom. Routledge, Abingdon (2020)

18. Papatheocharous, E., Nyfjord, J., Papageorgiou, E.: Fuzzy cognitive maps as decision support tools for investigating critical agile adoption factors. In: Fitzgerald, B., Conboy, K., Power, K., Valerdi, R., Morgan, L., Stol, K.-J. (eds.) LESS 2013. LNBIP, vol. 167, pp. 180–193. Springer, Heidelberg (2013). https://doi.org/10.1007/978-3-642-44930-7_12

19. Wohlin, C., Runeson, P., Höst, M., Ohlsson, M.C., Regnell, B., Wesslén, A.: Experimentation in Software Engineering. Springer, Heidelberg (2012). https://doi.org/10.1007/978-3-642-29044-2

20. Wiesche, M., Jurisch, M.C., Yetton, P.W., Krcmar, H.: Grounded theory methodology in information systems research. MIS Q. **41**(3), 685–701 (2017)

21. Höst, M., Regnell, B., Wohlin, C.: Using students as subjects-a comparative study of students and professionals in lead-time impact assessment. Empir. Softw. Eng. **5**(3), 201–214 (2000). https://doi.org/10.1023/A:1026586415054

22. Behutiye, W., Karhapää, P., Costal, D., Oivo, M., Franch, X.: Non-functional requirements documentation in agile software development: challenges and solution proposal. In: Felderer, M., Méndez Fernández, D., Turhan, B., Kalinowski, M., Sarro, F., Winkler, D. (eds.) PROFES 2017. LNCS, vol. 10611, pp. 515–522. Springer, Cham (2017). https://doi.org/10.1007/978-3-319-69926-4_41

Open Access This chapter is licensed under the terms of the Creative Commons Attribution 4.0 International License (http://creativecommons.org/licenses/by/4.0/), which permits use, sharing, adaptation, distribution and reproduction in any medium or format, as long as you give appropriate credit to the original author(s) and the source, provide a link to the Creative Commons license and indicate if changes were made.

The images or other third party material in this chapter are included in the chapter's Creative Commons license, unless indicated otherwise in a credit line to the material. If material is not included in the chapter's Creative Commons license and your intended use is not permitted by statutory regulation or exceeds the permitted use, you will need to obtain permission directly from the copyright holder.

Process Assessment

Setting the Scope for a New Agile Assessment Model: Results of an Empirical Study

Doruk Tuncel[1]([envelope]), Christian Körner[1], and Reinhold Plösch[2]

[1] Siemens AG, Munich, Germany
doruk.tuncel@siemens.com
[2] Johannes Kepler University Linz, Linz, Austria

Abstract. Agile software development methods have been increasingly adopted by many organizations at different organizational levels. Whether named agile adoption, agile transition, agile transformation, digital transformation or new ways of working, the success of embracing this change process mostly remains uncertain. This is primarily because there are many ways of evaluating success. Based on the existing agile assessment models, we developed a model of principles with associated practice clusters that serves as a core for a new agile assessment model that is capable of assessing agile organizations at different scale. Towards our ultimate goal to establish a lightweight, context-sensitive agile maturity model, we validated our initial findings in an expert interview study to identify improvement points, and ensure the at hand model's applicability, coherence and relevance. The results of the interview study show that the structure as well as the content of our assessment model fits with the experts' expectations and experience.

Keywords: Agile · Maturity assessment · Process improvement

1 Introduction

Agile software development methodology has been a well investigated topic over the past two decades. Its potential towards enabling more lean and customer oriented value creation processes makes it valuable for almost any organization. On the other hand, it is known that the success and potential impact of agile software development methodology is dependent on how it is put in practice. While it is clear that merely applying certain practices comes short in reaping the value of agile methodology, enforcing it to inappropriate organizational contexts or considering it as a silver bullet generates more harm than they help. In order to enable contextually appropriate adoptions, one important criterion is identifying the current state of an organization. Contextual appropriateness itself is a function of culture, complexity of problems at hand, form of the value to be delivered and potentially many other aspects. Therefore, in

© The Author(s) 2021
P. Gregory et al. (Eds.): XP 2021, LNBIP 419, pp. 55–70, 2021.
https://doi.org/10.1007/978-3-030-78098-2_4

order to evaluate an organization's current state with respect to the application of agile software development methodology, manifold aspects are required to be rigorously assessed. Yet, the questions including but not limited to how to structure such an assessment model so that it provides enough flexibility to be applicable to different organizational contexts, which aspects to consider in the evaluation without compromising from practical applicability, how to ensure objectivity of the results, how to identify improvement areas and guide organizations towards those improvement areas remain unanswered. Though there exist multitude of models and various methodologies towards achieving this goal, the existing models mostly lack both meticulous scientific and industrial validation, practical applicability and contextual appropriateness.

Our aim with this research endeavour is to tackle this unsolved, complex problem, without compromising from the aforementioned essential attributes. Tuncel et al. [1] state that there could be two approaches for model development. Based on our experience in evaluating the process maturity of development organizations, we could develop an assessment model for the agile software development methodology context. Or, we could assess existing agile maturity assessment models, identify their valuable components and concepts, learn from their mistakes and develop a model based on the existing scientific body of knowledge. We have been pursuing the latter approach. In this paper, we mainly explain the process of identifying five principles derived from the Agile Manifesto [2] as one of those valuable components of the existing assessment models. These are the condensed pillars of agile software development methodology, which are ideally capable of reflecting the reality of an organization with respect to their agility. Following up on this, we discuss the practice clusters we establish within each of these principle pillars. These principles and clusters in the end, form the structural boundaries of the proposed assessment model. In this process itself, we aim to act agile and iterate over the model elements multiple times. In this paper, we share the results of this first iteration, which is provided by means of expert interviews. Other parts of the assessment model, e.g., the questions for each cluster as well as the assessment and aggregation model are out of scope for this paper. In order to investigate the importance, relevance and completeness of the consolidated principles and clusters within this first iteration, we formulated the following research questions:

- RQ1: Do the pillars of principles sufficiently cover the relevant aspects of agility in practice?
- RQ2: Do the clusters of a principle sufficiently operationalize the principle?
- RQ3: Does the importance of clusters differ considering the organizational levels?

This paper is organized as follows. In Sect. 2 we provide the necessary background information in the theory behind assessment model construction, and summarize front-line studies that provide an assessment model. In Sect. 3, first, we elaborate on the research methodology. Second, establish the landscape for the structure of the proposed agile assessment model. Third, we discuss the validation procedure of the presented elements of the proposed agile assessment model. In Sect. 4, we share the results of the interview and objectively refer to the outcomes of the answers. In Sect. 5, we reflect on the results, share our key findings and discuss the potential threats to validity and our approach towards overcoming these limitations. Finally, in Sect. 6, we summarize our research and provide an outlook to the potential next steps to be taken.

2   Related Work

As discussed in Sect. 1, developing an agile assessment model that does not lack essential attributes is a challenging endeavour and there have been attempts towards this direction. It is important to highlight that, whether an assessment model or a maturity model, these models consist of multiple components: an overall structure such as which subject areas are to be asked for in an assessment, elements to look for within those subject areas, questions to find out about the state of these elements, a method for calculating the leveling structure and an aggregation mechanism. Since the scope of our research is establishing and validating the initial component mentioned above, this section discusses first, the existing studies that are relevant for establishing a structure for an assessment model, then, the pioneer studies that offer such a model structure themselves.

2.1   Model Development Approaches

De Bruin et al. [3] propose a structured generic framework for developing a maturity model. The framework consists of six distinct phases of model development, namely: *Scope, Design, Populate, Test, Deploy* and *Maintain*. Then, they discuss each of these phases in detail by means of exemplifying them over two well-established models. It is reflected by the authors that, the scope setting procedure of the model is followed by the actual design, both of which occur prior to populating the model.

Becker et al. [4] establish an eight step procedure for developing maturity models. This procedure provides not only the distinct phases but also the activity flow and the logic to be followed throughout the development process. The authors provide eight requirements for maturity model development, which are derived from the design science research guidelines provided by Hevner et al. [5]. The study highlights the importance of starting the model development procedure by comparing the model to be developed against the existing models, as well as following an iterative procedure for the entire development process.

Wangenheim, von et al. [6] highlight the relevance of the process of creating software process capability/maturity models (SPCMMs) for the field of software engineering. This relevance is motivated by means of discussing how harmful can the misuse of SPCMMs be for the organizations. Authors provide five distinct phases as *Knowledge identification, Knowledge specification, Knowledge refinement, Knowledge usage* and *Knowledge evolution*. These phases encompass total of sixteen steps including but not limited to defining the scope, developing a draft, validating the draft. It is explicitly mentioned that sound theoretical basis and proper evaluations of the models with respect to validity, reliability and generalizability are lacking in most of the models. This study concludes by noting the need for methodological support to enable model validations.

Maier et al. [7] mention the importance of maturity grids in terms of their capacity to enabling organizational capability assessments. Upon reviewing twenty four different grid structures, authors provide guiding reference points for maturity grid development and define four phases, and thirteen decision points corresponding to these phases. These four phases are *Planning*, *Development*, *Evaluation* and *Maintenance*. Moreover, they provide the applicable decision options for each of these decision points.

2.2   Assessment Models

Sidky et al. [8] propose one of the essential approaches for guiding organizations' adoption process of agile practices. To achieve that, authors define an agile adoption framework consisting of two components: The *agile measurement index* and the *four stage process* that together provide assistance for adopting agile practices. The provided measurement index is formed by agile *levels*, *principles*, *practices* and *indicators*. Five principles of the measurement index are the condensed formulations of twelve agile principles of the Agile Manifesto. Practices are the elements falling in the intersecting cells of the Level-Principle matrix. Five levels of on the other hand provide the different stages of adoption. The four stage process utilizes this measurement index. The model is explicitly highlighting the importance of *tailorability* of the five levels, by describing the challenges behind reaching a consensus on the assignment of practices to the levels. It is concluded that the framework received overall positive feedback, yet, has significant room for improvement.

Qumer and Henderson-Sellers [9] define an agile software solution framework that is built upon an agile conceptual aspect model, that is accompanied by an agile toolkit and a four dimensional analytical tool. Authors define a method core comprising five aspects, namely: *Agility*, *People*, *Process*, *Product*, *Tools*, and an *Abstraction* aspect to reflect an agile software development methodology. While the agile toolkit consists of seven main components, the provided analytical tool focuses on the following four dimensions: *Method scope*, *Agility characterization*, *Agile value characterization* and *Software process characterization*. To complement these two components of the framework for process adoption, authors establish the Agile Adoption and Improvement Model (AAIM). AAIM is built on the following three agile blocks: *Prompt*, *Crux* and *Apex* and six agile levels. This study emphasizes the relevance of having a model that is applicable to different situation specific scenarios in the domain of software engineering.

Fontana et al. [10] suggest a framework for maturing in agile software development that has its roots in the complex adaptive systems theory. While explicitly mentioning ambidexterity as a fundamental attribute towards maturity, the provided framework focuses on the outcomes rather than prescribing practices. The core role of people in software development organizations is explicitly acknowledged within the study. The contrast between exploitation and exploration is represented as an important element for balancing the specific outcomes and adopting new practices. Further, by means of a cross-case analysis, the authors name six pursued outcomes: *Practices, Team, Deliveries, Requirements, Product* and *Customer*. In conclusion, this study draws attention to the importance of allowing context-specific practices in the maturing process without compromising from the agile values.

3   An Assessment Model Proposal

As the focal point of this research, this section elaborates on the methodology behind the development procedure of the proposed agile assessment model, the overall structure of the model along with the definitions of core model elements. Finally, without going into the detailed results, it discusses the validation phase of the model.

3.1   Methodology

In order to construct a scientifically founded agile assessment model that is capable of serving the needs of the industry, we have formulated a fine combination of research methodologies that enables us to perform the necessary research activities in an effective manner. Towards this goal, we have initiated our research with a *Systematic Literature Review* based on backwards and forward snowballing described by Wohlin [11], the systematic literature review study allowed us identifying reusable components of the previously conducted researches, and the already established assessment models. We have published the results of this research in [1]. Following up on these research results, we conduct *Design Science Research* in accordance with Hevner et al. [5]. As described by the authors, developing the design artifact is the core activity of the design science research. In the context of our research, building the overall structure of the proposed agile assessment model maps to this core activity. This core activity is to be followed by an *Action Design Research* per Sein et al. [12]. Proceeding with an action design research implies conducting an *intervention*, however, it is out of the scope of this research and is not discussed to great extent.

3.2   Model Structure

The proposed agile assessment model consists of two fundamental elements: *principles* and *clusters*. Principles are, as the name suggests, a set of abstract notions that are essential to the agile software development methodology. Clusters on the other hand, are the semantic classifications of the practices of agile software development methodology within the principles. The proposed model has five principles and eighteen clusters within those principles. Its structure is established by the following procedure: Initially, principles that are capable of capturing and reflecting the agile reality of an organization are extracted from the twelve notable agile assessment models. These twelve models are the prominent models among the 40+ models we have examined in our previous research [1]. While establishing these principles, we considered the critical views on the principles of the Agile Manifesto in an alignment with Meyer [13] and the degree of acceptance of these principles in the scientific literature. As a result, for the initial structure of the proposed model, a condensed set of five principles that are essentially derived from the Agile Manifesto are constructed as-is, based on the well received proposal of Sidky et al. [8]. Following that, the practices of agile software development methodology that are either implicitly or explicitly mentioned within these twelve models analyzed in our literature study are systematically extracted. Because some of these twelve models (e.g., Turetken et al. [14]) build up on one other (e.g., Sidky et al. [8]), or some (e.g., Patel and Ramachandran [15]) reuse certain practices such as *"User stories are written."* from another (e.g., Nawrocki et al. [16]), the identified duplicates in collected practices are discarded. Additionally, since the scope of the proposed model is beyond any agile software development framework, in the cases where models developed specifically towards a certain framework (e.g., Turetken et al. [14]), the framework specific practices are as well left out. In the end, to form the preliminary structure of the proposed agile assessment model in this paper, the remaining practices were classified under five principles, and with respect to their conceptual proximity to each other, were clustered underneath those five practices. As discussed in Sect. 2, establishing this overarching model structure encompass the initial steps of the model development. The resulting structure can be depicted in Fig. 1.

Principles				
Embrace change to deliver customer value	**Plan and deliver software frequently**	**Human centricity**	**Technical excellence**	**Customer collaboration**
Lean Mindset	Value Delivery Planning	Psychological Safety	Testing	Customer Involvement
		Effective Communication	Continuous Improvement	
Change Orientation		Unit Empowerment		
Iterative & Incremental Value Delivery	Value Delivery Actualization	Unit Collaboration	Design & Coding Practices	Customer Decision Making
		Unit Autonomy	Data Driven Dev & Ops	
Flexibility in Value Delivery		Personal Growth		

(Row label: Clusters)

Fig. 1. Initial structure of the proposed model

3.3 Validation

As it is mentioned in Sect. 1, in order to obtain critical feedback on the proposed model structure, we conducted an interview study. The interview study involved six domain experts in agile software methodologies. The profiles of the interviewed experts are diversified from senior software developers, architects to senior agile coaches, senior process consultants to senior technical team leads, working in different development organizations, least of them having 7+ years of experience in the domain. The validation interviews focused on receiving feedback with respect to the completeness of the five agile principles, and the consolidated set of eighteen clusters positioned under these five principles. During the interviews, for each cluster, experts were systematically asked to evaluate 1) how well does the cluster fit to the principle it is positioned within, 2) whether the cluster is found to be fit into different principles as well, 3) whether the importance of a cluster vary with respect to different organizational scales, and 4) whether a clusters requires either a split or a merge with another cluster to establish a proper level of granularity. Following on top of these cluster specific questions, experts were additionally asked to comment on the completeness of these five principles with respect to their capacity to reflect the agile reality of an organization, as well as of these eighteen clusters with respect to their capacity to completely reflect the principle they are positioned under. In order to establish the context of a principle and a cluster, descriptions of each cluster (e.g., Value Delivery: The organization uses proper methods, techniques and tools for planning the delivery of value by means of realized user stories, epics or features.) are provided along with certain exemplary aspects (e.g., Release Planning, Collaborative Planning, Backlog Management, User Stories) to be associated with that cluster. While the results of this validation procedure and the key observations are reflected in Sects. 4 and 5 respectively, the complete list of cluster descriptions and exemplary aspects can be found at https://bit.ly/3eKj4im.

4 Results

The proposed model structure consists of five principles and eighteen clusters. In this section, first, we present the achieved results, grouped by each of the five principles. For each principle, the expert responses regarding the clusters within that principle are reflected. Particularly, the responses regarding the importance of a cluster with respect to the organizational scale are visualized by Figs. 2, 3, 4, 5 and 6. Second, we share the results regarding the overall structure of the proposed model under Sect. 4.6. Due to space limitations, results with relatively low information are provided at https://bit.ly/3eKj4im.

In the following figures, S refers to small organizational units such as agile teams, M refers to the medium level organizational units, which can be interpreted as project or product organizations consisting of multiple teams, and L refers to large organizational units. Depending on an organizational context, it is possible to perceive this level as the top level management of development organizations, where orchestration of multiple medium level organizational units are required. In agile frameworks addressing scale (e.g., SAFe, LeSS, Nexus) scaling starts from single teams, reach multiple teams or the entire organization. In order to abstract from specific agile frameworks and in order to avoid confusion regarding the terms, we use these more abstract terms small, medium and large. The coding mechanism of results in the following figures are as follows: *Very Important:* 5, *Important:* 4, *Neither/Nor:* 3, *Unimportant:* 2, *Very Unimportant:* 1 and *I don't know:* -, while E1 to E6 refer to the interviewed experts.

4.1 Embrace Change to Deliver Customer Value Principle

The results indicate that "Lean Mindset" cluster is an overarching cluster. This implies that it should be reflected under multiple principles. In fact, all of the interviewees explicitly stated that "Lean Mindset" should be reflected under at least two other principles. Additionally, interviewees highlight that the difference between the mindset and actual practice may not always be clear, in a way that one can have a lean or lean-agile mindset, yet fail to practice this mindset in real life scenarios. When it comes to "Change Orientation" one important point is, except one of the interviewees, there is an agreement that "Change Orientation" as well should be reflected under multiple principles. On the other hand, "Iterative and Incremental Value Delivery" is expected to be found also under "Planning and Delivering Software Frequently". This is highlighted by two of the interviewees by the response "Does not fit well", one of which also noted that the importance of this cluster is less when larger organizational scales are considered. Although there is no agreement with respect to its fitness to the principle it is positioned under, "Flexibility in Value Delivery" is found to be fit also under "Technical Excellence" by half of the interviewees.

	E1			E2			E3			E4			E5			E6		
	S	M	L	S	M	L	S	M	L	S	M	L	S	M	L	S	M	L
Lean Mindset	4	5	4	5	5	4	5	5	5	5	5	5	5	4	5	5	5	5
Change Orientation	5	4	4	5	5	4	5	5	5	5	5	5	5	5	5	4	4	4
Iterative & Incremental Value Delivery	4	5	5	5	5	5	5	4	3	5	5	4	5	5	4	5	5	5
Flexibility in Value Delivery	4	4	4	4	3	5	4	4	4	5	5	5	3	4	5	4	4	4

Expert = E, Small = S, Medium = M, Large = L   *Very Important = 5, Important = 4, Neither/Nor = 3, Unimportant = 2, Very Unimportant = 1, I don't know = "-"*

Fig. 2. Embrace change to deliver customer value

4.2 Plan and Deliver Software Frequently Principle

Based on the interview study outcomes, there are two particular observations regarding this principle. First, except one of the interviewees, both the cluster "Value Delivery Planning" and "Value Delivery Actualization" are found to be "Fit Very Well" in this principle. Second, all of the interviewees found

"Value Delivery Actualization" to be the most *important* for "Small" scale organizational units. While there is no general agreement about under which other principles to reflect these two clusters, an important result can be that "Value Delivery Actualization" is mostly perceived as in relation with "Technical Excellence", while "Value Delivery Planning" is associated with "Embrace Change to Delivery Customer Value".

	E1			E2			E3			E4			E5			E6		
	S	M	L	S	M	L	S	M	L	S	M	L	S	M	L	S	M	L
Value Delivery Planning	4	4	4	5	5	4	3	4	5	5	5	5	4	4	4	4	5	5
Value Delivery Actualization	5	4	5	5	4	3	5	4	3	5	5	3	5	5	5	5	4	4
Expert = E, Small = S, Medium = M, Large = L						*Very Important = 5, Important = 4, Neither/Nor = 3, Unimportant = 2, Very Unimportant = 1, I don't know = "-"*												

Fig. 3. Plan and deliver software frequently

4.3 Human Centricity Principle

One particular shared comment was that it is not easy to make a clear distinction between the clusters "Unit Empowerment" and "Unit Autonomy". Consequently, the idea to merge two clusters was prominently mentioned. Further, human related aspects were referred to as so essential yet overlooked aspects by multiple experts. As it can be observed from Fig. 4, all clusters are found to be at least "Important", especially on the scale of small organizational units.

	E1			E2			E3			E4			E5			E6		
	S	M	L	S	M	L	S	M	L	S	M	L	S	M	L	S	M	L
Psychological Safety	4	4	4	5	5	4	4	4	4	5	5	5	5	3	3	4	4	4
Effective Communication	5	4	4	5	5	5	4	4	4	5	4	4	5	3	3	5	5	5
Unit Empowerment	5	4	4	5	5	5	-	-	-	4	5	5	5	4	4	4	4	4
Unit Collaboration	4	4	4	5	5	5	4	4	4	5	5	3	5	5	5	4	4	4
Unit Autonomy	4	4	4	5	4	4	-	-	-	4	5	5	4	4	4	4	4	4
Personal Growth	5	4	3	5	5	3	5	5	5	5	4	4	-	-	-	5	5	5
Expert = E, Small = S, Medium = M, Large = L						*Very Important = 5, Important = 4, Neither/Nor = 3, Unimportant = 2, Very Unimportant = 1, I don't know = "-"*												

Fig. 4. Human centricity

4.4 Technical Excellence Principle

Regarding the four clusters under this principle, primary remark is that "Continuous Improvement" cluster is perceived as "Very Important" by almost all of the experts, irrespective of the organizational scale. Another important observation is that this cluster is expected to additionally be positioned under "Embrace Change to Deliver Customer Value", by all but one of the experts.

	E1			E2			E3			E4			E5			E6		
	S	M	L	S	M	L	S	M	L	S	M	L	S	M	L	S	M	L
Testing	5	5	4	5	5	2	5	4	3	5	4	3	4	4	4	5	5	4
Continuous Improvement	4	4	5	5	5	5	5	5	5	5	5	5	5	5	5	5	5	5
Design and Coding Best Practices	5	4	4	5	2	2	5	2	2	5	3	3	5	4	4	5	4	4
Data Driven Development & Operations	4	4	4	5	4	2	3	4	5	5	5	4	5	5	4	5	5	5

Expert = E, Small = S, Medium = M, Large = L   Very Important = 5, Important = 4, Neither/Nor = 3, Unimportant = 2, Very Unimportant = 1, I don't know = "-"

Fig. 5. Technical excellence

4.5 Customer Collaboration Principle

While both of the clusters under this principle are found to be "Fit Very Well" except one case for "Customer Involvement" where it is evaluated as "Fits Well"; half of the interviewee responses indicate an association with "Embrace Change to Deliver Customer Value" for both of these clusters. When it comes to the importance of a cluster with respect to the organizational scale, a pattern can be observed in Fig. 6. Specifically when the interviewees posed an answer, all of them agree that "Customer Decision Making" cluster is "Very Important" for middle level and larger organizational units, whereas its importance decrease as the organizational scale gets smaller.

	E1			E2			E3			E4			E5			E6		
	S	M	L	S	M	L	S	M	L	S	M	L	S	M	L	S	M	L
Customer Involvement	4	5	4	4	5	4	5	4	4	5	3	2	5	5	5	4	5	5
Customer Decision-Making	3	-	-	4	5	5	5	3	5	5	5	5	5	5	5	4	5	5

Expert = E, Small = S, Medium = M, Large = L   Very Important = 5, Important = 4, Neither/Nor = 3, Unimportant = 2, Very Unimportant = 1, I don't know = "-"

Fig. 6. Customer collaboration

4.6 Overall Structure

Figure 7 shows that the different backgrounds of the interviewees provide certain patterns in the results. Particularly, the importance of a cluster with respect to different organizational scales can be captured by the color transitions among the cells. The experts with consulting or coaching roles for example, seem to put more importance on the small organizational units, than the experts with software implementation focus. Based on the collected responses, the initial model structure is to be updated with "Change Orientation" and "Continuous Improvement" becoming overarching concepts. Further, "Unit Empowerment" and "Unit Autonomy" clusters are to be merged.

5 Discussion

Based on the results of our interview study, this section discusses the important findings under two groups: general findings and cluster specific findings. Then, it provides answers to the research questions. Finally, in Fig. 8, we share the updated structure of the proposed model after an iteration over the discussed findings. General findings touch to the important remarks with respect to the overall structure of the proposed model, whereas cluster specific findings reflect some of the important patterns observed regarding the clusters. Figure 7 is formed by merging the aforementioned tables in their order of presentation. This consolidated view is provided to allow the reader to observe certain vertical patterns that can be associated with expert profiles. The complete table reflecting the fitness of each cluster with respect to the principles they are positioned under, as well as whether they also fit under multiple principles can be found at the URL provided in the Sect. 4.

	E1			E2			E3			E4			E5			E6			AVG		
	S	M	L	S	M	L	S	M	L	S	M	L	S	M	L	S	M	L	S	M	L
C1.1	4	5	4	5	5	4	5	5	5	5	5	5	5	4	5	5	5	5	4.83	4.83	4.67
C1.2	5	4	4	5	5	4	5	5	5	5	5	5	5	5	5	4	4	4	4.83	4.67	4.50
C1.3	4	5	5	5	5	5	5	4	3	5	5	4	5	5	4	5	5	5	4.83	4.83	4.33
C1.4	4	4	4	4	3	5	4	4	4	5	5	5	3	4	5	4	4	4	4.00	4.00	4.50
C2.1	4	4	4	5	5	4	3	4	5	5	5	5	4	4	4	4	5	5	4.17	4.50	4.50
C2.2	5	4	5	5	4	3	5	4	3	5	5	3	5	5	5	5	4	4	5.00	4.33	3.83
C3.1	4	4	4	5	5	4	4	4	4	5	5	5	5	3	3	4	4	4	4.50	4.17	4.00
C3.2	5	4	4	5	5	5	4	4	4	5	4	4	5	3	3	5	5	5	4.83	4.17	4.17
C3.3	5	4	4	5	5	5	-	-	-	4	5	5	5	4	4	4	4	4	4.60	4.40	4.40
C3.4	4	4	4	5	5	5	4	4	4	5	5	3	5	5	5	4	4	4	4.50	4.50	4.17
C3.5	4	4	4	5	4	4	-	-	-	4	5	5	4	4	4	4	4	4	4.20	4.20	4.20
C3.6	5	4	3	5	5	3	5	5	5	5	4	4	-	-	-	5	5	5	5.00	4.60	4.00
C4.1	5	5	4	5	5	2	5	4	3	5	4	3	4	4	4	5	5	4	4.83	4.50	3.33
C4.2	4	4	5	5	5	5	5	5	5	5	5	5	5	5	5	5	5	5	4.83	4.83	5.00
C4.3	5	4	4	5	2	2	5	2	2	5	3	3	5	4	4	5	4	4	5.00	3.17	3.17
C4.4	4	4	4	5	4	2	3	4	5	5	5	4	5	5	4	5	5	5	4.50	4.50	4.00
C5.1	4	5	4	4	5	4	5	4	4	5	3	2	5	5	5	4	5	5	4.50	4.50	4.00
C5.2	3	-	-	4	5	5	5	3	5	5	5	5	5	5	5	4	5	5	4.33	4.60	5.00

Fig. 7. Importance of clusters with respect to the organizational scales

5.1 General Findings

Both Principle and Cluster Completeness are Highlighted. Although some additional remarks and suggestions were provided by the interviewees, all of the experts appreciated the completeness of the model elements.

Descriptive Texts and Exemplary Aspects Help Defining the Boundaries. Experts provided positive feedback on being given clear cluster descriptions, example practices, artifacts and aspects associated with clusters so that they can easily establish the context of a cluster.

There Is No "One, All Agreed Positioning" of the Clusters. The concepts and practices of the agile software development methodology are perceived very differently based on the background and experience of the individuals.

In Fig. 7, we observe that most of the average cluster values are greater than or equal to *4.00*. This is expected as the underlying elements of the model are extracted from the scientific literature. Where the average values fall under *4.00*, it can be observed that it is caused by the distance of the larger organizational units to the implementation level concerns of software development. Even though there is no agreement on a single model structure, the experts provided great insights towards improving the proposed model to capture the reality of an organization. These findings show that the initially proposed model structure was too simplistic for reflecting the reality.

5.2 Cluster Specific Findings

Technical Excellence Clusters Act as a Prerequisite for Frequent Delivery. Technical excellence is mostly interpreted as the first step towards making frequent delivery possible, as frequent delivery implies a certain level of automation, and involves making architectural decisions.

Technical Excellence Clusters are Perceived as Relatively Less Important for Higher Level Organizational Units. As technical excellence clusters are reflecting more the implementation level concerns, their importance is perceived to decrease as the scale of the organization increase. The lower importance score of the technical clusters on higher levels were therefore not surprising for us.

Customer Collaboration Clusters Contribute to Planning. Especially for large organizational units, customer collaboration is commented to be very important, and is perceived as an enabler of the delivery planning activities.

Human Centricity Clusters are Well Perceived. In almost all of the interviews, human centricity clusters received positive feedback. It is often commented that, people play a central role almost in any process, and if the aim of a model is to capture the reality with respect to agile, people should never be overlooked.

RQ1: Do the Pillars of Principles Sufficiently Cover the Relevant Aspects of Agility in Practice? The principles are evaluated to be complete in terms of reflecting the world of agile. Only one of the experts stated that communicating the purpose of agile transformation and the role of management should be reflected in this structure more explicitly.

RQ2: Do the Clusters of a Principle Sufficiently Operationalize the Principle? The clusters are evaluated to be sufficient and complete in terms of spanning the principles they are positioned under. Only one of the experts mentioned that the budgeting aspects may be necessary to position under a principle appropriately.

RQ3: Does the Importance of Clusters Differ Considering the Organizational Levels? From Fig. 7, we observe that the importance of clusters differ with respect to the organizational scale. This is an important finding as it can help conducting contextually appropriate assessments, where the scale of the organization is considered as a component of the organizational context.

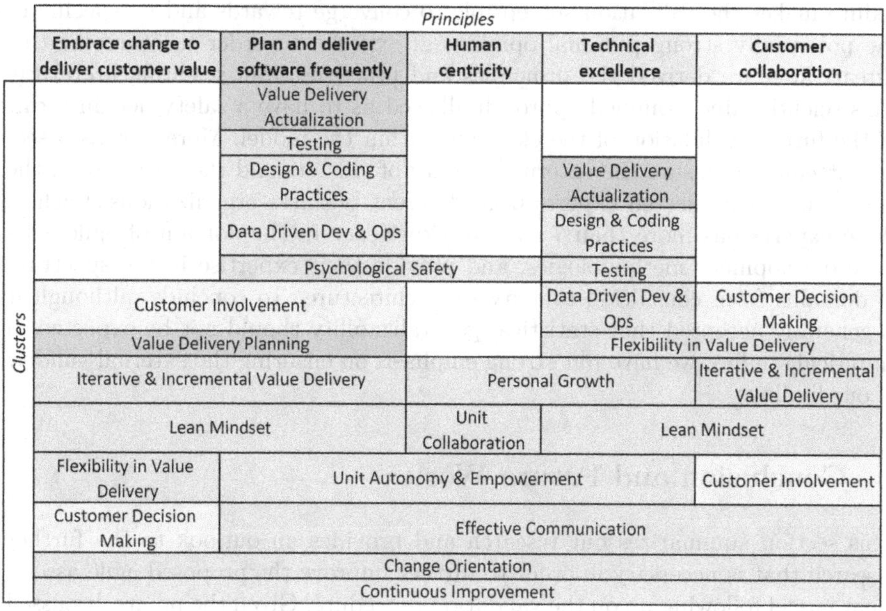
Principles
Embrace change to deliver customer value
Plan and deliver software frequently
Human centricity
Technical excellence
Customer collaboration
Clusters
Value Delivery Actualization
Testing
Design & Coding Practices
Data Driven Dev & Ops
Value Delivery Actualization
Design & Coding Practices
Psychological Safety
Testing
Customer Involvement
Data Driven Dev & Ops
Customer Decision Making
Value Delivery Planning
Flexibility in Value Delivery
Iterative & Incremental Value Delivery
Personal Growth
Iterative & Incremental Value Delivery
Lean Mindset
Unit Collaboration
Lean Mindset
Flexibility in Value Delivery
Unit Autonomy & Empowerment
Customer Involvement
Customer Decision Making
Effective Communication
Change Orientation
Continuous Improvement

Fig. 8. Updated structure of the proposed model

5.3 Threats to Validity

In this section, we discuss the validity threats and our attempts to ensure a high quality of research by keeping these threats minimal. We are aware of the four validity threats namely Construct Validity, External Validity, Internal Validity and Reliability as defined, and tailored to the software engineering domain by Yin [17] and Runeson et al. [18] respectively. However, as our methodology is not a case study research, not all four of these validity threats are covered in this section. Rather, we concentrate on the following two aspects as they are found to be more relevant for our methodology:

Construct Validity reflects how properly the examined concept represents the ideas of the researchers. Therefore, should there be any misunderstandings between the researchers and the interviewed parties with respect to the definitions or concepts that are being discussed, they should be addressed. In our interview study, in order to proactively avoid potential misunderstandings, we provided descriptive texts for each cluster, as well as exemplary practices falling under that particular cluster. This approach allowed us to establish the boundaries and the context of the inspected cluster. As our interview partners positively commented on the cluster descriptions and exemplary aspects, we can assume that we were able to properly tackle this threat to validity.

External Validity refers to the generalizability of the derived results from a research activity. In our research, validation of the consolidated agile principles and agile practices is performed by means of expert interviews. This procedure makes the validation susceptible to converge towards and be specific to the potentially strong personal opinions of experts. In order to overcome this threat, first, we derived the principles and practices from scientific literature. This scientifically grounded approach allowed us to have a safety net, in terms of the further validation of the elements within the model. Moreover, as a second attempt to ensure the external validity of clusters and the structure of the model, we have selected experts from different business organizations. Each of these experts has more than 7 years of experience in the domain of agile software development methodologies, and provide their expertise in the spectrum of domains from consulting to software architecture. To conclude, although it is generally accepted that statistical generalizability should not be expected in empirical studies, we have put strong emphasis on ensuring the external validity of our findings.

6   Conclusion and Future Work

This section summarizes our research and provides an outlook to the further research that is necessary in order to further improve the proposed agile assessment model following up on the validation procedure. Given the points discussed under Sect. 4 and Sect. 5, there is an overall positive feedback to the proposed elements of the assessment model, and this provides a promising outlook for the future of our research. Our research motivates the need towards building an agile assessment model based on an in depth, comparative analysis of the existing models. While learning from the relatively weaker aspects of the existing models, we established our model structure based on principles of the Agile Manifesto. The clusters of practices are also reflecting approximately twenty years of scientific analysis of agile software development activities starting from Nawrocki et al. [16], to Laanti [19].

Our endeavour towards iterative and incremental development of this model requires us to frequently consult experts and receive continuous feedback on the evolving elements of the proposed model. As discussed in Sect. 2 to a great extent, establishing the boundaries and the overall structure of the assessment model is an important step of assessment model development which needs to be followed by populating the assessment matrix with practices. In our context, this maps to identifying which practices should go under which clusters, which practices should be discontinued or marked as irrelevant for contemporary development activities of the organizations. In the following steps, it will be necessary to further refine the practice clusters and establish boundaries across the principles for the clusters that are relevant for multiple principles. Once the overall structure such as which subject areas are to be asked for in an assessment, and which elements are to be looked for within those subject areas sufficiently identified, a method for calculating the leveling structure, as well as the appropriate questions to find out about the state of these elements to be looked for need to be clarified. As the next step, we will develop questions for all clusters and validate them with detailed interviews with a focus on completeness and suitability for agile assessments. Upon completing these remaining phases, we will develop an aggregation mechanism so that meaningful outcomes can be retrieved when an assessment is conducted.

These activities are planned as part of an action design research described by Sein et al. [12]. By means of an action design research, we will be able to not only employ the proposed assessment model in real business environment, but also receive feedback regarding the methodology behind the assessment.

References

1. Tuncel, D., Körner, C., Plösch, R.: Comparison of agile maturity models: reflecting the real needs. In: 2020 46th Euromicro Conference on Software Engineering and Advanced Applications (SEAA), pp. 51–58. IEEE (2020)
2. Beck, K., et al.: Manifesto for agile software development (2001)
3. De Bruin, T., Rosemann, M., Freeze, R., Kaulkarni, U.: Understanding the main phases of developing a maturity assessment model. In: Australasian Conference on Information Systems (ACIS), pp. 8–19. Australasian Chapter of the Association for Information Systems (2005)
4. Becker, J., Knackstedt, R., Pöppelbuß, J.: Developing maturity models for it management. Bus. Inf. Syst. Eng. 1(3), 213–222 (2009)
5. Hevner, A.R., March, S.T., Park, J., Ram, S.: Design science in information systems research. MIS Quart. 28, 75–105 (2004)
6. von Wangenheim, C.G., Hauck, J.C.R., Zoucas, A., Salviano, C.F., McCaffery, F., Shull, F.: Creating software process capability/maturity models. IEEE Softw. 27(4), 92–94 (2010)
7. Maier, A.M., Moultrie, J., Clarkson, P.J.: Assessing organizational capabilities: reviewing and guiding the development of maturity grids. IEEE Trans. Eng. Manage. 59(1), 138–159 (2011)
8. Sidky, A., Arthur, J., Bohner, S.: A disciplined approach to adopting agile practices: the agile adoption framework. Innovations Syst. Softw. Eng. 3(3), 203–216 (2007)
9. Qumer, A., Henderson-Sellers, B.: A framework to support the evaluation, adoption and improvement of agile methods in practice. J. Syst. Softw. 81(11), 1899–1919 (2008)

10. Fontana, R.M., Meyer, V., Jr., Reinehr, S., Malucelli, A.: Progressive outcomes: a framework for maturing in agile software development. J. Syst. Softw. **102**, 88–108 (2015)
11. Wohlin, C.: Guidelines for snowballing in systematic literature studies and a replication in software engineering. In: Proceedings of the 18th International Conference on Evaluation and Assessment in Software Engineering, pp. 1–10 (2014)
12. Sein, M.K., Henfridsson, O., Purao, S., Rossi, M., Lindgren, R.: Action design research. MIS Quart. **28**, 37–56 (2011)
13. Meyer, B.: Agile! The Good, the Hype and the Ugly. Springer, Heidelberg (2014)
14. Turetken, O., Stojanov, I., Trienekens, J.J.: Assessing the adoption level of scaled agile development: a maturity model for scaled agile framework. J. Softw. Evol. Process **29**(6), e1796 (2017)
15. Patel, C., Ramachandran, M.: Agile maturity model (AMM): a software process improvement framework for agile software development practices. Int. J. Softw. Eng. IJSE **2**(1), 3–28 (2009)
16. Nawrocki, J., Walter, B., Wojciechowski, A.: Toward maturity model for extreme programming. In: Proceedings 27th EUROMICRO Conference. 2001: A Net Odyssey, pp. 233–239. IEEE (2001)
17. Yin, R.K.: Case study research and applications. Sage (2018)
18. Runeson, P., Host, M., Rainer, A., Regnell, B.: Case study research in software engineering: Guidelines and examples. Wiley (2012)
19. Laanti, M.: Agile transformation model for large software development organizations. In: Proceedings of the XP2017 Scientific Workshops, pp. 1–5 (2017)

Open Access This chapter is licensed under the terms of the Creative Commons Attribution 4.0 International License (http://creativecommons.org/licenses/by/4.0/), which permits use, sharing, adaptation, distribution and reproduction in any medium or format, as long as you give appropriate credit to the original author(s) and the source, provide a link to the Creative Commons license and indicate if changes were made.

The images or other third party material in this chapter are included in the chapter's Creative Commons license, unless indicated otherwise in a credit line to the material. If material is not included in the chapter's Creative Commons license and your intended use is not permitted by statutory regulation or exceeds the permitted use, you will need to obtain permission directly from the copyright holder.

Towards a Standardized Questionnaire
for Measuring Agility at Team Level

Hanna Looks[1(✉)], Jannik Fangmann[2], Jörg Thomaschewski[2], María-José Escalona[1],
and Eva-Maria Schön[3]

[1] University of Seville, Seville, Spain
`hanna.looks@iwt2.org, mjescalona@us.es`
[2] University of Applied Sciences Emden/Leer, Emden, Germany
`j.fangmann@ux-researchgroup.com,`
`joerg.thomaschewski@hs-emden-leer.de`
[3] University of Applied Sciences (HAW), Hamburg, Germany
`eva-maria.schoen@haw-hamburg.de`

Abstract. Context: Twenty years after the publication of the agile manifesto, agility is becoming more and more popular in different contexts. Agile values are changing the way people work together and influence people's mindset as well as the culture of organizations. Many organizations have understood that continuous improvement is based on measurement.

Objective: The objective of this paper is to present how agility can be measured at the team level. For this reason, we will introduce our questionnaire for measuring agility, which is based on the agile values of the manifesto.

Method: We developed a questionnaire comprising 36 items that measure the current state of a team's agility in six dimensions (*communicative, change-affine, iterative, self-organized, product-driven* and *improvement-oriented*). This questionnaire has been evaluated with respect to several expert reviews and in a case study.

Results: The questionnaire provides a method for measuring the current state of agility, which takes the individual context of the team into account. Furthermore, our research shows, that this technique enables the user to uncover dysfunctionalities in a team.

Conclusion: Practitioners and organizations can use our questionnaire to optimize collaboration within their teams in terms of agility. In particular, the value delivery of an organization can be increased by optimizing collaboration at the team level. The development of this questionnaire is a continuous learning process with the aim to develop a standardized questionnaire for measuring agility.

Keywords: Agile · Questionnaire · Measurement of agility · Agile values · Team level

1 Introduction

In more and more industries, agile values [1] are changing the way people work together and influence people's mindsets. This can be seen in the increasing spread of agile process models [2]. The establishment of the term Agile in software development began

© The Author(s) 2021
P. Gregory et al. (Eds.): XP 2021, LNBIP 419, pp. 71–85, 2021.
https://doi.org/10.1007/978-3-030-78098-2_5

with the Agile Manifesto in 2001 [3]. As a reaction to the influence of the increasing trend of digitalization in software development, the Agile Manifesto defines the values and principles for a new approach to the development of digital products, which differs from traditional software development [3]. Agile transformation is understood as a development away from traditional process models towards agile process models in the development of digital products [4]. In the 1980s, Takeuchi and Nonaka [5] had already stated that a sequential phases approach to product development is not well suited because of the lack of flexibility. Digitalization leads to an increasing dynamic of user requirements, which in turn leads to ever shorter development cycles and shorter product launch times. These developments impact the way in which users are involved in the development process [4, 6]. In response to these changes, the solution approach postulated in the Agile Manifesto requires a shift in the focus of software development from process and project to people and product [1].

Agility is a mindset that must be transferred to the specific context of its user, and so, strongly depends on the individual situation. The emergence of an agile way of working takes place here in the context of agile transformation through the adaptation of agile values [1]. An important part of the Agile mindset is continuous improvement based on feedback. For this purpose, measurement is pursued in many subject areas. Research has already dealt with the measurement of agility in recent years. Many of the approaches are concerned with measuring the process using artefacts and workflows [7]. However, the Agile values are not taken into account by these approaches. Agile is more than a process; hence it is important to start with people working together to measure agility.

In this paper we present our questionnaire for measuring agility. Our research is guided by the following research question:

'How can agility be measured at the team level?'

Our understanding of agility is influenced by the agile values [1]. We decided to focus on the team level because the team is responsible for value delivery in agile product development [8].

Our questionnaire was developed by means of scientific methods. Therefore, the current state of research in the field of measuring agility must be sufficiently considered. For this reason, a literature review was conducted. This literature review serves as the starting point of the construction process for the questionnaire, which must consistently follow the rules of science in order to be able to make generalizable statements about the reality of experience.

The paper is structured as follows: Sect. 2 provides an overview of related work.

Section 3 presents the research method used to develop the questionnaire to measure agility. Section 4 presents the results including the complete questionnaire. Section 5 discusses the significance of the results and limitations. At the end, Sect. 6 concludes with a summary of this paper and our future research projects.

2   Related Work

We used a literature review to identify models for measuring agility. We looked at models that measure agility across the levels of organization, team, and individual to obtain a comprehensive picture of related work. Furthermore, we analyzed related work in terms of their methodology for measuring agility. The results are presented in the following.

On the one hand, we identified and evaluated seven maturity models [7, 9–14]. to measure agility in the development of digital products. On the other hand, we evaluated two questionnaires [15, 16].

The authors of the models justify their creation primarily with the realization that no suitable model for agile maturity levels had yet been established at the time of creation [7, 11, 14]. In this respect, it is evident that the identified models are in an early phase of development and have not been consistently and actively developed since their creation [17]. So far, none of the maturity models examined has been sufficiently evaluated and empirically proven.

We can conclude that further conceptual and empirical research is required to enable valid application of the models [16, 17]. In general, these publications make it clear that there is a need for structured approaches to support agile transformation. This view is confirmed in other sources [3, 16]. The need for agile transformation support along with the lack of validation of existing models confirms the need for research. The Agile Manifesto was used as a basis for developing the identified maturity models [7, 9, 10]. In general, the determination of the agile maturity level in the identified models is largely independent of the process model; it is based on the basic concept of agility [17]. Although they originated independently, many of the maturity models examined have a comparable structure. However, it can be seen that the maturity models emerged against fundamentally different theoretical backgrounds and intentions [17]. Accordingly, the requirements that must be achieved with increasing maturity levels are strongly related to the individual context in which the models were defined. Therefore, no uniform, hierarchical model of the requirements for agility across the maturity models could be gained from the analysis of the maturity models [14]. In addition to the context-dependent applicability, the different theoretical backgrounds in the creation of the models examined also mean that the results are not comparable across models when applied [17]. Even though all maturity models depict agility and most have a similar number of maturity levels, it cannot be said that users of different models with the same maturity level are equally advanced in the agile transformation.

The questionnaires (see [15, 16]) studied offer an approach to determining progress in agile transformation that is independent of maturity levels. The scales defined by the questionnaires correspond to the construct of process fields in the maturity models. They delineate different sub-areas of the domain of agility from each other [18]. A hierarchical prioritization of the queried agility requirements is, therefore, not necessary.

The analysis of the identified models has shown that the models each show different ways to achieve agile maturity, while the questionnaires aim to determine agile maturity.

3 Research Method

This paper presents our questionnaire for measuring agility at the team level. Our aim is to develop a standardized questionnaire to measure agility. The results of the measurement should enable suitable measures to be derived and prioritized and the agile transformation to be driven forward in a targeted manner, taking into consideration the agile values.

This section first explains the development of the questionnaire. The development of the questionnaire was carried out by considering the research question *'How can agility be measured at the team level?'*. We, therefore, define the requirements below:

- Determining of a representative overall impression of the current state of agility at the team level
- Focusing on agile values independent of the application of methods
- Supporting the agile transformation process
- Covering all dimensions of the concept of agile transformation
- Talking up the least possible time and effort for testing (maximum 10 min)
- Considering the user-specific context of the participant

The aforementioned requirements were derived from the issues we identified in the related work (see Sect. 2). In order to be able to advance the agile transformation in a targeted manner with appropriate measures, a comprehensive overall impression of the current state of agility is required. By focusing on the agile values, the application of the questionnaire is not limited by the use of a specific agile approach. Furthermore, the need for a short testing time is justified by the conception, that the measurement of agility needs to be done in an agile way. We think that a complex and time-consuming method for measuring agility is in conflict with the concept of agility itself. To take into account, that every agile transformation differs based on the specific context, in which the transformation takes part, this specific context needs to be assessed in the questionnaire.

The development of the questionnaire is a continuous learning process. In the beginning, we started with a literature review (see Sect. 2) and an expert survey in order to identify a list of potential items for our questionnaire (see Sect. 3.1). Then, after the first version of the questionnaire was created, we conducted a pretest (see Sect. 3.2). Afterwards, we adapted the questionnaire to the context of public administration and evaluated it (see Sect. 3.3). We also conducted another expert survey to review the comprehensibility of the items and the assignment to the six defined dimensions of agility (see Sect. 3.4).

3.1 Initial Construction of the Questionnaire

The maturity models and questionnaires for implementing and measuring agile transformation identified in the literature review (see Sect. 2) form the starting point for the construction of the questionnaire. Each of these models defines elementary questions for assessing the current state of agile transformation, which are referred to as indicators in the following. The 539 indicators identified were completely reworded in the construction of the questionnaire so that they could be considered as potential items. After sorting out duplicate and irrelevant indicators, the remaining 386 indicators were assigned to agile values. Afterwards, the indicators defining a common behavior were grouped. These groups were then combined and reformulated into a potential item that reflects the underlying behavior of the assigned indicators. This process resulted in 83 possible candidate items of the questionnaire (see Fig. 1).

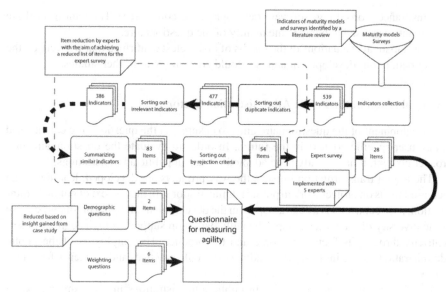

Fig. 1. Process of construction of the questionnaire

Through an empirical selection based on an expert survey with five experts the 28 most relevant items were selected as assessment questions for the questionnaire. The aim of these assessment questions is to evaluate the current state of agility.

These 28 items were then assigned to the defined six dimensions of agility (see Sect. 4.1). The illustration of this mapping is shown in Sect. 4.3.

The assessment of agility through the assessment questions is initially independent of the specific context of the questionnaire user. In order to take the user-specific context into account, weighting questions were added to the assessment questions. Furthermore, demographic questions to capture the demographic situation of the user were included in the questionnaire. Based on the implementation of a case study, the demographic questions were reduced from five to two questions (see Sect. 4.2). The result of the construction process is a questionnaire comprising 36 items.

3.2 Pretest

Subsequent to the construction of the questionnaire, a pretest was conducted. The pretest represents a prototypical testing of the questionnaire before the actual data collection is carried out; it is an indispensable prerequisite for preparing the main survey [19].

This pretest serves to determine the quality of the items and dimensions as a result of the construction process of the questionnaire. For this pretest, the authors constructed an online version of the questionnaire in the German language. The online questionnaire contains all three groups of questions demographic questions, assessment questions, and weighting questions, and was extended with an introduction that clarifies the context of use for the participants, it contains all three groups of questions. Sixty participants from different companies took part in the pretest. The companies belong to different industries (e.g. insurance, consulting, software development, e-commerce). The data from these participants was used to analyze the quality of the questionnaire.

The statistical evaluations of the results of this pretest confirmed that we were on the correct path in our development and, so, could continue with further studies.

3.3   Evaluation in the Public Administration Sector

The development of the questionnaire aims to ensure that the questionnaire can be used in any user-specific context in the future. In order to evaluate the questionnaire in a broader context, it has already been adapted for use in public administrations.

The digital transformation impacts the way products are developed, leadings to an increased focus on project work in public administrations. In the context of public administration, user-centricity is a central aspect in the development of digital products because of the diversity of the target group. The agile paradigm supports a high degree of user-centricity through its focus on people and the product. The employees of the public administration increasingly show a readiness for agile practices and implicitly for topics of user involvement.

For the use of the questionnaire in public administrations in Germany, an expert survey was conducted with 26 experts in three iterations, with the aim of adapting the wording of the items to the user-specific context. Based on the expert survey conducted, it was shown that the questionnaire can be adapted to the user specific context. Furthermore, the dimension *team-centered* was also renamed *self-organized*. This renaming will now be adopted for the dimension in the following. The adaptations showed that the development of the questionnaire is a continuous learning process; further adaptations are necessary.

After adapting the questionnaire to the context of public administration, we were able to apply the questionnaire in a first case study to three teams of a public administration in Germany and successfully determine the current state of agility within these teams.

The results of the survey show a representative overview of the current state of agility at the team level. The case study also showed that due to team sizes between five and eight team members, the anonymity of the survey based on individual demographic questions could no longer be guaranteed. Therefore, the items of the demographic questions were reduced (see Sect. 4.2).

3.4   Expert Survey

During a further expert survey in two iterations, the items of the assessment questions of the questionnaire were reviewed again and linguistically adapted. In the first iteration, five experts were asked about the comprehensibility of the items. They were furthermore, given the task to assign the items to one or more of the six dimensions of agility, as we defined them (see Sect. 4.1). In this first iteration, four of the 28 items of the assessment questions were rated as not clearly understandable. Furthermore, the items were not clearly assigned to the dimensions. These results were carried over into a second iteration. Within the second iteration, the four items that were not clearly understandable could be adjusted in their wording in conversation with six agile experts. The experts judged the divergent assignment of the items to the dimensions to be dependent on the linguistic understanding of the items, the ambivalence of the items and the experience horizon of the experts from the first iteration. This divergent assignment shows the relevance of the need for further research.

4 Results

The following section presents our questionnaire to measure agility at team level. Owing to the adaptations already carried out, the questionnaire presented in this paper is a Version 2.0. Three groups of questions were defined: demographic questions, assessment questions, and weighting questions. The 36 defined items (see Sect. 3.1) were assigned to these three question groups.

4.1 Defining Six Dimensions of Agility

In order to develop a suitable questionnaire that takes agile values into account, we defined six dimensions of agility. For the definition of the dimensions, the agile values were compared with the traditional values. Based on the agile expression of the defined value pairs, the six dimensions *communicative, change-affine, iterative, self-organized, product-driven*, and *improvement-oriented* have been defined for the questionnaire. The construction was based on a mixed strategy with aspects of intuitive, rational, criteria-oriented, and factor-analytical construction. These dimensions may change in the future as we identify the need for them, based on future study results.

The meaning of the six dimensions for the agile approach - as distinguished from the plan-based approach in respect of the development of the questionnaire - is defined as follows:

Communicative

For the sequential processing of the plan, the plan-based approach defines a formal process that must be strictly followed in the implementation of the plan. In the agile transformation, this focus shifts. Here, the focus is on direct communication, both within the development team and with the customer.

Change-Affine

In the plan-based approach, a change in requirements represents an unforeseen deviation from the plan. This can only be integrated into the plan with great effort and, so, it results in a negative attitude towards changes. In the agile approach, the product and requirements are reviewed by the customer in several feedback cycles in order to avoid developing the product without taking the customer's needs into account. Identified changes are seen as adding value to the product for the customer, resulting in an open attitude towards change.

Iterative

Since a change in requirements is not expected in the plan-based approach, the product is created through the linear processing of the initially defined plan. In contrast, the agile approach provides for iterative development with regular reassessment of open requirements. The requirements that have to be implemented in the iteration are processed by the team in accordance with the pull principle.

Self-organized
The plan-based approach is characterized by a strong hierarchy-centricity in respect of project management. A leading authority takes the decisions in the project and delegates the tasks to the development team. In the agile approach, the development team itself accepts a high degree of responsibility in the project. The team works in a self-organized way and can take decisions independently of a leading authority.

Product-Driven
The plan-based approach is characterized by a high degree of documentation. In the agile approach, less value is placed on documentation. The focus here is on the product to be created. Much of the documentation can be replaced by direct communication. The close cooperation, therefore, enables a stronger product centricity, with consideration of the customer's benefit.

Improvement-Oriented
The strong orientation towards the project plan results in the plan-based approach in the fact that deviations from the plan must be answered for. The resultant apportionment of blame can be avoided in the agile approach through constant cooperation. Regular retrospectives are used to constantly try to improve the project approach in order to generate a product with high customer benefit.

4.2 Demographic questions

In order to capture the demographic context of the participants, five demographic questions were first constructed. The case study showed that because of the size of a team, anonymity in the survey results cannot be maintained (see Sect. 3.3). Based on these findings from the case study, the demographic questions were reduced to Item 1 and Item 2 (see Table 1).

Table 1. Demographic questions

ID	Item
1	How would you assess your competence in the field of agile development of digital products?
2	How would you describe the way you think and act in your daily work?

These demographic questions can be used to verify whether the self-assessment of competence and working methods correlates with the results of the survey.

In the questionnaire, the demographic questions are asked at the beginning of the survey, since they are a suitable introduction to the survey.

4.3 Assessment Questions

The 28 items selected by the experts in the construction process (see Sect. 3.1) were assigned to the previously defined dimensions (see Sect. 4.1), as shown in Table 2.

These items are used in the questionnaire to assess the agility of a team. The first column of the following tables defines a unique abbreviation for each item, which is used to reference the items.

Table 2. Assessment questions

ID	Dimension	Item
3	Communicative	Each team member is aware of the tasks of the other team members
4	Communicative	The source code is considered a collective property by the entire team
5	Communicative	The team meets on a scheduled basis several times a week to exchange information directly
6	Communicative	Communication involves all team members
7	Communicative	All project stakeholders know the current progress of the product development
8	Communicative	The customer or his representative can be contacted directly at any time in the project
9	Communicative	Requirements are gathered from the customer in collaboration with the team
10	Communicative	Team members are provided appreciation for their work
11	Change-affine	Proposed changes in the requirements can be adapted by the customer during the project
12	Change-affine	Each iteration is completed with the delivery of the working product to the customer
13	Change-affine	Changed requirements are seen as an added value of the product for the customer and not as an additional workload
14	Change-affine	The customer regularly inspects the working product with regard to the realization of the business value
15	Iterative	The autonomous assignment of tasks is not restricted by organizational procedures
16	Iterative	The developers determine their tasks autonomously from the open requirements
17	Iterative	Projects can be started without fully defining the requirements at the beginning of the project
18	Iterative	Detailed project planning is only available for the next iteration

(continued)

Table 2. (*continued*)

ID	Dimension	Item
19	Self-organized	The scope of work for an iteration is decided by the team
20	Self-organized	The team is accountable for its actions
21	Self-organized	Decisions regarding the execution of their own work can be made by the team without the involvement of a managing authority
22	Self-organized	The entire team actively collaborates on project planning
23	Product-driven	Productive working time is used for work on the product
24	Product-driven	The customer is directly participating in all project decisions
25	Product-driven	All subject matter experts are actively involved in the identification of the requirements
26	Product-driven	Documentation is critically reviewed for its value
27	Improvement-oriented	In regular retrospectives, the approach of the project is reflected with the aim of improvement
28	Improvement-oriented	All team members actively participate in continuous improvement in the project
29	Improvement-oriented	Sights gained from retrospectives are turned into concrete improvement measures
30	Improvement-oriented	Improvements can be explored experimentally during the project

Except for the *communicative* dimension, which comprises eight items, all dimensions include four items. The items of each dimension form a psychometric scale. According to Döring and Bortz [20], a psychometric scale is a summary of items that together measures a characteristic of a complex construct. By forming a scale, the theoretical construct described by the dimension can be captured more precisely than by querying it with a single item [20].

The items are formulated as statements. For every statement the participant is asked to indicate the extent to which the behaviour required by the items apply to thinking and acting in his or her current developmental environment. According to Moosbrugger and Kelava [21], a discretely graded rating scale is suitable for answering this type of question. Regarding the scale points, a 7-point Likert scale was chosen. On the scale, the participant is asked to choose between the extremes *'totally agree'* and *'totally disagree'*. The individual scale points are verbalized as follows: *totally agree, agree, rather agree, neutral, rather disagree, disagree, totally disagree.*

The scale has an odd number of scale points, which means that neutral middle category is present. The participant is, therefore, not forced to give a tendency, as would be the case with a scale with an even number of scale points [19]. With an uneven number of scale points, however, there is a risk that the mean category will not be used exclusively in the sense of the mean characteristic expression, but also if comprehension problems occur or the answer is refused. This mixture of response behaviour, known as confounding, is to be relativized by the additional option of no response on the response scale [21].

Regarding scale points, a number of five or seven is suggested in the literature for odd scales [19, 22]. A fewer number of scale points leads to a loss of information, as the participant cannot give the answer with sufficient differentiation [19]. More scale points can lead to cognitive overload, as the participant is no longer able to differentiate meaningfully between the response options [21]. Based on the results of Finstad [22], it was decided to use the higher differentiability of a 7-point scale.

4.4 Weighting Questions

In order to fulfil the objective of taking the user-specific context into account, the questionnaire was supplemented with weighting questions. For each of the six dimensions of the questionnaire, an additional item was defined that asks about the importance of the dimension for the user. Accordingly, the items of the scales can be weighted in a manner specific to the context. For the formulation of the weighting questions, a concise description of the behaviour of the team required by the dimension was chosen.

The questions are listed in Table 3. As with the assessment questions, a unique abbreviation is given.

Table 3. Weighting questions

ID	Dimension	Item
31	Communicative	The agile team should communicate frequently and directly with each other
32	Change-affine	The agile team should react quickly and flexibly to volatile requirements
33	Iterative	The agile team should develop the product in several iterations
34	Self-organized	The agile team should operate autonomously as a self-organized team
35	Product-driven	The focus of the agile team should be on the product to be created
36	Improvement-oriented	The agile team should continuously improve the development process

Analogous to answering the assessment questions, the weighting questions are rated on a 7-point Likert scale. In contrast to the assessment questions, however, the questions do not ask for agreement but for importance. For this reason, the naming of the scale points for the weighting questions is chosen as follows: *particularly important, important, rather important, neutral, rather unimportant, unimportant, particularly unimportant*. To preclude any confusion, the scale was also supplemented here with the option of no answer.

We have learned in a case study that it is valuable to have an introductory workshop before carrying out the questionnaire. On the one hand, the team can build a shared understanding as regards the objectives of the questionnaire and to define common goals among the team. On the other hand, it is helpful in terms of reducing bias during the questionnaire study, because the dimensions can be discussed in order to build a shared understanding regarding the wording and meaning.

5   Discussion and Limitations

In the previous sections, we presented our questionnaire for measuring agility at the team level as well as the construction process of our questionnaire. In the following, we want to discuss the strengths and weaknesses of the questionnaire.

During our journey to create our questionnaire, we conducted several studies (see Sects. 3.2, 3.3 and 3.4) and discussed it with many experts. We learned that our questionnaire is able to assess the agile values with the assistance of the six dimensions (*communicative, change-affine, iterative, self-organized, product-driven, improvement-oriented:* see Sect. 4.1). Moreover, the additional weighting questions allow us to include the respective context of the respondent as well as define the objective of the survey. In our case study, we learned that we can analyze how the current state of agility is perceived. For example, one study showed that a team has very different perceptions in respect of the understanding of agility and agile working. The difference in these perceptions in cooperating teams leads to misconceptions about the way of work. Such a work environment can lead to a breakdown of trust and commitment between teams, which furthermore leads to dysfunctionalities according to Lencioni [23].

We also found that the implementation of the survey must be accompanied by an expert. The implementation of the questionnaire should be carried out in a moderated fashion. On the one hand, it is important to reach a shared understanding of the objective. On the other hand, it is important to interpret the results correctly and derive measures based on the measurement. Furthermore, the moderated implementation of the questionnaire causes a stronger analysis of the contents and, so, leads to a reflection of one's own work as well as the work in the team. For this reason, we are currently working on a process model for the application of the questionnaire [24, 25]. In summary, this means that practitioners and companies can use the questionnaire to optimize collaboration within their teams. Optimizing collaboration has a positive effect on the value delivery of the team and, hence, on the success of a company.

In addition, our questionnaire for measuring agility has some limitations. The expert survey has shown that the items of the assessment questions (see Sect. 4.3) cannot be clearly assigned to the defined dimensions. This ambiguous assignment of the items to the defined dimensions can be caused by the different kinds of linguistic understanding of the items, the environment, the experts' horizon of experience, or also the ambiguity of the items. The expert surveys showed that adjustments with regard to the linguistic formulation were repeatedly necessary. We are currently in the process of conducting further studies, in which we will investigate the assignment of the items to the dimensions by means of statistical analysis.

6   Conclusion and Future Work

This paper presented an overview of the current state of research on the development of a questionnaire to measure agility at the team level. Our questionnaire for measuring agility includes 36 items, assigned to these three question groups (2 demographic questions, 28 assessment questions, and 6 weighting questions). In order to develop a suitable questionnaire that takes the agile values into account, we used the six dimensions *communicative, change-affine, iterative, self-organized, product-driven*, and *improvement-oriented*.

Firstly, we provided an overview of the related work. We identified and analyzed seven maturity models and two questionnaires for measuring agility based on a literature review. In addition, the research method for the development of the questionnaire was specified.

We presented our research method, including the initial construction of the questionnaire, a pretest, a case study, and further expert surveys.

By conducting the expert surveys, an optimization in the wording of the developed items of the assessment questions was already achieved. The pretest and the case study already show that the questionnaire is suitable for measuring agility at the team level and that the current state of agility can be captured. Furthermore, the case study showed that the results of the questionnaire can be used to identify dysfunctionalities in teams.

In future work, we want to create a standardized tool for supporting the agile transformation of an organization. We are already conducting further studies on this in Spain. On the one hand, the aim is to develop a standardized questionnaire for measuring agility. Conducting the expert survey and the case study shows that the development of this instrument is a continuous learning process. Further research is required to develop this instrument into a standard. On the other hand, we want to elaborate on our process model for using this questionnaire within the agile transformation.

Acknowledgements. This research is partially supported by NICO (Nuevas Iniciativas para el Aseguramiento Temprano de la Calidad Funcional y no Funcional en Procesos y Productos Software Orientados al Usuario) (PID2019-105455GB-C31), which is funded by Spanish Ministry of Science, Innovation and Universities.

References

1. Beck, K., et al.: Manifesto for Agile Software Development (2001). https://agilemanifesto.org
2. Version One Inc.: 14th Annual State of Agile Report (2020)
3. Ozcan-Top, O., Demirörs, O.: assessment of agile maturity models: a multiple case study. In: Woronowicz, T., Rout, T., O'Connor, R.V., Dorling, A. (eds.) SPICE 2013. CCIS, vol. 349, pp. 130–141. Springer, Heidelberg (2013). https://doi.org/10.1007/978-3-642-38833-0_12
4. Schön, E.-M., Winter, D., Escalona, M.J., Thomaschewski, J.: Key challenges in agile requirements engineering. In: Baumeister, H., Lichter, H., Riebisch, M. (eds.) XP 2017. LNBIP, vol. 283, pp. 37–51. Springer, Cham (2017). https://doi.org/10.1007/978-3-319-57633-6_3
5. Takeuchi, H., Nonaka, I.: The new new product development game. Harvard Bus. Rev. **64** (1986)

6. Schön, E.-M., Thomaschewski, J., Escalona, M.J.: Lean user research for agile organizations. IEEE Access **8**, 129763–129773 (2020)
7. Sidky, A., Arthur, J., Bohner, S.: A disciplined approach to adopting agile practices: the agile adoption framework. Innov. Syst. Softw. Eng. **3**, 203–216 (2007)
8. Schwaber, K., Sutherland, J.: The Scrum Guide (2020)
9. Qumer, A., Henderson-Sellers, B., McBride, T.: Agile adoption and improvement model. In: Proceedings European and Mediterranean Conference on Information Systems 2007 (2007)
10. Packlick, J.: The Agile Maturity Map A Goal Oriented Approach to Agile Improvement. Agile 2007.13–17 Aug. 2007, Washington, D.C. IEEE Computer Soc, Los Alamitos, California [u.a.] (2007)
11. Patel, C., Ramachandran, M.: Agile maturity model (AMM): a software process improvement framework for agile software development practices. Int. J. Softw. Eng. IJSE **2**(1), 3–28 (2009)
12. Benefield, R.: Seven dimensions of agile maturity in the global enterprise: a case study. In: 43rd Hawaii International Conference on System Sciences (HICSS), 2010; Honolulu, Hawaii, 5–8 January 2010. IEEE, Piscataway, NJ (2010)
13. Yin, A.P.G.: Scrum Maturity Model. Dissertacao para obtencao do Grau de Mestre em Engenharia Informática e de Computadores. Technical report, Universidade Técnica de Lisboa, Lissabon (2011)
14. Fontana, R.M., Meyer, V., Reinehr, S., Malucelli, A.: Progressive outcomes: a framework for maturing in agile software development. J. Syst. Softw. **102**, 88–108 (2015)
15. So, C., Scholl, W.: Perceptive agile measurement: new instruments for quantitative studies in the pursuit of the social-psychological effect of agile practices. In: Abrahamsson, P., Marchesi, M., Maurer, F. (eds.) XP 2009. LNBIP, vol. 31, pp. 83–93. Springer, Heidelberg (2009). https://doi.org/10.1007/978-3-642-01853-4_11
16. Gren, L., Torkar, R., Feldt, R.: The prospects of a quantitative measurement of agility: a validation study on an agile maturity model. J. Syst. Softw. **107**, 38–49 (2015)
17. Leppänen, M.: A comparative analysis of agile maturity models. In: Coady, J., Schneider, C., Linger, H., Barry, C., Lang, M., Pooley, R. (eds.) Information Systems Development. Reflections, Challenges and New Directions, pp. 329–343. Springer New York, New York, NY (2013). https://doi.org/10.1007/978-1-4614-4951-5_27
18. Maier, A.M., Moultrie, J., Clarkson, P.J.: Assessing organizational capabilities: reviewing and guiding the development of maturity grids. IEEE Trans. Eng. Manage. **59**, 138–159 (2012)
19. Porst, R.: Fragebogen. Ein Arbeitsbuch. Springer VS, Wiesbaden (2014). https://doi.org/10.1007/978-3-658-02118-4.pdf
20. Döring, N., Bortz, J.: Forschungsmethoden und Evaluation in den Sozial- und Humanwissenschaften. Springer, Heidelberg (2016). https://doi.org/10.1007/978-3-642-41089-5.pdf
21. Moosbrugger, H., Kelava, A. (eds.): Testtheorie und Fragebogenkonstruktion. Springer, Heidelberg (2012). https://doi.org/10.1007/978-3-642-20072-4
22. Finstad, K.: Response interpolation and scale sensitivity: evidence against 5-point scales. J. Usability Stud. **5**, 104–110 (2010)
23. Lencioni, P.: The five dysfunctions of a team. Pfeiffer, San Francisco, California (2012)
24. Fangmann, J., Looks, H., Thomaschewski, J., Schön, E.-M.: Agile transformation in e-government projects. In: 15th Iberian Conference on Information Systems and Technologies, Sevilla, Spain, pp. 1–4 (2020)
25. Looks, H., Fangmann, J., Thomaschewski, J., Schön, E.-M.: Towards a process model for agile transformation in e-government projects. J. Inf. Syst. Eng. Manage. (2021)

Open Access This chapter is licensed under the terms of the Creative Commons Attribution 4.0 International License (http://creativecommons.org/licenses/by/4.0/), which permits use, sharing, adaptation, distribution and reproduction in any medium or format, as long as you give appropriate credit to the original author(s) and the source, provide a link to the Creative Commons license and indicate if changes were made.

The images or other third party material in this chapter are included in the chapter's Creative Commons license, unless indicated otherwise in a credit line to the material. If material is not included in the chapter's Creative Commons license and your intended use is not permitted by statutory regulation or exceeds the permitted use, you will need to obtain permission directly from the copyright holder.

The Impact of Agile Transformations on Organizational Performance: A Survey of Teams, Programs and Portfolios

Christoph Johann Stettina[1]([⊠]), Victor van Els[1], Job Croonenberg[2], and Joost Visser[1]

[1] Leiden Institute of Advanced Computer Science,
Leiden University, Leiden, The Netherlands
`c.j.stettina@liacs.leidenuniv.nl`
[2] Tilburg School of Economics and Management,
Tilburg University, Tilburg, The Netherlands

Abstract. While many organizations embark on agile transformations, they can lack insight into the actual impact of these transformations across organizational layers. In this paper, we collect new and study existing evidence on the impact of agile transformations on organizational performance across teams, programs and portfolios. We conducted an international survey collecting the perceptions of agile coaches, transformation leads and other relevant roles, and we correlated levels of agile maturity to the perceptions on dimensions of organizational performance. Based on 134 responses from 29 countries across 16 industries, (1) we consolidated understanding of the benefits of agile transformations based on prior evidence and our data from a more diverse and larger sample, (2) we identified the dimensions impacted by agile transformations as being productivity, responsiveness, quality, workflow health and employee satisfaction & engagement and (3) we traced specific benefits on those dimensions to individual organizational layers of teams, programs and portfolios, showing the magnitude of impact of each dimension per layer. Overall, we can conclude that agile transformations have a variety of strong organizational benefits. This aggregated evidence allows reflection on transformation trends, but also enables organizations to optimize their agile transformation efforts.

Keywords: Agile transformations · Agile portfolio management · Software development · Organizational performance

1 Introduction

While many organizations embark on an agile transformation to make their businesses more agile and responsive, the actual impact of those transformation efforts is often not well understood. Agile transformations are a relatively new and complex organizational phenomenon. Initially developed and applied

© The Author(s) 2021
P. Gregory et al. (Eds.): XP 2021, LNBIP 419, pp. 86–102, 2021.
https://doi.org/10.1007/978-3-030-78098-2_6

within individual teams and initiatives with a focus on software development, organizations have begun to apply it at an enterprise level, impacting multiple organizational layers such as teams [6,27], programs and portfolios [28], as well as multiple business domains such as HR, finance and sales [21].

While agile transformations are frequently thought to provide better alignment with client needs, better involvement of business and users, as well as better and more transparent planning [28], their impact is historically understood from the perspective of an agile software development capability due to their roots in that domain [6]. Current studies consider their impact only on individual levels, mostly within teams and individual organizations. For practitioners, this is problematic, as it is difficult to understand the expected benefits and how those benefits relate to the necessary investments required to adopt agile ways of working.

In this paper we report on our international study, presenting for the first time a view on the impact of agile transformations across the domains of portfolio, programs and teams. To academia we present a model of agile maturity and organizational performance, depicting how organizational performance is impacted through growth of agile maturity across the levels of portfolios, programs and teams during agile transformations. To practice we provide examples of what impact organizations can expect from undertaking an agile transformation.

2   Related Work

In this section we will briefly elaborate on the definition and history of agile transformations with their associated challenges, and then discuss extant literature on the impact of agile transformations on organizational performance. This will transition into the research question as posed in the following section.

2.1   Agile Transformations and Their History

In order to overcome the challenges of adoption and achieve the benefits of agile methods in the context of larger enterprises, organizations embark on a Agile Transformation Process [8,13]. The development and adoption of agile at scale, agile project and portfolio management can be historically described in at least four successive stages:

(1) Team-level agile: At first, in the late 1990s, a number of frameworks and methods were created to deal with an increasing number of failing software development projects. The academic roots lie with Takeuchi and Nonaka [29], whose product development game was translated and expanded into frameworks such as Scrum [24] and XP. Today these frameworks are known under the umbrella of agile methods, facilitating shortened feedback loops and better aligning work with business needs.

(2) Cross-team and program-level agile: The success of Scrum leading up to 2000 brought about the desire to execute larger initiatives in an agile way. However, as Scrum was originally designed for initiatives or projects with an optimal team size of 5–9 individuals, organizations began experimenting with ways to coordinate several agile teams to deliver initiatives requiring larger workforces.

This led to the creation of Scrum of Scrums. Other frameworks focusing on smaller organizations have been developed, such as Nexus, which limits itself to 80 people.

(3) Enterprise agile: An increasing adoption of Scrum in organizational settings, while successful on the one hand, challenged the existing roles and responsibilities in organizations applying these frameworks. As Scrum requires more interaction between users, sponsors and teams, it often clashes with standard organizational structures and workflow [5]. Hence, as of approximately 2010, frameworks began appearing that allowed the embedding of large-scale agile IT initiatives into enterprises, the most prominent being the Scaled Agile Framework (SAFe) [12], LeSS (Large-Scale Scrum) and the Spotify model.

(4) Business agility: From 2018 onwards, companies and framework creators adjusted their thinking from IT-driven to organization-wide agility [1]. While the term can be traced back to earlier academic literature [16], terms such as agile finance, agile marketing, agile sales and agile HR began appearing later [21].

2.2 Understanding Individual Transformation Journeys

Strategies Employed: Frameworks tend to have ideal implementation roadmaps, but the implementation strategies actually employed may vary. For example, there is a team-per-team transformation, a department-per-department implementation and a 'big bang' approach to full organizational change. Further, a new department or even company can be set up to be agile-native. Different companies approach this in different ways, and therefore achieve different results.

Challenges Involved: When undergoing agile transformations, commonly reported challenges are (1) resistance to change, (2) difficulty of implementation resulting from vague terminology and a lack of clear guidance from literature and (3) the integration of non-development functions, e.g. projects being iterative means funding needs to be iterative, which is not always the case [5,18].

Agile Maturity Across Differing Organizational Layers: Companies have transformed to become agile to varying degrees across different organizational layers, including teams, programs and portfolios. All three layers are addressed by the SAFe framework [12], but other frameworks such as LeSS, the Spotify model and the business agility framework do not necessarily acknowledge them.

The SAFe layers can be summarized as follows [12]: *Team level*: a set of teams responsible for the development of User Stories based on Features identified at the Program level. *Program level*: a team of teams building upon a set of 5–12 teams, responsible for the development of Features to be developed by the underlying teams. *Portfolio level*: the portfolio management team defines the strategic themes, translates those into a portfolio-backlog, and allocates it to respective program layers as appropriate. Thus, based on the scaling principle, the program layer builds on multiple underlying teams. While portfolios build on multiple programs respectively, they apply a different workflow in which the programs within the portfolio might be competing for resources [28].

Progress in becoming agile can be measured in terms of agile maturity, using the five levels identified and proposed by Laanti [14], as shown in Fig. 1.

	Beginner	Novice	Fluent	Advanced	World-class
Portfolio	Prioritized portfolio Work identified as Epics, owner nominated Backlog tool support	Portfolio work is continuous Systematic and fast rolling decision-making Agile metrics	Options thinking in portfolio decision-making Measuring feedback, guidance based on data collected and trends	Detecting and utilizing fast business opportunities Agility part of values and company strategy	Ability to innovate new businesses that increase client competitiveness
Program	Agile projects / programs Incremental planning and execution Agility to embrace change	Agile release trains in use Agile roles in use, defined and carry responsibility Increment demos guide future development Organized for lean-agile way-of-working Value stream thinking	Agile budgeting and cost follow-up Networked leadership Systematically speeding up production releases Agile metrics Acceptance tests planned	Continuous positive feedback from customers from last deliveries Ability to create systems and services previously impossible	Ability to respond rapidly to challenging customer needs Networked, empowered, self-controlled, adaptive organization
Team	Fast fixes as needed Scrum in use Dedicated build environment Version control	Automated testing, integration and deployment efforts	Test-first approach Systematically removing impediments	No errors released, production code practically error-free	Production releases multiple times per day

Fig. 1. Transformation maturity model based on Laanti [14]

2.3   The Impact of Agile Transformations

Practitioner literature promises high-impact numbers in decent alignment with reported metrics. For example, SAFe presents the following benefits [12]: 10–50% happier, more motivated employees, 30–75% faster time-to-market, 20–50% increase in productivity, 25–75% defect reduction[1]. However, these figures are currently supported only by anecdotal evidence from supplied case studies with limited reproducibility, as reported without e.g. sample size or calculation methodology. Additionally, practitioner frameworks generally report qualitative improvements as opposed to strict metrics.

More academically, previous research by Laanti [15] outlines a model to evaluate organizational improvements, and applies it to measure the perceived benefits of agile. In this research, Laanti collects agreement with statements that claim, for example, quality improvement as a result of agile transformations on a seven-point scale, as presented in Table 1. Reported values show an average reported mean of 5, suggesting some, though limited, agreement. The natural limitations of this are that degree of improvement is not measured, and a lack of differentiation is made between organizational levels. Olszewska [20] provides a quantitative analysis of performance in agile contexts. Both find positive results, and in combination with other studies, agile has started being associated with factors such as (1) improved quality [25], (2) added value [22], (3) faster time-to-market, (4) better responsiveness to change [15,20] and (5) lower development cost [30]. Past studies have the shortcoming of being limited to case studies, or not adjusting for the penetration of agile throughout different organizational levels. Concretely, solely IT being agile as opposed to the entire organization being agile may result in different organizational improvements.

---

[1] In the most recent 5.1 version of the SAFe framework, the impact is presented as 30%, 75%, 35% and 50%, respectively resembling the means of the original ranges.

3   Research Question

Extant literature suggests adopting agile methods across the layers of an organization, meaning pursuing an agile transformation is associated with improved organizational performance. However, empirical support is scarce, primarily researching agile at team level. Past research has not considered agile presence at different organizational levels, and practitioner frameworks even go so far as to claim that adopting agile methods is associated with equal performance improvement at all levels, meaning the team, program and portfolio level. This research aims to fill that gap by investigating organizational performance associated with agile transformations at those differing levels. As such, the research question of this paper is: *What are the benefits of undergoing an agile transformation?*

4   Methodology

In order to both answer our research question and attain a suitable level of external validity, data from a wide range of agile practitioners was needed. Hence, we developed a survey to obtain a suitable sample size. Surveys are easy to distribute, thus facilitating sample size, and are self-administered, thus minimizing desirability biases through anonymity [11].

4.1   Survey Design

In order to answer our research question, we designed a survey in five segments: (1) Context; (2) Agile transformation; (3) Agile maturity; (4) Organizational performance; and (5) Satisfaction. To improve survey quality, multiple versions of the survey were tested and subjected to expert input. This resulted in adjusted questions to ensure all participants were able to answer.

(1) Context: The survey first gathers relevant descriptive information to verify representativeness of the sample. It includes questions on the participant's role in the organization and its transformation, as well as the company's size and industry.

(2) Agile transformation: This section first verifies whether the company has completed an agile transformation, or is in the process of one, or plans to transform in the future. Second, it explores what strategy was employed to initiate the transformation, and what transformation framework was utilized. Third, the scope of the initiative is assessed, verifying how much of the organization is transforming.

(3) Agile maturity: Laanti [14] presents a maturity model distinguishing three common organizational levels in agile: portfolio, program and team. If sufficient effort is put in, companies move through these levels from beginner, novice, fluent, advanced to eventually world-class. What needs verification is as follows: as companies scale their agility, will the benefits of agility scale as well? Similarly, as companies level up their agility, will the benefits follow? Participants were asked to rank their company in terms of proficiency for each organizational level.

(4) Organizational performance: To evaluate the impact of the agile transformation, participants were asked to input their perceived percentile improvements on the following metrics, as adopted from Laanti [15]: effectiveness of development; quality of the product; transparency of development; increased collaboration; work being more fun; work being more organized; work being more planned; autonomy of development teams; earlier detection of bugs/errors/defects; work being less hectic. These measures were employed to facilitate comparison with existing literature.

(5) Transformation satisfaction: Satisfaction with the transformation was evaluated on a seven-point Likert scale with the following question: *How satisfied are you with the results of the transformation (so far)?*

4.2   Data Collection

The survey was distributed through online communities on platforms such as LinkedIn and personal networks. Furthermore, to ensure sample representativeness, relevant practitioners were approached directly, simultaneously targeting relevant companies and ensuring a variety of seniority level. The collection period spanned three weeks from 11 July to 21 August 2018. During this time frame, 264 people started the survey, and 134 completed it, resulting in a response rate of 51%.

5   Results

5.1   Descriptive Statistics

Roles of Participants: The principal roles of participants within the different transformations as reported were Agile Program Coach (26.12%) and Transformation Manager/Lead (21.64%). Other roles were Team Coach (21.64%), Transformation sponsor (8.21%) and DevOps coach (5.22%).

Size of Organizations: Most participants are employed in large organizations. This means that most companies in this sample have more than 50,000 employees (38.06%). The next largest group of respondents (23.88%) work within companies with an employee number of between 1,001 and 5,000. The remaining respondents were from companies with fewer than 1,000 employees (19.4%), between 20,001 and 50,000 employees (9.7%) and between 5,001 and 20,000 employees (8.96%).

Industry: A large proportion of the participants come from three specific industries. These industries are software (21.64%), financial services (17.91%) and professional services (15.67%). The probable reason for these higher percentages is that the agile way of working is more prevalent within these industries. The remaining responses were from workers in the following industries: telecoms (6.72%), utilities (5.97%), health care (4.48%), retail (4.48%), government (3.73%), manufacturing (3.73%), consumer products (2.99%), public services (2.24%), transportation (2.24%), insurance (0.75%), media & entertainment (0.75%), internet services (0.75%) and education (0.75%).

5.2   Transformation Details

Transformation Strategy: Participants were asked about the strategy used to implement large-scale agile within their company. Most companies used the bottom-up (team-by-team) strategy (42.54%), whereas others used the department-by-department strategy (29.1%), the big-bang strategy (11.94%), the new department strategy (7.46%) and the new company strategy (0.75%). Eight per cent of the participants said they used another strategy or no strategy at all.

Agile Frameworks Applied: The largest group of participants reported using the Scaled Agile Framework®(SAFe®) (42.11%). Other participants reported the use of Scrum of Scrums (19.55%), internally created methods (14.29%), Enterprise Scrum (3.01%), Large-scale scrum (2.26%), Lean management (2.26%) and Nexus (0.75%). Other participants responded they used another or no framework for the transformation (15.79%).

Capital Investment: The largest group of participants indicated that the transformation had needed an investment of between €500,000 and €2 million (26.72%). The other participants responded that the investment needed was between €2 and €10 million (25.19%), between €100,000 and €500,000 (16.03%), less than €100,000 (14.5%), more than €50 million (9.16%) and between €10 and €50 million (8.4%).

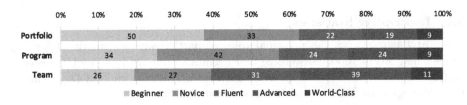

Fig. 2. Agile maturity across portfolio, program and team layers

Maturity: As seen in Fig. 2, on team level the biggest group of participants assessed their company as being at advanced level (29%). The other participants estimated that their organization was fluent at team level (23%), novice at team level (20%) and beginner at team level (19%). A smaller group estimated it to be at world-class level (8%). On program level, the biggest group of participants estimated their company to be at novice level (32%). The other participants estimated that their organization was at beginner on program level (26%), fluent on program level (18%), advanced on program level (18%) and world-class on program level (7%). On portfolio level the biggest group of participants estimated their company at beginner level (38%). The other participants estimated that their organization was at novice level (25%), fluent at portfolio level (17%), advanced at portfolio level (14%) and world-class at portfolio level (7%).

Table 1. Perceived impact of agile transformation on various metrics associated with dimensions of organizational performance. Mean and three quartiles are reported for our own data. For comparison (discussed in Sect. 6.2), reported means are reproduced from Laanti [15] and Olszewska [20], and reported ranges from SAFe [12]. Laanti reported on a seven-point Likert scale, rather than improvement percentage.

	Survey data				[15]	[20]	SAFe [12]
	Mean	Q1	Q2	Q3	Mean	Mean	Range
Productivity							20–50%
Increases the effectiveness of development	60%	40%	69%	81%	4.97		
Features / Money spent (Hustle metric)						483%	
Responsiveness							
Improves time-to-market	67%	49%	72%	90%			30–75%
Customer service request turnaround time						24%	
Lead time per feature						64%	
Quality							
Improves the quality of the product	61%	47%	70%	81%	4.70		
Enables the earlier detection of defects	67%	50%	71%	89%	4.77		
Number of external Trouble Reports (TR)						−188%	
Avg # days of Open External TR						31%	
Defect reduction							25–75%
Workflow health							
Number releases per time						400%	
Number of days between commits						38%	
Makes work more organized	57%	32%	59%	81%			
Makes work more planned	55%	31%	55%	80%	4.50		
Employee satisfaction & Engagement							10–50%
Makes work more fun	63%	44%	70%	84%	4.61		
Makes work less hectic	49%	21%	50%	73%	3.64		
Increases the autonomy of development teams	64%	50%	70%	82%	4.86		
Increases collaboration	75%	60%	79%	91%	5.04		
Increases the transparency of development	70%	50%	75%	91%	5.13		

Satisfaction with Transformation: The biggest group of participants was moderately satisfied with the results of the transformation (38.06%). Other groups of participants were slightly satisfied (20.9%), extremely satisfied (18.66%), slightly dissatisfied (8.21%), neither satisfied nor dissatisfied (7.46%), moderately dissatisfied (3.73%) and extremely dissatisfied (2.99%).

Organizational Impact: Our results regarding perceived impact of agile transformations on various dimensions of organizational performance are reported in Table 1. For each dimension, the perceived impact on one or more associated metrics was measured. For these, we show the mean impact, as well as the impact at first, second and third quartile of the distribution. The second quartile (median) reflects the central tendency, which is highest for *Increases collaboration* at 75% improvement and lowest for *Makes work less hectic* at 50% improvement. The first and third quartiles capture the inter-quartile range (IQR) showing smallest dispersion for *Increases collaboration* with IRQ $= 91\% - 60\% = 31\%$ and largest dispersion for *Makes work less hectic* with IQR $= 73\% - 21\% = 52\%$.

Portfolio	Program	Team	Metric	Dimension
0.450*	0.511*	0.487*	Increases the effectiveness of development	Productivity
0.373*	0.381*	0.382*	Improves time-to-market	Responsiveness
0.322*	**0.450***	0.450	Increases the quality of the product	Quality
0.357*	0.437*	0.413*	Enables the earlier detection of defects	
0.263*	0.356*	0.263*	Makes work more planned	Workflow health
0.303*	0.379*	0.305*	Makes work more organized	
0.121	0.212*	0.225*	Makes work more fun	
0.426*	0.363*	0.359*	Makes work less hectic	Employee satisfaction & engagement
0.298*	0.350*	0.372*	Increases the autonomy of development teams	
0.279*	0.297*	0.244*	Increases collaboration	
0.237*	0.319*	0.332*	Increases the transparency of development	

*= p < .05

Fig. 3. Correlations between maturity at different organizational layers and metric improvement per dimension. In bold we show the strongest correlations (above 0.45).

5.3   Correlation Analysis

The model shown in Fig. 3 shows the correlations of agile maturity on a particular layer with organizational performance per metric. Pearson correlations were used to allow for significance testing and due to the linearity of the expected relationship between maturity and performance. Except *Makes work more fun*, all metrics correlated with agile maturity are significant at $P<0.05$ across all organizational levels. The strongest correlations, and thus the largest improvements associated with improved agile maturity, are as follows: *Increases the effectiveness of development* with coefficients between 0.45 and 0.51; *Enables the earlier detection of defects* improving between 0.36 and 0.44; improvements in *Makes work less hectic* between 0.36 and 0.43. Notably, no metrics seem to respond uniformly across organizational levels. In terms of the proposed research question, all metrics seem to undergo relevant improvements as a result of undergoing an agile transformation.

6 Discussion

Our discussion starts with general observations (6.1), and then goes into separate dimensions (6.2) and organizational layers (6.3).

6.1 The Impact of Agile Transformations: General Observations

We now discuss the impact of agile transformations, comparing our data with existing literature, beginning with general observations, and continuing with a discussion of the individual dimensions in Sect. 6.2. To allow comparison of results across existing studies and our data, we grouped the metrics of Laanti [15], Olszewska [20] and SAFe [12] into a hierarchical classification in Table 1.

Our data suggests that agile transformations positively impact organizational performance across all employed metrics. An observation one can make while looking at Table 1 is that all studies report rather large improvements.

Further, one can observe that the impact differs per organizational layer. For example, an increased maturity on program level shows the strongest impact, correlating with the dimensions of Productivity, Quality and Workflow health (see Fig. 3). Most notably, increasing agile maturity at the program level has a correlation coefficient of 0.511 with *Increases the effectiveness of development,* and one of 0.450 with *Increases the quality of product,* as shown in Fig. 3. The weakest correlation is found with *Makes work more fun* at the program level at 0.212. Satisfaction with the transformation is positively associated with performance benefits, except for the *Improves time-to-market* metric. However, dissatisfied respondents still report an average performance improvement of 45%. The highest satisfaction shows an average performance improvement of 77%. This is in line with previous research finding that satisfaction with change predicts performance benefits of that change, while asserting that agile transformations in and of themselves are beneficial.

Comparing our data to the results of Laanti [15], Olszewska [20] and SAFe [12], one can observe that reported performance improvements vary significantly. We identify three potential interpretations of this cross-study variance. A rather obvious explanation is that the applied metrics differ and the measurements have been taken differently across the various studies. An increased acceptance and maturity of agile methods in practice could be another potential explanation. Yet another reason could be that the impact is contextual and varies greatly across the surveyed organizations. Previous studies and professional reports (cf. State of Agile Survey [26] and Business Agility Report [1]) indeed indicate an increase in acceptance and adoption of agile methods in practice.

6.2   Impacted Metric Dimensions

We will now continue to discuss the individual metrics presented in Table 1 and their measurements.

Overall, our results correlate with previous findings that organizational performance improves as a result of agile transformations. Differences can be found, however, in the magnitude of this improvement, with Olszewska occasionally reporting very high numbers [20]. These differences may be caused by the differences in sample, since both Laanti and Olszewska report findings from within a single organization. Furthermore, comparison is challenging due to different scales and operationalization of concepts. Notwithstanding these differences, the benefits of agile transformations are confirmed through improved replication across a larger sample.

We will now continue to discuss the impact of agile transformations across the five identified dimensions of (1) Productivity, (2) Responsiveness, (3) Quality, (4) Workflow health and (5) Employee satisfaction & engagement, with their respective metrics as illustrated in Fig. 3.

Productivity: Defined as total output divided by total input, improvements in productivity come from both efficiency and effectiveness [2]. Factors influencing productivity in software development can be categorized into product (e.g. complexity, size), process (e.g. maturity) and development environment (e.g. languages, development tools) [17,31]. SAFe reports a 50% improvement in productivity in general. On *Increases the effectiveness of development*, our reported improvements almost double Laanti's results.

Responsiveness: Responsiveness here refers to quickness of response to either customer or market demand [2]. Responsiveness in software development is generally associated with a mature use of agile practices and processes [23] and team configuration (e.g. application of feature teams with an end-to-end responsibility over a (sub)product [19]). We report similar *Time-to-market* improvements at 67% as SAFe's 20–70%, though without a range, which suggests our results may be higher. More concretely, Olszewska reports an improvement of 24% and 64% on *Customer service request turnaround time* and *Lead time per feature* respectively. This shows that responsiveness can be expected to improve, but depending on operationalization, different results may be achieved.

Quality: Defined as a measure of excellence, both product and development quality fall under this category [2]. In software development, the ISO 25010 standard delineates two overarching categories: product quality and quality in use. These have eight and five categories respectively, which in turn have 31 and 11 sub-categories [10]. While the complexity of quality may therefore not be fully covered in existing agile literature, results seem to unite in finding benefits of agile transformations. Laanti reports a fair degree of agreement on *Increases the quality of the product* (4.70/7) and *Enables the earlier detection of defects* (4.70/7), which is mirrored by our results of 61% and 67% respectively. The *Increases the quality of the product* and *Enables the earlier detection of defects* reported here fall into the range reported by SAFe under defect reduction, as does Olszewska's *Average days of open external reports* (31%). Notably, the *Number of external trouble reports* worsened, meaning increased, with 188% as reported by Olszewska [19]. This may have been caused by the increased number of releases, since there would be more opportunities for trouble reports to be logged within the same time frame.

Workflow Health: Workflow refers to the way that work is organized, or the sequence of steps in a work process [2]. A workflow can be called healthy, when the work is well organized and planned, in which case individual tasks are executed and (intermediate) products are delivered at a steady pace. Thus, the notion of workflow health concerns the internals of the work process, which is linked to, but distinct from, the other categories such as employee satisfaction or productivity. The results presented here correlate with existing literature in emphasizing the benefits to be achieved by pursuing an agile transformation. A transformation *Makes work more organized* by 55%, and Laanti reports agreement on improvements here (4.50). Olszewska's metric of the *Number of days between commits* reports a slightly lower improvement of 38%. Olszewska also reports an impressive improvement in *Number of releases per time* of 400%. Important to distinguish is that increases in *Number of releases per time* are affected not only by workflow health, but also by the size of an individual release. In agile software development, individual pieces of work are to be small, suggesting the workflow health improvement, its presence implicitly agreed upon, may not reach 400%.

Employee Satisfaction and Engagement: This section here follows the definition: employees being happy and actively engaged with their job due to the job itself and the overall working conditions [2]. Higher satisfaction and engagement leads to higher individual performance, and literature has found a positive relationship with firm growth as well as retention rates [3,9]. *Increases collaboration* and *Increases the transparency of development* are the highest evaluated metrics in Laanti's study as well as ours. Interestingly, all metrics except *Makes work less hectic* (49%) exceed the range given by SAFe of 10–50%. *Makes work less hectic* is also the only metric where participants reported a negative impact, with 3.61 [15].

Customer Satisfaction: The table notably does not include this concept, which is a limitation of our data set as well as of existing agile literature. A faster time-to-market is not valuable if what is delivered is not valued by customers.

6.3   The Relevance of Organizational Layers

In this subsection we will discuss the correlation of impact with reported maturity across teams, programs and portfolios. Figure 3 presents the results of the correlation analysis between the maturity model and the impact dimensions.

While the impact dimensions discussed by Laanti [15], Olszewska [20] and SAFe [12] generally do not discriminate between organizational layers, looking at the types of metrics used, it can be assumed that those metrics are most applicable at the program and team layers. Due to the absence of portfolio-level metrics (e.g. portfolio performance metrics such as maximizing the portfolio's overall economic value, strategic alignment and portfolio balance, or satisfaction metrics such as decision effectiveness [4]), for the sake of comparability, we will therefore discuss the impact on the program and team layers.

Following our analysis, we see that the perceived impact on performance is not consistent across organizational levels, meaning that performance improvement at the portfolio level is not equal to that at the team or program levels.

Notably, only the *Makes work less hectic* improvement increases when scaling from program to portfolio level. All other metrics' improvement is decreased to varying degrees. Since scaling agile to the portfolio level is a relatively new phenomenon, the associated complexity may not allow the benefits to actualize to their full extent. Another explanation may be that intrinsic differences in the benefits of agile at the portfolio and program level exist. The portfolio level oversees several programs whereas the program level is, simply put, a group of teams. Making a parallel with a portfolio of business units is useful. The coordination costs of having multiple business units is well established in literature, and significant changes in the business unit operation necessitate adjustments in how the portfolio is managed. This would suggest that scaling agile to the portfolio layer adds a degree of complexity that companies may not be equipped to manage. This interpretation is supported by the fact that the lowest agile maturities are reported at the portfolio level. Further, at the portfolio level, different metrics matter, e.g. *Improves time-to-market* is likely to be valued higher than *Enables the earlier detection of defects*. The program level is a group of teams, suggesting that improvements as a result of an agile transformation should follow the same mechanisms. However, the portfolio is not a sum of programs and follows a different scaling mechanism [28]. For these reasons, it is not unusual for performance improvement at the portfolio level to be perceived differently (i.e. lower) than at the program and team level.

6.4   Limitations

Although we applied a rigorous method when designing the questionnaire and collecting the data, multiple limitations are present in the current paper. Particularly, in survey-based research, three main types of bias can be found and are discussed here: sampling bias, response bias and non-response bias.

Sampling bias is the bias related to the way respondents are selected. We note that the majority of responses stem from participants who tend to be responsible for agile transformations (e.g. Agile Program Coaches and Transformation Managers and Leads), which may lead to self-selection bias, but also to more high-quality answers, as those participants are expected to have the best overview of the transformation. We addressed sampling bias by sharing the survey with different communities rather than those purely involved with agile methods. Nevertheless, self-selection bias might have occurred as a result of the research being an online survey. Responses from additional business stakeholders and software developers affected by the transformation would be a valuable addition to future research.

Response bias can be encapsulates friendliness bias and social desirability bias. As perceptions rather than concrete improvements ('hard-data') were collected, the results are open to potentially biased responses. The scale used for organizational performance could be a source of bias as it was presented as a 0%–100% range. This may have deterred participants from selecting 0, and also did not allow participants to indicate a decrease in performance. However, results are somewhat robust since participants who reported low satisfaction with their agile transformation still reported a minimum performance increase of 40%. As the survey was anonymous, we further believe that response bias due to socially desirable answers was mitigated.

Non-response bias is a bias where participants are unwilling to take or complete the survey, resulting in under-representation of specific viewpoints. With a rather high response rate of 51%, we believe that the non-response bias is limited. Still, negative opinions are under-represented, at under 10% of participants. This may suggest that overall, transformations go smoothly, but might also indicate that the dissatisfied group is under-represented in this paper.

7   Conclusions

In this paper we have presented the results of our empirical study on the impact of agile transformations on organizational performance. Based on an international survey with 134 participants from varying industries and nationalities, we discuss the perceived benefits.

The contribution of this paper is threefold: (1) we consolidated understanding of the benefits of agile transformations based on prior evidence and our data from a more diverse and larger sample; (2) we identified the dimensions impacted by agile transformations as being *productivity, responsiveness, quality, workflow health* and *employee satisfaction*; and (3) we traced specific benefits on those metric dimensions to individual organizational layers of teams, programs and portfolios, showing the magnitude of impact of each metric per layer.

First, by comparing existing quantitative results with both academic and practitioner literature, we conclude that agile transformations indeed result in widespread organizational performance improvements. Importantly, depending on the operationalization of a specific concept, exact results will vary between studies. However, the identified dimensions are confirmed to be positively impacted by the pursuit of an agile transformation with limited dependence on the selected metrics. Second, based on existing literature, including input for the described comparison, a comprehensive overview of the impacted dimensions is established. From an investigation of the non-agile literature, we posit the unsurprising notion that different metrics are appropriate at different layers. A particularly strong candidate is strategic alignment of projects at the portfolio level. Further, we point out the lack of further, customer-facing metrics, e.g. customer satisfaction. Third, besides the applicability of individual metrics, we confirm that the benefits of agile maturity on specific metrics differ according to the organizational layer. For example, workflow health sees practically equal improvements at the team and portfolio level, but notably higher improvements at the program level.

Overall, the level of granularity in understanding these performance benefits is improved by acknowledging organizational layers and the differences of performance benefits of agile transformations between them. A more fine-grained understanding of the impact at different dimensions and layers achieved through our research opens the possibility of building an integrated model of maturity, impacted metrics and organizational layers, where inter-dependencies within and across these topics can be investigated. This facilitates a potential adoption and growth model for organizational agility to optimize transformation paths for impact. A very recent publication [7] that presents a multi-factorial model of developer productivity seems to have independently taken a similar approach to ours, in the way it looks at various dimensions and organizational layers, and discusses similar metrics to ours. While the authors of that research take the notion of productivity as their focal point, our perspective is agile transformation, where productivity is just one of various dimensions.

We conclude that agile transformations positively impact organizational performance, with reported improvements in many cases going way beyond 30% across the reported dimensions.

Acknowledgment. The authors would like to thank the survey participants and anonymous reviewers for contributing to this study.

References

1. Business Agility Institute: The Business Agility Report: Responding to disruption, 3rd edition (2020)
2. Cambridge University Press: Cambridge Online Dictionary. https://dictionary.cambridge.org/. Accessed 12 Jan 2021
3. Coffman, C., Gonzalez-Molina, G.: Follow this path: How the world's greatest organizations drive growth by unleashing human potential. Hachette+ ORM (2002)
4. Cooper, R.G., Edgett, S.J., Kleinschmidt, E.J.: New product portfolio management: practices and performance. J. Prod. Innov. Manage. Int. Publ. Prod. Dev. Manage. Assoc. **16**(4), 333–351 (1999)
5. Dikert, K., Paasivaara, M., Lassenius, C.: Challenges and success factors for large-scale agile transformations: a systematic literature review. J. Syst. Softw. **119**, 87–108 (2016)
6. Dybå, T., Dingsøyr, T.: Empirical studies of agile software development: a systematic review. Inf. Softw. Technol. **50**(9–10), 833–859 (2008)

7. Forsgren, N., Storey, M.A., Maddila, C., Zimmermann, T., Houck, B., Butler, J.: The space of developer productivity: there's more to it than you think. Queue **19**(1), 20–48 (2021)
8. Gandomani, T.J., Zulzalil, H., Ghani, A.A.A., Sultan, A.B.M., Parizi, R.M.: The impact of inadequate and dysfunctional training on agile transformation process: a grounded theory study. Inf. Softw. Technol. **57**, 295–309 (2015)
9. Griffeth, R.W., Hom, P.W., Gaertner, S.: A meta-analysis of antecedents and correlates of employee turnover: update, moderator tests, and research implications for the next millennium. J. Manage. **26**(3), 463–488 (2000)
10. International Organization for Standardization: ISO/IEC 25010:2011 systems and software engineering - systems and software quality requirements and evaluation (SQuaRE) - system and software quality models (2011)
11. Joinson, A.: Social desirability, anonymity, and internet-based questionnaires. Behav. Res. Methods Instrum. Comput. **31**(3), 433–438 (1999)
12. Knaster, R., Leffingwell, D.: SAFe 5.0 Distilled: Achieving Business Agility with the Scaled Agile Framework. Addison-Wesley Professional, Boston (2020)
13. Korhonen, K.: Evaluating the impact of an agile transformation: a longitudinal case study in a distributed context. Software Qual. J. **21**(4), 599–624 (2013)
14. Laanti, M.: Agile transformation model for large software development organizations. In: Proceedings of the XP2017 Scientific Workshops, p. 19. ACM (2017)
15. Laanti, M., Salo, O., Abrahamsson, P.: Agile methods rapidly replacing traditional methods at Nokia: a survey of opinions on agile transformation. Inf. Soft. Technol. **53**(3), 276–290 (2011)
16. Mathiassen, L., Pries-Heje, J.: Business agility and diffusion of information technology (2006)
17. Maxwell, K.D., Forselius, P.: Benchmarking software development productivity. IEEE Softw. **17**(1), 80–88 (2000)
18. Moe, N., Dingsøyr, T., Dybå, T.: Overcoming barriers to self-management in software teams. IEEE Softw. **26**, 20–26 (2009)
19. Olsson, H., Sandberg, A., Bosch, J., Alahyari, H.: Scale and responsiveness in large-scale software development. IEEE Softw. **31**(5), 87–93 (2013)
20. Olszewska, M., Heidenberg, J., Weijola, M., Mikkonen, K., Porres, I.: Quantitatively measuring a large-scale agile transformation. J. Syst. Softw. **117**, 258–273 (2016)
21. Oprins, R.J.J., Frijns, H.A., Stettina, C.J.: Evolution of scrum transcending business domains and the future of agile project management. In: Kruchten, P., Fraser, S., Coallier, F. (eds.) XP 2019. LNBIP, vol. 355, pp. 244–259. Springer, Cham (2019). https://doi.org/10.1007/978-3-030-19034-7_15
22. Petersen, K., Wohlin, C.: The effect of moving from a plan-driven to an incremental software development approach with agile practices. Empir. Softw. Eng. **15**(6), 654–693 (2010). https://doi.org/10.1007/s10664-010-9136-6
23. Recker, J., Holten, R., Hummel, M., Rosenkranz, C.: How agile practices impact customer responsiveness and development success: a field study. Proj. Manage. J. **48**(2), 99–121 (2017)
24. Schwaber, K.: Scrum development process. In: Sutherland, J., Casanave, C., Miller, J., Patel, P., Hollowell, G. (eds.) Business object design and implementation, pp. 117–134. Springer, London (1997) https://doi.org/10.1007/978-1-4471-0947-1_11
25. Sfetsos, P., Stamelos, I.: Empirical studies on quality in agile practices: a systematic literature review. In: 2010 Seventh International Conference on the Quality of Information and Communications Technology, pp. 44–53. IEEE (2010)

26. State Of Agile: Digital.ai 14th annual state of agile report (2020). https://stateofagile.com/#ufh-i-615706098-14th-annual-state-of-agile-report/7027494

27. Stettina, C.J., Heijstek, W.: Five agile factors: helping self-management to self-reflect. In: Proceedings of European Software Process Improvement Conference (EuroSPI) (2011)

28. Stettina, C.J., Hörz, J.: Agile portfolio management: an empirical perspective on the practice in use. Intl. J. Project Manage. **33**(1), 140–152 (2015)

29. Takeuchi, H., Nonaka, I.: The new new product development game. Harvard Business Review (1986)

30. Van Solingen, R.: Measuring the ROI of software process improvement. IEEE Softw. **21**(3), 32–38 (2004)

31. Wagner, S., Ruhe, M.: A systematic review of productivity factors in software development. arXiv preprint arXiv:1801.06475 (2018)

Open Access This chapter is licensed under the terms of the Creative Commons Attribution 4.0 International License (http://creativecommons.org/licenses/by/4.0/), which permits use, sharing, adaptation, distribution and reproduction in any medium or format, as long as you give appropriate credit to the original author(s) and the source, provide a link to the Creative Commons license and indicate if changes were made.

The images or other third party material in this chapter are included in the chapter's Creative Commons license, unless indicated otherwise in a credit line to the material. If material is not included in the chapter's Creative Commons license and your intended use is not permitted by statutory regulation or exceeds the permitted use, you will need to obtain permission directly from the copyright holder.

Measuring Software Delivery Performance Using the Four Key Metrics of DevOps

Marc Sallin[1]([⊠]) [iD], Martin Kropp[1] [iD], Craig Anslow[2] [iD], James W. Quilty[2] [iD],
and Andreas Meier[3] [iD]

[1] University of Applied Sciences and Arts Northwestern Switzerland,
Windisch, Switzerland
`martin.kropp@fhnw.ch`
[2] Victoria University of Wellington, Wellington, New Zealand
`{craig,james.quilty}@ecs.vuw.ac.nz`
[3] Zurich University of Applied Sciences, Wintherthur, Switzerland
`meea@fhnw.ch`

Abstract. The Four Key Metrics of DevOps have become very popular for measuring IT-performance and DevOps adoption. However, the measurement of the four metrics deployment frequency, lead time for change, time to restore service and change failure rate is often done manually and through surveys - with only few data points. In this work we evaluated how the Four Key Metrics can be measured automatically and developed a prototype for the automatic measurement of the Four Key Metrics. We then evaluated if the measurement is valuable for practitioners in a company. The analysis shows that the chosen measurement approach is both suitable and the results valuable for the team with respect to measuring and improving the software delivery performance.

Keywords: DevOps · Agile · Metrics · Four Key Metrics ·
IT-performance · Case study

1 Introduction

More and more organizations are adopting DevOps to accelerate delivery speed and improve quality of their software products [1]. The term DevOps first appeared in 2009 in social media coined by Patrick Debois [2]. Bass et al. define the term in their book as *"a set of practices intended to reduce the time between committing a change to a system and the change being placed into normal production, while ensuring high quality"* [3]. Companies state that the measurement of DevOps progress is seen as important but also as very difficult [4]. The State of DevOps report, first published in 2014, provides a view into the practices and capabilities that drive high performance in software delivery [5]. The researchers found that only four key metrics (FKM) differentiate between low, medium, high, and elite performers: Lead time for change, deployment frequency, time to restore service, and change failure rate [6]. These four metrics help organizations

© The Author(s) 2021
P. Gregory et al. (Eds.): XP 2021, LNBIP 419, pp. 103–119, 2021.
https://doi.org/10.1007/978-3-030-78098-2_7

and teams to determine whether they are improving the overall IT-performance. As they are strongly correlated with well-known DevOps practices they are also known as DevOps metrics [5].

The FKM in the State of DevOps report is based on surveys. While a survey approach has the advantage that you can raise highly focused questions, and address a clear target audience, it also comes with several disadvantages: the absence of a clear definition of the measurement, no continuous data, subjective answers, offline data capture and analysis, and extra effort and cost to generate the data. On the other side, using system data provides the advantage that these data are instantly available (e.g. the number of User Stories done in a Sprint), and can be captured and analysed automatically. However, these data may not be complete with respect to the required DevOps aspects (e.g., cultural measures) [7]. This work aims to address these disadvantages by automatically measuring the FKM and evaluate if the automatic measurement of the FKM is of value for practitioners with respect to improving their performance.

We defined two research questions to be answered by this study.

RQ1 How can the FKM be automatically measured?
RQ2 How valuable is the approach to automatically measure the FKM for software development teams?

RQ1 was answered using a multivocal literature review [8] to include both state-of-the-art and -practice literature. To answer RQ2 the findings of RQ1 were operationalized using a prototype. The prototype was used by a development team in an industrial context at Swiss Post and we asked the members of the development team to participate in a survey.

2   The Four Key Metrics (FKM)

This chapter explains the origin of the FKM, describes their original definition and explains why they gained a high popularity in industry. While DevOps has become very popular in industry [1, p. 18] to bring development and operation close together and deploy new software faster into operation, it was unclear how you can measure the improvement in DevOps.

Forsgren et al. searched for a performance measurement of software teams which focus on global outcome in DevOps. That means, in the basic sense of DevOps, firstly, a measurement that does not pit development against operations, by rewarding development for throughput and operations for stability and secondly, focus on outcomes, not output. That means, do not reward people for putting in large amounts of work, but rather measure results that add business value. They found that four key metrics differentiate between low, medium, high, and elite performers [9]. Forsgren et al. defined the metrics as follows:

Deployment Frequency: addresses minimizing the batch size in a project (reducing it is a central element of the Lean paradigm). As this is hard to measure in software, they took the deployment frequency of software to production as a proxy.

Lead Time for Change: defined as *"the time it takes to go from code committed to code successfully running in production"*. Shorter time is better because it enables faster feedback and course correction as well as the faster delivery of a fix to a defect.

Time to Restore Service: as failure in rapidly changing complex systems is inevitable the key question for stability is how long it takes to restore service from an incident from the time the incident occurs (e.g., unplanned outage, service impairment)?

Change Failure Rate: the percentage of changes for the application or service which results in degraded service or subsequently required remediation (e.g., lead to service impairment or outage, require a hot fix, a rollback, a fix-forward, or a patch).

In recent years, the FKM have gained large attention and popularity in industry and are applied by many known companies, like Zalando, RedGate, HelloFresh, PBS or Contentful. The publication of Forsgren's book "Accelerate: The Science of Lean Software and DevOps" in 2018 which summarizes their research [10], and the recommendation of ThoughtWorks in 2019 to adopt the FKM in their technology radar [11] has further increased the popularity of the FKM. The DevOps Trends Survey for 2020 carried out by Atlassian shows that nearly half of the respondents leverage the four key metrics [4, p. 24].

3   Multi-vocal Literature Review

Despite interest from industry [4], at the time of writing there is no research which suggests/summarizes how to automatically measure the FKM. To be able to define a broadly accepted definition for the automatic measurement we investigated what other researchers and practitioners did in this area. Usually systematic literature review (SLR) studies are conducted to capture the state of a research topic. However, SLRs focus mainly on research contribution and do not include grey literature from practice (GL) [8]. As a large majority of software practitioners do not publish in academic forums, we also included GL to make sure we get the result of the current state-of-practice in this field. Furthermore, the very current perspective, the relevance for practitioners and the low volume of published research indicates that not only formal literature should be used to cover a topic [8].

The multivocal literature review was conducted according to the guideline of Garousi et al. [8] which considers also the popular SLR guidelines by Kitchenham and Charters [12]. Literature was included if any of the inclusion and none of the exclusion criteria are met (see Table 1).

3.1   Systematic Literature Review

The publications of Forsgren et al. (i.e., the book "Accelerate" and the "State of DevOps Reports") are listed in Google Scholar and Research Gate. For the SLR,

Table 1. Multivocal literature review inclusion and exclusion criteria.

Inclusion	Exclusion
Contains more detailed definition than Forsgren et al.	Is not written in English or German
Contains information about automatic measurement or tooling	Is not text (e.g., YouTube, or Webinar)
Contains experience report about the automatic measurement	Is a book

the relevant/related research was identified using snowballing starting from their publications. All 93 unique articles which cited the literature about the FKM published by Forsgren et al. were retrieved by following the cited links. Citations from books were not included. 21 articles are not written in English or German and hence were excluded. Only 7 of the 72 remaining articles treated the topic "metrics" and none of them contained more information about the FKM than already presented by Forsgren et al. As no articles from the SLR were included, no data could be extracted and used in the synthesis.

3.2   Gray Literature Review

For the gray literature review (GLR) Google was used as search engine because pilot searches have shown that there is no more narrow scope for the source of information (e.g. only StackOverflow or Medium) which returns results. A pilot search was conducted to find which keywords are used when people are talking about the FKM. This was done by retrieving articles which talk about one of the four metrics (search for "deployment frequency", "lead time for change", "time to restore service" and "change failure rate") and screening the articles to see how the authors bring them into the context of the FKM. As a result, the following search terms were defined to be used for the GLR.

- DevOps metrics
- DevOps metrics accelerate
- DevOps metrics DORA
- four key metrics DevOps
- accelerate metrics definitions

In contrast to the searches within the formal literature, gray literature search returns an exhaustive number of results. Thus, stopping criteria need to be defined [8]. Google has a ranking algorithm which aims to return relevant articles ordered by priority. That means, the most relevant articles are at the top and the following stopping criteria were applied.

- *Theoretical saturation:* As soon five articles in a row did not match the "Is about this topic & contains information" inclusion criteria, the next five articles were screened by only looking at their title. If they were not relevant, the search was ended.

– *Effort bounded:* After reviewing 100 results for a search term, the search was ended.

Initially, 115 articles/search results were retrieved and screened. 43 out of those 115 were not about the topic and 5 were not in text form. 16 unique articles remain which either include a definition or an experience report.

3.3   Results

This section presents the results of the multivocal literature review. The full list of retrieved literature is provided online.[1]

Deployment Frequency: 7/16 articles contain a definition for deployment frequency. As this metric is already well defined by Forsgren et al. as *deployment of software to production*, the definitions do not widely diverge. They have in common that "number of deployments/releases in a certain period" are counted. Some state that they only count successful deployment (but successful is not defined) and some explicit mention that they count deployments to production. For the purposes of automated measurement, a deployment is defined as a new release[2] As this is a speed metric, every deployment attempt is counted as deployment even if it was not successful.

Lead Time for Change: 9/16 articles contain a definition for lead time for change. Like the deployment frequency, the definition of Forsgren et al. does not leave much room for interpretation although some deliberately took approaches diverging from that of Forsgren et al. All suggestions based on the original FKM definition measure the time a commit takes until it reaches production, the only difference is how they aggregate (i.e., mean, median, p90 etc.). Today it is default practice to use a version control system for source code. To make an adjustment to the software system a developer has to alter source code and to put it under version control. Hence, the commit[3] is defined as the "change". Thus, the lead time is given by the time span between the timestamp of the commit and the timestamp of the deployment, as defined in Sect. 3.3.

Time to Restore Service: 8/16 articles contain a definition for time to restore service. Five of them define the time to restore service as mean time for closing an incident in a certain period. One suggests using chaos engineering (i.e., introduce a failure and measure how long it takes until it gets discovered and resolved), there is a suggestion to periodically poll the "status" and record how long it takes when the status indicates degradation until the degradation gets restored (but do not mention from where the status is taken). The last suggestion made by two articles assumes that the time to restore service should

---

[1] https://1drv.ms/x/s!ApmGN3k-vuHI1ZxB8z9SnoO0r0t_vw?e=qAuxgW.

[2] A delivered version of an application which may include all or part of an application. [13, p.296].

[3] Depending on the used version control system this is called e.g. "commit" or "check-in".

be calculated for failed releases and thus suggests identifying "fix releases" and measuring how long it takes from one release to the following "fix release". The reasons for a failure are manifold, and frequently rely on human interpretation of what constitutes "failure" and "fix", which makes it difficult to fully automate this metric. Provided that a team has an incident management, the calculation via incidents is an interesting approach. Since the incident creation could also be automated, this approach allows a mixture of manual and automated failure recognition. For this work, we define the time to restore as the time between incident creation to closing the incident, like this is stated by the majority of articles found. This choice was made because there is already an incident management in place, which can be used to gather the data and this seems so far to be the most reliable source of data.

Change Failure Rate: 9/16 articles contain a definition for change failure rate. The different suggestions are listed below.

– Percentage of releases that were followed by a "fix release".
– Count of hot fixes in commit messages.
– Detect failures by using monitoring metrics and divided by deployments.
– Manually mark a deployment as successful or not.
– Count rollbacks divided by deployments.

To measure change failure rate, first, it has to be defined what a change is. In all identified articles a change is indicated by a deployment. Accordingly, the change failure rate is the ratio of change failures to deployments (see Sect. 3.3). The next challenge is to identify a failure and attribute it to a change. Unlike for the time to restore service, the incident management cannot be used for failure detection as, according to Forsgren et al., a change failure includes all cases where subsequent remediation was required.[4] Especially for development teams with a good software delivery performance, the team itself will be responsible for the deployment and any resulting failures will be fixed immediately without an incident ever existing. As we assume a low change failure rate in the context of our case study of Swiss Post, we decided to use for our measurements the manual classification of a deployment as a failure by the development team.

Summary: The velocity metrics are more precisely defined and thus the automatic measurement is easier and more straightforward to derive. This is also reflected in the articles found. With the toolchain used by the development team, the measurement of the speed metrics can be completely automated. The stability metrics are less well defined, and unlike the velocity metrics, the boundaries can be drawn less precisely. The literature provided various approaches, but the approaches that would have allowed a fully automated measurement do not capture all relevant aspects of the metrics. For this reason, we have chosen to use only partial automation for measuring the stability metrics. We assume that the change failures are less manifold than failures in general and thus suggest

---

[4] This could be, for example, an automated rollback which is never visible in the incident management system.

the creation of a taxonomy of change failures, which will be the enabler for tools and concepts to automatically detect them.

4 Measure the Four Key Metrics

Based on the earlier definitions Sect. 3 an application was built to measure the FKM automatically. The prototype application is divided into two main parts (green) and several data sources (blue). One is the collector, and the other is the aggregator. The collector is responsible to gather the necessary raw data, transform them and write them in a not compressed manner to the storage of the aggregator (i.e., do no calculations like average). The aggregator enables different calculations and visualizations. This separation aims to enable the usage of different collectors (e.g., for applications which are built and deployment with another toolchain) and to keep the flexibility of having different ways of calculating the metrics (e.g., use the median instead of the mean or use other time periods). The Fig. 1 shows the components of the prototype.

The collector part was implemented using Jenkins[5] (Host/Execute in regular intervals) and PowerShell[6] (collection logic). The aggregator part was Splunk[7] (use an index as storage, do calculations using the Splunk Query Language and visualization with a dashboard). The resulting UI is shown in Fig. 2.

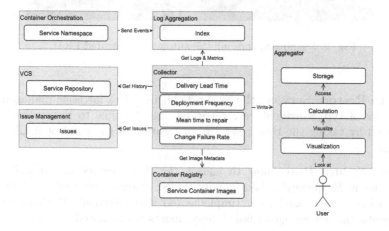

Fig. 1. Concept of prototype to measure the FKM. (Color figure online)

Deployment Frequency: the deployments are detected by using the pulled event from OpenShift, which is logged if a Docker image is pulled from a registry. Those events are sent to Splunk from where the collector gets the data.

---

[5] https://www.jenkins.io (25.04.2021).

[6] https://github.com/PowerShell/PowerShell (25.04.2021).

[7] https://www.splunk.com/ (25.04.2021).

Lead Time for Change: the deployments are collected like described in "Deployment Frequency". The logged event contains the name of the Docker image and the version. The comm it hash from which the Docker image was built is retrievable from Artifactory by using the Docker image name and version. The source code repository URL is also attached as metadata to the Docker image. With the commit hash of the current deployment and the last deployment, as well as the repository URL, all commits which were newly deployed to production are retrieved and the lead time for each commit is calculated.

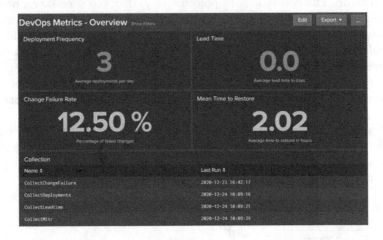

Fig. 2. Dashboard showing the automatic measured FKM.

Time to Restore Service: the Scrum team uses Jira for issue management. Jira issues of type "incident" are retrieved and the time to restore service is calculated by taking the time passed from creation of the incident until it was resolved.

Change Failure Rate: how to collect the deployments was described in "Deployment Frequency". Additionally, failed changes are registered by the team, using a web-based form (implemented with Jenkins). With those two ingredients, the percentage of failed deployments is calculated.

5   Case Study

To investigate the RQ2 "How valuable is the approach to automatically measure the FKM for software development teams?", we conducted a survey after the development team had worked with the prototype for three weeks. For this, the prototype was presented and explained to the team. They decided to look at the metrics once a week as part of an already existing meeting and discuss them.

5.1   Case Description

The study was conducted at the Informatics/Technology function unit of Swiss Post Ltd. Swiss Post Ltd is the national postal service of Switzerland. The group consists of strategic subsidiaries which operate in the core markets of Swiss Post Ltd and function units which are affiliated to Swiss Post Ltd. [14].

In 2019 the Informatics/Technology function unit had around 1200 full-time equivalent employees with about 330 software developers. The unit runs only projects for internal customers i.e., the IT department does not offer services for customers outside of the group. The Scrum team consisting of 10 people looked at in this study is located in the Informatics/Technology function unit and works for Logistics Services in the area of parcel sorting. Logistics Services is one of the subsidiaries of Swiss Post Ltd and is among other things responsible for parcel sorting and delivery. In 2020 Logistics Services delivered 182,7 million parcels [15]. The Informatics/Technology function unit is under pressure, that new products should be delivered earlier to the customer, and IT must be able to react faster to changes in the environment. At the same time, the customer expects consistently high quality. To achieve these goals Informatics/Technology function unit is undergoing an agile transformation. Beside adopting agile methodologies like Scrum and Kanban, DevOps practices are being introduced as part of this agile transformation. The Informatics/Technology function unit is mainly organized project driven but the Scrum team which participated in this study is a stable product team. In 2020 they started to work on a new software system, which is one of the core systems for the sorting of parcels. The team also started to invest in their tool-chain (Fig. 3) and began adopting certain DevOps practices. However, so far, no actions have been taken by the management and the team to measure the progress of the transformation process and the DevOps practices with respect to its improvements; so the team is also not able to track the progress of improvements.

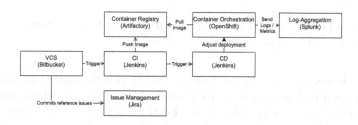

Fig. 3. The toolchain used by the Swiss Post Scrum team.

5.2   Methodology

The research question was divided into sub questions to be answered by the survey. In order to be valuable, a metric should be valid, this concern was addressed by the sub questions one and two. A metric is considered valuable if the team can act on it i.e. it leads to effects. This was addressed by sub question three. The sub question four aimed to capture the subjective perspective of the team onto the value of the automatically measured FKM.

1. Are the FKM a valid way of measuring the speed and stability for software delivery?
2. Can the FKM be used as an indicator for advancing DevOps adoption?
3. What is the effect of measuring the FKM on the teams?
4. Does the development team find value in measuring the FKM?

The survey consisted of four parts: demographics, metric measurement, effect of metric measurement and usefulness of metrics. In the metric measurement part, the participants were asked for their opinion about the FKM and if they think that the metrics as defined by Forsgren et al. measure what they claim to. Furthermore, they were asked how good the automatic measurement implementation reflects what the metrics should measure. The effect of the metric measurement part asked what effects, if any, they expect if the metrics would be measured long term.[8] Finally, the participants were asked how likely they would recommend another team to use the automatic metrics measurement and what metric they consider the most important to be automatically measured.[9]

The questions and our analysis is principally based on Likert scales, and is therefore a quantitative approach based on self-reported experience and perception. After each Likert scale question, there was the possibility to optionally explain the rating in free text.

Six out of ten team members participated in the survey. Among them are four developers and two software architects, aged between 25 and 44. Four of the participants stated that they already knew about the FKM before they were introduced by us.

5.3   Results

This section presents the results of the survey about the automatic metrics measurement. The results are provided online.[10]

Metrics Measurement. Figure 4 shows what the participants think about the metrics defined by Forsgren et al. In general, the participants agree (statement 1: 2× strongly agree, 4× agree) that the FKM are a valid way of measuring the speed and stability for software delivery. The two speed metrics are generally seen as a valid way of measuring the software delivery performance (statement 2: 2× strongly agree, 3× agree, 1× disagree). There is slightly less agreement about the stability metrics (statement 3: 1× strongly agree, 3× agree, 2× somewhat

---

[8] The measurement period was to short to ask for effects that have already occurred.
[9] The full survey can be retrieved here https://1drv.ms/b/s!ApmGN3k-vuHI1ZVZuj-pZY76IvhC_Q?e=AaxwMe.
[10] https://1drv.ms/x/s!ApmGN3k-vuHI1ZtdjwlKBlPYInsY2g?e=V2aBMD.

agree). The FKM were explicitly picked to make sure teams do not trade-off quality for speed. However, it seems there is a piece missing as the participants are sceptical about the stability metrics showing when a team does this trade-off (statement 4: 1× strongly disagree, 1× somewhat agree, 2× agree, 1× strongly agree).

For the implementation of the automatic measurement there was broad agreement that the measurement of the speed metrics is sufficient and moderate agreement about the stability metrics (see Fig. 5).

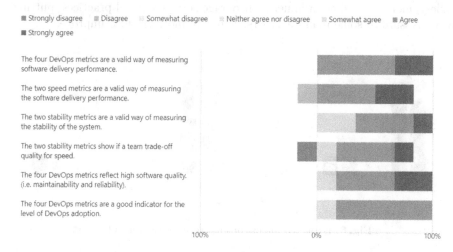

Fig. 4. Participants agreement about the validity of the FKM, as originally defined by Forsgren et al.

Fig. 5. Participants agreement about whether the implemented automation is able to capture the correct measurement.

Effect of Metric Measurement. Figure 6 the answers to the expected effects are shown. The left part shows the answers to the question whether the participant expect an effect on the team and/or on the personal behavior. The left side shows what kind of effect they expect.

The described effects expected for the personal behavior were: Pay more attention to get the pull requests merged quickly, greater use of feature flags, better root cause analysis, more team spirit, feeling more responsible for the work, source of motivation to improve. The effects expected for the team behavior were: More attention for the software delivery process, less deployment pain and anxiety, more relaxed environment, encourage some technical practices, putting some pressure to some team members, source of motivation to improve.

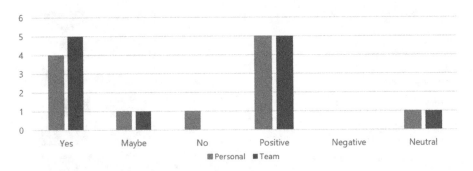

Fig. 6. Expected effects of long term measurement.

Usefulness of the Metrics. The question "On a scale from 1–10, how likely are you to recommend the metrics measurement to another team?" was answered with an average score of 8.3 (max: 10, min: 6, sd: 1.5). The participants ranked the Lead Time for Change as the most important metric to be automatically measured, followed by Change Failure Rate, Time to Restore Service and the Deployment Frequency on the fourth rank. The participant with the value of six explained this score in the free text answer. He wrote that he thinks the most teams do not yet have the mindset nor the tools to start measuring.

6   Discussion

6.1   RQ1: How to Automatically Measure the FKM?

This question was addressed with a multivocal literature review. We identified no scientific literature which investigated the automatic measurement of the FKM. The gray literature review revealed sixteen articles which described aspects of the automatic measurement. Nine of them were published in 2020, three in 2019 and one in 2018, which we explain with the growing interest in DevOps.

The definitions by Forsgren et al. for the stability metrics (change failure rate and time to restore service) are not as clear as the definitions of the speed metrics (deployment frequency and lead time for change) and therefore the suggestions for how to perform the measurement are more diverse for the stability metrics than for the speed metrics. How to automatically measure the speed metrics only differs in detail but still, they are context sensitive i.e., some practices applied by a team can have influence on the definition used and also the measurement implementation (e.g., feature flags, canary releases or Blue/Green deployments).

Worth to mention is the fact that automatic measurement is only possible if the processes are automated. That means only teams which already invest in their automation will be able to use the automatic measurement. Thus, a team might start with tracking their FKM with a survey to get a baseline [7] and as they advance, they switch to an automatic measurement.

6.2   RQ2: How Valuable Is the Approach to Automatically Measure the FKM for Software Development Teams?

We addressed this question with a prototype and a survey. The sub questions to this research question are discussed in the following sections.

Are the FKM a Valid Way of Measuring the Speed and Stability for Software Delivery? In general the participants agreed that the metrics defined by Forsgren et al. are valid. There was slightly more agreement about the speed than the stability metrics. This might be the case because the speed metrics are easier to measure and more clearly defined. Participants are skeptical about the stability metrics showing when a team trade-off quality against speed. A possible reason is that the metrics will show this trade-off not in short but in long term. If a team decides to not constantly refactor the code base, in the short term they will be faster and not lose stability. However, in the mid to long term the technical dept will lead to lower pace and to lower stability [16]. Another reason is that change failure rate and time to restore service do not capture all quality aspects. Lets imagine a team skips all regression test non-critical parts of the system. They get faster but more bugs are discovered in production, which makes the perceived quality of users lower. But the stability metrics will not show this if the bugs do not lead to failures. Although the stability metrics are valid to capture the stability of a system, each system has other quality attributes which should not be traded-off for speed. As they are individual, each team might define additional metrics to capture these attributes.

Can the FKM Be Used as an Indicator for Advancing DevOps Adoption? This question was addressed with a statement with a Likert scale rating. The participants generally agreed but not strongly. The reason gets unveiled when looking at the free text answers. There is general agreement that the FKM are good representatives of DevOps adoption but do not cover every aspect. One aspect mentioned is the provisioning of infrastructure. A DevOps team might be fast with existing services but slow when creating a new one. That might be fine if it's a very rare event, otherwise it should be optimized as well. In his article, Cochran talks about his research about "developer feedback loops" and mention metrics which might not be covered by the FKM like "Find root cause for defect", "Become productive on new team", "Launch a new service in production" [17]. However, there is a need to consider that Forsgren et al. do not postulate that the FKM cover all aspects but say that they are sufficient to divide the teams into clusters. Thus, it would have to be examined whether the high/elite performers correlate with efficient developer feedback loops.

What Is the Effect of Measuring the FKM on the Teams? The participants mostly agreed that they see value in automatically measuring the FKM and expect that the long-term measurement will lead to positive effects on the personal and on the team behavior. But they also state that the FKM do not cover all aspects which are considered as important for quality, speed, and DevOps in general (see also the sections above). It was mentioned that the intrinsic motivation of getting better will let the team take the necessary actions to improve the metrics. The intrinsic motivation is important because one should be well aware of Goodhart's law which states that "When a measure becomes a target, it ceases to be a good measure." [18]. It is not recommended to give a development team the goal of improving metrics and rewarding them with external incentives. Furthermore, a team might need to be guided to improve their FKM. The participants who have a noticeable amount of experience in software engineering, agile and some experience with DevOps only moderately agree that they are able to influence the FKM (2× somewhat agree, 3× agree, 1× strongly agree) and that they know which practices and techniques correlate with each of the DevOps metrics (3× somewhat agree, 2× agree, 1× strongly agree).

Does the Development Team Find Value in Measuring the FKM? From the stated expected positive effects and the high recommendation score the conclusion follows, that the team sees value in measuring the FKM. However, this have to be seen in the context of this team. One of the participants states that he belief that a team has to have already the "right" mindset to get a value from the measurement. If a development team which want to improve it's software delivery performance and/or DevOps adoption the automatic measurement of the FKM are a valuable tool.

The metric with ranked with the highest priority to be measured was the lead time for change. That one with the next was change failure rate. Which indicates that there is the motivation to see how fast one can deliver, however, stability should not suffer as a result.

6.3 Limitations

We are aware that the study has several limitations. The SLR part of the MLR returned no results i.e., no scientific literature but only gray literature was included. The lack of scientific literature is maybe due to the applied methodology (i.e., there are articles, but they are not listed to cite the origin articles used for snowballing). The definitions found are presented in gray literature, those articles are usually less reliable as they do not apply scientific methods, not provide many details and are representing the subjective view of the author. Furthermore, it is possible that important gray literature was not included because a GLR is not exhaustive but certain the stopping criteria are applied.

The research was carried out as a case study. The sample size was small and homogeneous. Participants of the survey were already high performers according to FKM and had already invested into their CI/CD processes, else the automatic measurement wouldn't have been possible. Hence, the results of the study are not representative and generalization is only possible to a limited extent. Furthermore, the study is highly context specific to the Swiss Post environment, which also limits the generalization. But might still be helpful to companies with similar setups. Due to time constraints, the duration in which the team made use of the metrics was too short to ask about perceived effects and we asked about expected effects. It has to be considered that those effect might not show up as expected.

6.4 Summary

The findings indicate that the suggested automatic measurement of the FKM is a good starting point and a valuable tool for intrinsically motivated software development teams, which want to improve software delivery performance and show their DevOps adoption. But the FKM do not cover every aspect e.g. the developer feedback loops are not covered. Hence, it is important that the development team does not only focus on improving the measurements.

6.5 Outlook

The study found that it is possible to meaningful measure the FKM automatically and the software developers team see it as valuable, the prototype going to be rolled out for all development teams at Swiss Post (i.e., all teams which create containerized applications will be able to use it). Professionals and researchers outside of Swiss Post might adapt the suggested definitions and ways to automatically measure the FKM, to build tools for measuring the FKM in their context.

7 Conclusions

In this work we investigated how the four key metrics defined by Forsgren et al. can be measured automatically and if practitioners think that the metrics are valuable. We conducted a multivocal literature review to reveal how the four key metrics are measured by different companies in the industry and in other research projects. Based on those findings, we created a prototype to automatically measure the metrics. The prototype was used by a Scrum team at Swiss Post for three weeks. Afterwards, we collected their experience by using a survey.

The participants of the survey stated that they think that the FKM are a valid measurement for software delivery performance and that they would recommend the automatic measurement for another team. However, they also stated that the FKM are not capturing every important aspect e.g. how fast can infrastructure be provisioned. Despite of the maturity of the team in terms of experience with Agile, DevOps, software engineering and their ranking according to the FKM, it was discovered that the participants only moderately agreed that they think they are able to influence the metrics and that they know what practices to apply to improve. This finding suggests that especially less mature team need guidance to be able to improve on the FKM as they are a lagging measurement and do not directly suggest any actions.

References

1. StateOfAgile: 14th annual STATE OF AGILE REPORT. Technical report 14 (2020)
2. Mezak, S.: The Origins of DevOps: What's in a Name? (2018)
3. Bass, L., Weber, I., Zhu, L.: DevOps: A Software Architect's Perspective, 1st edn. Addison-Wesley Professional (2015)
4. Atlassian: 2020 DevOps Trends Survey. Technical report, Atlassian (2020)
5. PuppetLabs: 2014 State of DevOps Report. Technical report, PuppetLabs (2014)
6. PuppetLabs: 2019 State of DevOps Report. Technical report, PuppetLabs (2019)
7. Forsgren, N., Kersten, M.: DevOps metrics. Queue **15**(6), 19–34 (2017)
8. Garousi, V., Felderer, M., Mäntylä, M.V.: Guidelines for including grey literature and conducting multivocal literature reviews in software engineering. arXiv (2017)
9. Forsgren, N., Smith, D., Humble, J., Frazelle, J.: Accelerate: State of DevOps. Technical report, DORA (2019)
10. Forsgren, N., Humble, J., Kim, G.: Accelerate: The Science of Lean Software and DevOps. 1st edn. IT Revolution Press (2018)
11. ThoughtWorks: ThoughtWorks Technology Radar - Four Key Metrics (2019)
12. Kitchenham, B.A., Charters, S.: Guidelines for performing Systematic Literature Reviews in Software Engineering. Technical Report EBSE 2007–001, Keele University and Durham University Joint Report (2007)
13. ISO/IEC, IEEE: ISO/IEC/IEEE 24765:2010 - Systems and software engineering - Vocabulary. Iso/Iec Ieee 2010 (2010). 410
14. Group Struture - Swiss Post (2020)
15. Swiss Post: Post verzeichnet Allzeitrekord von 182,7 Millionen Paketen (2021)
16. Behutiye, W.N., Rodríguez, P., Oivo, M., Tosun, A.: Analyzing the concept of technical debt in the context of agile software development: a systematic literature review. Inf. Softw. Technol. **82**, 139–158 (2017)
17. Cochran, T.: Maximizing Developer Effectiveness (2021)
18. Strathern, M.: 'Improving ratings': audit in the British University system. Eur. Rev. **5**(3), 305–321 (1997)

Open Access This chapter is licensed under the terms of the Creative Commons Attribution 4.0 International License (http://creativecommons.org/licenses/by/4.0/), which permits use, sharing, adaptation, distribution and reproduction in any medium or format, as long as you give appropriate credit to the original author(s) and the source, provide a link to the Creative Commons license and indicate if changes were made.

The images or other third party material in this chapter are included in the chapter's Creative Commons license, unless indicated otherwise in a credit line to the material. If material is not included in the chapter's Creative Commons license and your intended use is not permitted by statutory regulation or exceeds the permitted use, you will need to obtain permission directly from the copyright holder.

Large-scale Agile

Evolution of the Agile Scaling Frameworks

Ömer Uludağ[1(✉)], Abheeshta Putta[2], Maria Paasivaara[2,3],
and Florian Matthes[1]

[1] Technische Universität München, München, Germany
{oemer.uludag,matthes}@tum.de
[2] Aalto University, Espoo, Finland
{abheeshta.putta,maria.paasivaara}@aalto.fi
[3] LUT University, Lappeenranta, Finland
maria.paasivaara@lut.fi

Abstract. Over the past decade, agile methods have become the favored choice for projects undertaken in rapidly changing environments. The success of agile methods in small, co-located projects has inspired companies to apply them in larger projects. Agile scaling frameworks, such as Large Scale Scrum and Scaled Agile Framework, have been invented by practitioners to scale agile to large projects and organizations. Given the importance of agile scaling frameworks, research on those frameworks is still limited. This paper presents our findings from an empirical survey answered by the methodologists of 15 agile scaling frameworks. We explored (i) framework evolution, (ii) main reasons behind their creation, (iii) benefits, and (iv) challenges of adopting these frameworks. The most common reasons behind creating the frameworks were improving the organization's agility and collaboration between agile teams. The most commonly claimed benefits included enabling frequent deliveries and enhancing employee satisfaction, motivation, and engagement. The most mentioned challenges were using frameworks as cooking recipes instead of focusing on changing people's culture and mindset.

Keywords: Agile scaling frameworks · Large-scale agile · Survey

1 Introduction

Ever since the creation of the Agile Manifesto in 2001, practitioners and academics have devoted a great deal of attention to agile software development methods [1]. Initially, they were designed for small, co-located, and self-organizing teams that develop software in close collaboration with business customers using short iterations [2]. Hence, agile methods have been primarily applied to projects within the so-called *'agile sweet spot'*, i.e., small and co-located teams of less than 50 persons with easy access to the user and business

© The Author(s) 2021
P. Gregory et al. (Eds.): XP 2021, LNBIP 419, pp. 123–139, 2021.
https://doi.org/10.1007/978-3-030-78098-2_8

experts and that develop non-life-critical software [3]. Given the successful adoption of agile methods in small organizations and projects, also many large software organizations have begun to adopt these methods [4]. However, the adoption of agile methods outside the agile sweet spot poses significant challenges to organizations, such as coordination challenges in multi-team environments [5]. To resolve issues associated with the adoption of agile methods in large-scale organizations and projects, several agile scaling frameworks, such as Large Scale Scrum (LeSS)[1] and Scaled Agile Framework (SAFe)[2], have been created both by some custodians of existing agile methods and by others who have worked with companies to scale agile methods to their settings [4, 6, 7]. As large organizations face growing pressures and expectations to become more agile, and the agile scaling frameworks claim to provide off-the-shelf solutions to scaling, their adoption has rapidly increased in industry, as confirmed by the yearly non-scientific survey on the state of agile development conducted by VersionOne [6–8].

Not only is there a growing interest in adopting agile scaling frameworks from an industrial perspective [8], but there is also a growing academic interest to study the adoption of these frameworks [6]. A systematic mapping study by Uludağ et al. [6] uncovered the topic of agile scaling frameworks as a major research stream in the field of large-scale agile development, with a total of 16% of all published studies related to large-scale agile development. The existing literature on the scaling frameworks mainly investigates how individual frameworks are adopted based on case studies (cf. [9]) followed by a comparison of the frameworks based on their underlying characteristics based on literature reviews (cf. [10]). However, the existing literature on agile scaling frameworks disregards the following topics: (i) providing a comprehensive overview of agile scaling frameworks and their evolution, (ii) studying the reasons behind creating these frameworks, and (iii) investigating the benefits and (iv) challenges of adopting these frameworks. To address this research gap, we conducted a survey with the creators/methodologists of known agile scaling frameworks and aim to answer the following research questions (RQs):

- *RQ1: How did the agile scaling frameworks evolve over the years?*
- *RQ2: What are key reasons behind creating of agile scaling frameworks?*
- *RQ3: What are the claimed benefits of adopting agile scaling frameworks?*
- *RQ4: What are the claimed challenges of adopting of agile scaling frameworks?*

The remainder of this paper is structured as follows. In Sect. 2, we provide an overview of related work. In Sect. 3, we portray the research design of our paper. Section 4 presents the result of our survey. In Sect. 5, we discuss our main findings and limitations and conclude our study with a summary of our results and remarks on future research.

---

[1] https://less.works/, last accessed on: 03-10-2021.

[2] https://www.scaledagileframework.com/, last accessed on: 03-10-2021.

2   Background and Related Work

The successful adoption of agile methods in small teams ignited a new passion among firms to start using agile methods in large projects, even beyond software development, across the enterprise [11]. This phenomenon is often referred as *'large-scale agile development'* [12]. In line with Dikert et al. [5], we understand the term *'large-scale agile development'*, as the application of agile methods in large multi-team settings consisting of 50 persons or more, or at least six teams.

Over the past two decades, software engineers and researchers have devoted a great deal of attention to agile software development [13]. Within few years, various agile methods appeared on the landscape, such as Extreme Programming and Scrum, to name a few [1]. Figure 1 presents the various agile methods, their interrelationships, and their evolutionary paths [13].

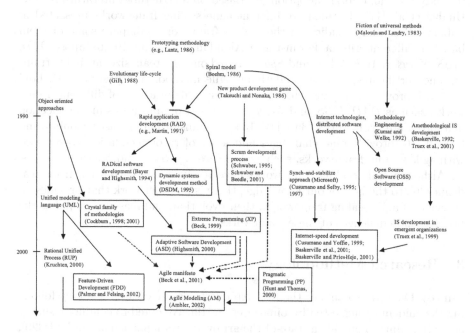

Fig. 1. Evolutionary map of agile methods [13]

Agile methods adhering to varying degrees to the tenets of the Agile Manifesto[3] share some common characteristics, e.g., iterative and incremental development and focus on small releases [1]. The ideal context of applying agile methods in software projects lies within the so-called *'agile sweet spot'*, i.e., small and co-located teams of less than 50 persons with easy access to the user and business experts and that develop non-life-critical software [3]. However, applying agile methods both for larger projects or in larger companies [5], i.e., scaling agile

---

[3] http://agilemanifesto.org/, last accessed on: 03-10-2021.

methods, involves two significant challenges. First, the scaling of agile methods entails additional scaling and complexity factors that summon *'bitter spot'* conditions for agile methods, such as a large number of teams, geographical distribution, entrenched culture, or formal governance structures [14]. Second, present agile methods do not provide sufficient guidance on dealing with these scaling and complexity factors [15]. Thus, custodians of existing agile methods and consultants that have worked with companies in scaling agile to their settings have proposed several agile scaling frameworks over the last years to address the limitations of the agile methods in large organizations and projects [6,7,10]. These frameworks incorporate predefined workflow patterns to deal with issues related to large number of teams, inter-team coordination, and customer involvement [10,16].

Due to the importance of this topic to companies, researchers have started to study the frameworks' adoption [6]. Based on a structured literature review, Uludağ et al. [17] identified 20 different agile scaling frameworks presented in Table 1[4]. Secondary studies on the scaling frameworks compare some of them based on different criteria. For instance, Alqudah and Razali [10] juxtapose *DAD*, *LeSS*, *Nexus*, *RAGE*, *SAFe*, and *Spotify* based on, e.g., team size, available training and certificates, and the underlying agile methods and practices. Diebold et al. [18] provide a map visualizing underlying agile practices of different frameworks, such as *DAD*, *LeSS*, and *Nexus*, to support organizations in the selection of appropriate frameworks. Based on 13 agile transformation cases, Conboy and Carroll [16] provide nine challenges and a set of recommendations associated with agile scaling frameworks, such as *LeSS*, *Nexus*, *S@S*, and *Spotify*.

Although agile scaling frameworks have received some attention from academics [6], to the best of our knowledge, there is no other work that provides an overview of agile scaling frameworks, their evolution, and reasons, as well as the benefits and challenges of these frameworks.

3   Research Methodology

Survey Design. To answer the research questions, we created a survey following the guidelines suggested by Linåker et al. [19]. We opted to conduct a survey as it often aims to provide a state-of-the-art overview on particular methods [20], such as agile scaling frameworks. As a large part of our survey consists of closed-ended questions to quantitatively analyze the agile scaling frameworks, we used a survey as it is a suitable means to provide a quantitative description of the data [20]. The questionnaire consisted of four sections with a total of 22 questions[5]. The first section included questions on the framework background, e.g., reasons

---

[4] We extended the table by Uludağ et al. [17] by adding a column to show the scaling levels of the frameworks and expanded the list of the frameworks by two additional frameworks: *HSD* and *Parallel* as their methodologists approached us during two agile conferences (see Sect. 3). We set the names of agile scaling frameworks whose methodologists participated in our survey in bold.

[5] Questionnaire link: https://bit.ly/2ZPl69S.

Table 1. Overview of agile scaling frameworks based on [17]

Framework	Methodologist	Organization	Publ. date	Category	Scaling level
Dynamic Systems Development Method Agile Project Framework for Scrum (DSDM)	Arie van Bennekum	DSDM Consortium	1997	Framework	Portfolio
Crystal Family (Crystal)	Alistair Cockburn		1998	Set of methods	Team
Scrum of Scrums (SoS)	Jeff Sutherland; Ken Schwaber	Scrum Inc	2001	Mechanism	Program
Large Scale Scrum (LeSS)	Craig Larman; Bas Vodde	LeSS Company B.V	2007	Framework	Enterprise
Gill Framework (Gill)	Asif Qumer; Brian Henderson-Sellers	Adapt Inn	2008	Framework	Enterprise
Enterprise Transition Framework (ETF)	-	agile42	2011	Framework	Enterprise
Mega Framework (Mega)	Rafael Maranzato; Marden Neubert; Paula Heculano	Universo Online S.A	2011	Framework	Portfolio
Scaled Agile Framework (SAFe)	Dean Leffingwell	Scaled Agile Inc	2011	Framework	Enterprise
Disciplined Agile Delivery (DAD)	Scott Ambler	Disciplined Agile Consortium	2012	Framework	Enterprise
Enterprise Agile Delivery and Agile Governance Practice (EADAGP)	Erik Marks	AgilePath	2012	Set of practices	Enterprise
Spotify Model (Spotify)	Henrik Kniberg; Anders Ivarsson; Joakim Sundén	Spotify	2012	Model	Enterprise
Recipes for Agile Governance in the Enterprise (RAGE)	Kevin Thompson	Cprime	2013	Framework	Portfolio
Continuous Agile Framework (CAF)	Andy Singleton	Maxos LLC	2014	Framework	Program
Enterprise Scrum (eScrum)	Mike Beedle†	Enterprise Scrum Inc	2014	Framework	Enterprise
eXponential Simple Continuous Autonomous Learning Ecosystem (XSCALE)	Peter Merel	Xscale Alliance	2014	Set of principles	Enterprise
Holistic Software Development (HSD)	Mike MacDonagh; Steve Handy	Holistic Software Consulting Ltd	2014	Framework	Enterprise
ScALeD Agile Lean Development (SALD)	Peter Beck; Markus Gärtner; Christoph Mathis; Stefan Roock; Andreas Schliep	-	2014	Set of principles	Enterprise
FAST Agile (FAST)	Ron Quartel	Cron Technologies	2015	Set of methods	Program
Lean Enterprise Agile Framework (LEAF)	-	LeanPitch Technologies	2015	Framework	Enterprise
Nexus (Nexus)	Ken Schwaber	Scrum.org	2015	Framework	Program
Parallel Agile (Parallel)	Doug Rosenberg; Brarry Boehm; Matt Stephens; Charles Suscheck; Shobha Dhalipathi; Bo Wang	Parallel Agile Inc	2016	Set of methods	Enterprise
Scrum at Scale (S@S)	Jeff Sutherland; Alex Brown	Scrum Inc	2018	Framework	Enterprise

behind the framework creation and the claimed benefits and challenges. The second section presented questions about framework evolution, e.g., the framework version history. In the third section, we aimed to capture the lean and agile foundations behind the framework, e.g., agile practices adopted to develop the framework. In the final section, we collected information on compatibility between the frameworks. The questions were compiled based on previous studies [8,17] and the Ask Matrix[6].

Survey Validation. Two experienced researchers validated the questionnaire from the software engineering research group at TU Munich. Their suggestions on length, language, and the order of questions were incorporated.

Data Collection. We collected data between August 2017 and September 2019 using the online tool *Unipark*[7]. We used various approaches to reach out to the inventors or organizations, i.e., methodologists, that created the frameworks shown in Table 1. First, we sent out the questionnaire link to 22 methodologists by email. Second, we contacted some of the methodologists in two of the leading agile conferences: XP 2019[8] and Agile 2019[9], and emailed them the survey link. Third, we reached a few methodologists via LinkedIn[10] by sending a personal message with the survey link. We received responses from 15 creators.

Data Analysis. We imported the survey data related to our four research questions to excel sheets. The first two authors analyzed data for all research questions individually by following Corbin and Strauss's coding guidelines [21]. We started with breaking down the data into meaningful entities, i.e., open codes. Later, based on the constant comparison of similarities and differences, we grouped the open codes into higher categories of codes called axial codes. Finally, both authors had a few discussions to compare the open and axial codes from their analysis. The majority of the codes matched between the two authors, and only a few adjustments were made by mutual agreement.

4   Results

4.1   RQ1: Evolution of the Agile Scaling Frameworks

Figure 2 shows a time-based overview of the 15 agile scaling frameworks whose methodologists participated in our survey. Grey rectangles (▬) indicate the *start of development* of a framework, whereas green rectangles (▬) show *current versions* and blue rectangles (▬) symbolize *intermediate versions*. Figure 2 also shows two types of dependencies between the frameworks and their versions: Dashed arrows indicate the influence between different frameworks, whereas solid arrows show a predecessor relationship.

---

[6] http://www.agilescaling.org/ask-matrix.html, last accessed on: 03-10-2021.

[7] https://www.unipark.com/en/, last accessed on: 03-10-2021.

[8] https://www.agilealliance.org/xp2019/, last accessed on: 03-10-2021.

[9] https://www.agilealliance.org/agile2019/, last accessed on: 03-10-2021.

[10] https://www.linkedin.com/, last accessed on: 03-10-2021.

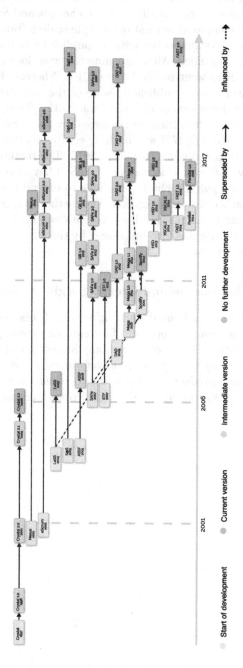

Fig. 2. Evolution of agile scaling frameworks

According to our survey data, *Crystal* is the first created agile scaling framework which development started in 1997. *Nexus, eScrum,* and *S@S* were also relatively early designed compared to most other agile scaling frameworks. However, it took the methodologists almost ten years to publish these frameworks, e.g., by publishing their official guides. Although nine frameworks were created before 2010, only three of them went public before 2010. Whereas, between 2011 and 2018, twelve frameworks were published. None of the methodologists indicated stopping the further development of their frameworks. Most frameworks have multiple versions, whereas four frameworks have only one version, namely *Nexus, LeSS, Spotify,* and *XSCALE*. *Gill* was initially created as the *ASSF* framework (2005-2008), which then evolved into *Gill* in 2012. The methodologists of *Mega* indicated that *Mega 1.0* was a derivative of *SoS*. They also stated that *Mega 2.0* was influenced by *Spotify* including the idea to extend the adoption of agile practices to other parts of the organization. The methodologists of *Spotify* found inspiration from Craig Larman's and Bass Vodde's two books (cf. [22, 23]), that later became *LeSS*. *Spotify* was also influenced by the Program Increment Planning events of *SAFe* (cf. [24]).

4.2   RQ2: Key Reasons Behind Creating Agile Scaling Frameworks

Table 2 presents 12 reasons behind creating scaling frameworks based on our survey. These reasons were grouped into four categories: complexity, customer, market, and organization. The most commonly stated reasons were: *improving the agility/adaptability of the organization, improving the collaboration of agile teams working on same product, improving the coordination of agile teams working,* and *improving the synchronization of agile teams working on same product.*

Table 2. Reasons behind the creation of agile scaling frameworks

Reason category	Reason	Reported in
Complexity	Dealing with increased complexity	ETF, SAFe
	Descaling large product organizations in smaller independent entities	eScrum, XSCALE
Customer	Delivering higher business value	LeSS
	Improving customer involvement	eScrum
Market	Improving the agility/adaptability of the organization	DAD, Gill, HSD, SAFe, S@S, Spotify
	Dealing with changing environments	LeSS
Organization	Improving the collaboration of agile teams working on same product	Nexus, Parallel, SAFe, S@S
	Improving the coordination of agile teams working on same product	Crystal, Nexus, S@S
	Improving the synchronization of agile teams working on same product	FAST, Nexus, SAFe
	Enabling the information/communication flow between agile teams	Crystal, Mega
	Scaling agile to more people/teams/higher organizational levels	LeSS, SAFe
	Managing dependencies between agile teams	eScrum

4.3   RQ3: Benefits of Adopting Agile Scaling Frameworks

Table 3 presents 30 claimed benefits of adopting scaling frameworks based on our survey. These benefits were grouped into two categories, namely: business/product and organization/culture. The most commonly mentioned benefits were: *enabling frequent product deliveries, enhancing employee satisfaction/motivation/engagement, improving software quality, providing customer/ business value, improving the collaboration of agile teams working on same product, improving the coordination of agile teams working on same product, improving the synchronization of agile teams working on same product.*

4.4   RQ4: Challenges of Adopting Agile Scaling Frameworks

Table 4 presents 22 challenges of adopting scaling frameworks based on our survey. These challenges were grouped into three categories: implementation, organization/culture, and scope. The most commonly mentioned challenges were: *using frameworks as cooking recipes* and *using frameworks without understanding for what reasons they should be applied.*

Table 3. Claimed benefits of adopting agile scaling frameworks

Benefit category	Benefit	Reported in
Business/Product	Enabling frequent product deliveries	FAST, Parallel, SAFe, S@S, Spotify
	Improving software quality	Mega, Parallel, SAFe
	Providing customer/business value	LeSS, Mega, S@S
	Enabling continuous improvement	ETF, Spotify
	Enabling continuous integration	Mega, Nexus
	Enabling shorter feedback cycles	FAST, Nexus
	Enabling better adaptability to changing market conditions	S@S
	Enabling faster time-to-market	SAFe
	Enabling the release of working products every Sprint	Nexus
	Improving customer satisfaction	eScrum
	Improving efficiency	Gill
	Minimizing software production costs	Parallel
Organization/Culture	Enhancing employee satisfaction/motivation/engagement	eScrum, FAST, Mega, SAFe, S@S, Spotify
	Fostering the creation of autonomous teams	eScrum, FAST, S@S
	Improving the collaboration of agile teams working on same product	Crystal, Mega, S@S
	Improving the coordination of agile teams working on same product	Crystal, Mega, S@S
	Improving the synchronization of agile teams working on same product	Crystal, Mega, S@S
	Enabling enterprise agility	LeSS, S@S
	Fostering innovation	FAST, Gill
	Improving agile mindset and understanding	DAD, ETF
	Improving accountability	Nexus
	Improving organizational performance	Spotify
	Improving team cohesion	Mega
	Improving transparency	Nexus
	Improving workflows	HSD
	Enabling better understanding of the organization and its vision	DAD
	Enabling the prioritization of company bottlenecks	XSCALE
	Fostering servant leadership	FAST
	Reducing headcount	FAST
	Resolving organizational impediments	S@S

Table 4. Claimed challenges of adopting agile scaling frameworks

Challenge category	Challenge	Reported in
Implementation	Implementing is difficult due to framework complexity	eScrum, HSD
	Missing familiarization with framework	eScrum, Nexus
	Implementation overhead	SAFe
	Misconception due to unconventional agile practices	FAST
	Insufficient guidance	Crystal
	Insufficient guidance regarding lean practices	Mega
Organization/Culture	Using frameworks as cooking recipes	DAD, HSD, SAFe, Spotify
	Using frameworks without understanding for what reasons they should be applied	ETF, Nexus, Spotify
	Lack of management buy-in	SAFe, S@S
	Moving away from agile	Parallel, SAFe
	Moving back from agile to traditional management approaches	ETF, LeSS
	Change resistance	LeSS
	Implementation is difficult in command and control-style organizations	FAST
	Implementation is difficult in traditional organizations	FAST
	Involving non-development units is difficult	Gill
	Implementation is difficult due to remaining power structures	LeSS
	Changing the mindset of the organization is difficult	ETF
Scope	Implementation is limited to team level	Mega
	Implementation is not suitable for monolithic applications	Mega
	Insufficient guidance regarding product backlog management	Mega
	Insufficient guidance regarding managers and specialist positions	LeSS
	Requiring co-location of agile teams	FAST

5   Discussion and Conclusions

5.1   Key Findings

RQ1: How did agile scaling frameworks evolve over the years?
By comparing the evolution map of agile scaling frameworks in Fig. 2 with the evolutionary map of agile methods by Abrahamsson et al. [13], we observed two notable parallels. First, similar to the movement of agile methods, the movement to agile scaling frameworks emerged from parallel innovation both by some inventors of existing agile methods and by consultants who supported organizations in scaling the agile methods. Second, likewise to agile methods, agile scaling frameworks have been continuously emerging and evolving after the movement started. This trend will likely continue as the methodologists of agile scaling frameworks seem to be committed to improving them in the future. Although the evolution map visualizes several agile scaling frameworks, users have concentrated on a few frameworks [25], particularly on *SAFe* and *SoS* [8]. The most recent State of Agile survey [8] confirms this by stating that 35% of their respondents adopted *SAFe* and 16% used *SoS*. A similar observation can be made for agile methods, as 58% of the respondents of the State of Agile survey use Scrum, making it the most commonly used agile method [8].

RQ2: What are key reasons behind creating of agile scaling frameworks?
In total, we found 12 reasons behind the creation of 15 agile scaling frameworks. The reasons identified in our survey fall into either the category of improving the current state of the organization or dealing with the organization's prevalent challenges. Both look similar to reasons that trigger an organizational change [26]. Several reasons, e.g., *improving the collaboration and coordination agile teams working on same product* and *dealing with changing environments* were found in previous studies on large-scale agile development [27,28]. Other reasons related to the scaling of agile methods, such as *dealing with increased complexity* and *scaling agile to more people*, were also reported in [9,29–31]. However, to our knowledge, two reasons found in our survey related to *descaling large product organizations into smaller independent entities* and *improving customer involvement* were not reported by the extant literature on agile development. Surprisingly, several popular reasons for agile, e.g., improving productivity, improving visibility, and improving predictability, were not reported as reasons [8]. As the questionnaire's question was about the main reasons of creating a framework, these earlier mentioned reasons can be some of the implicit reasons behind the creation of the 15 agile scaling frameworks.

RQ3: What are the claimed benefits of adopting agile scaling frameworks?
In total, we identified 30 claimed benefits. The majority of these claimed benefits were similar to the benefits of agile adoption in general found from recent studies on agile method, e.g., State of Agile survey [8]. However, the most common benefit of agile, namely improved productivity [8], was not mentioned by any methodologists. We also identified benefits related to *reducing headcount* and *fostering servant leadership*, which were not found in the previous literature on

large-scale agile development. More research on benefits is needed to establish scientific evidence of using these frameworks in the industry. It is also crucial to understand which practices have contributed to these benefits.

RQ4: What are the challenges of adopting agile scaling frameworks?
We identified 22 challenges from 15 scaling frameworks. To our knowledge, none of the framework's official websites has given information related to the difficulties encountered while adopting these frameworks. The most common challenges identified in our study, i.e., *using frameworks as cooking recipes* and *using frameworks without understanding for what reasons they should be applied*, were not reported by previously published empirical studies. The majority of the challenges found in our study, e.g., *change resistance, moving away from agile, implementation is difficult due to remaining power structures*, and *lack of management buy-in*, were already reported in previously published studies on scaling frameworks [16,32–34] and large-scale agile development [5,35]. The challenges look similar to agile transformation challenges in general. Hence, using an agile scaling framework is not a silver bullet for scaling agile in large organizations, but a starting point for an agile transformation [33]. Several methodologists mentioned that leaders and change agents should focus on changing people's culture and mindset, rather than using frameworks only as cooking recipes.

5.2   Limitations

We discuss the limitations of our study through the threats, as suggested by Wohlin et al. [36].

Construct Validity. This threat is concerned whether the questions presented in the questionnaire represent the attributes being measured. Two survey experts thoroughly checked the questionnaire and evaluated its' understandability, clarity, and readability to counteract this threat. Moreover, the questions were compiled based on previously published studies in the realm of agile software development.

External Validity. This threat is about the generalizability of the results. We aimed to collect responses from all existing scaling frameworks. Out of 22 frameworks, we received responses from 15 methodologists. We could not get responses from the methodologists of seven frameworks despite contacting them several times via email. Thus, this threat could not be completely mitigated. However, we received responses from the most widely adopted scaling frameworks, such as *SAFe, LeSS, DAD*, and *Spotify* [8].

Internal Validity. This threat is concerned with factors that can affect the relationship between the research process and survey results, i.e., the cause and effect relationship. We contacted the methodologists via emails found from the frameworks' official websites. We received confirmation from most methodologists after they filled in the survey, which ensured that the right persons answered the survey. We also met some methodologists during the agile conferences personally and asked them to answer the survey.

Conclusion Validity. This threat deals with the ability to conclude from survey data. The data was coded independently by two researchers. Both researchers compared the codes and drew conclusions together to avoid misinterpretation and misunderstanding of the data.

5.3   Conclusions

Large-scale agile development has received significant interest by practitioners and academics over the last years [37]. As organizations are driven by pressures to scale and to react fast, agile scaling frameworks are increasingly prevalent in contemporary software organizations [7,8], sparking a growing academic interest in studying the adoption of these frameworks [6]. Although there is a body of knowledge on agile scaling frameworks, less research has been conducted to provide an overview of these frameworks and their evolution, study the reasons behind creating these frameworks, and investigate the benefits and challenges of adopting these frameworks. We surveyed the methodologists behind the agile scaling frameworks to address this research gap.

Our study provides an overview of 22 agile scaling frameworks of which 15 were covered by our survey. Our study extends extant literature by providing a map on agile scaling frameworks with their evolutionary paths. Although many methodologists started creating their first frameworks between 2001 and 2011, most guides on these frameworks were published later on. Our findings show a cluster of framework publications between 2011 and 2018, confirming the rising industry interest in scaling the agile methods. We identified 12 reasons behind the creation of the agile scaling frameworks. We revealed two new reasons which were not reported by the existing literature on agile development: *descaling large product organizations into smaller independent entities* and *improving customer involvement*. Further, the methodologists claimed 30 different benefits of adopting their frameworks related to business, product, organizational, and cultural aspects. The methodologists also reported two new benefits which were not described in the previous literature: *reducing headcount* and *fostering servant leadership*. The methodologists recognized 22 challenges in the adoption of the frameworks of which two were newly discovered in our study, i.e., *using frameworks as cooking recipes* and *using frameworks without understanding for what reasons they should be applied*.

We encourage researchers to investigate further how contextual factors, such as complexity, multi-product development, or agile maturity, impact a scaling framework's selection. We call for cross-case analyses to compare the adoption of agile scaling frameworks based on common comparison characteristics.

References

1. Dingsøyr, T., Nerur, S., Balijepally, V., Moe, N.B.: A decade of agile methodologies: Towards explaining agile software development. J. Syst. Softw. **85**(6), 1213–1221 (2012). Special Issue: Agile Development

2. Kettunen, P.: Extending software project agility with new product development enterprise agility. Softw. Process Improv. Practice **12**(6), 541–548 (2007)
3. Boehm, B.: Get ready for agile methods, with care. Computer **35**(1), 64–69 (2002)
4. Dingsøyr, T., Moe, N.B., Fægri, T.E., Seim, E.A.: Exploring software development at the very large-scale: a revelatory case study and research agenda for agile method adaptation. Empir. Softw. Eng. **23**(1), 490–520 (2017). https://doi.org/10.1007/s10664-017-9524-2
5. Dikert, K., Paasivaara, M., Lassenius, C.: Challenges and success factors for large-scale agile transformations: a systematic literature review. J. Syst. Softw. **119**, 87–108 (2016)
6. Uludag, Ö., Philipp, P., Putta, A., Paasivaara, M., Lassenius, C., Matthes, F.: Revealing the state-of-the-art in large-scale agile development: A systematic mapping study. arXiv preprint arXiv:2007.05578 (2021)
7. Carroll, N., Conboy, K.: Applying normalization process theory to explain large-scale agile transformations. In: Proceedings of the 14th International Research Workshop on IT Project Management, January 2019
8. VersionOne: 14th Annual State of Agile Survey (2020). https://stateofagile.com/#ufh-i-615706098-14th-annual-state-of-agile-report/7027494. Accessed 03 Oct 2021
9. Pries-Heje, J., Krohn, M.M.: The safe way to the agile organization. In: Proceedings of the XP2017 Scientific Workshops, pp. 1–4. ACM, May 2017
10. Alqudah, M., Razali, R.: A review of scaling agile methods in large software development. Int. J. Adv. Sci. Eng. Inf. Technol. **6**(6), 828–837 (2016)
11. Paasivaara, M., Behm, B., Lassenius, C., Hallikainen, M.: Large-scale agile transformation at ericsson: a case study. Empir. Softw. Eng. **23**(5), 2550–2596 (2018)
12. Dingsøyr, T., Fægri, T.E., Itkonen, J.: What is large in large-scale? *A Taxonomy of Scale for Agile Software Development*. In: Jedlitschka, A., Kuvaja, P., Kuhrmann, M., Männistö, T., Münch, J., Raatikainen, M. (eds.) PROFES 2014. LNCS, vol. 8892, pp. 273–276. Springer, Cham (2014). https://doi.org/10.1007/978-3-319-13835-0_20
13. Abrahamsson, P., Warsta, J., Siponen, M.T., Ronkainen, J.: New directions on agile methods: a comparative analysis. In: Proceedings of the 25th International Conference on Software Engineering, pp. 244–254. IEEE, May 2003
14. Ambler, S.W.: agile software development at scale. In: Meyer, B., Nawrocki, J.R., Walter, B. (eds.) CEE-SET 2007. LNCS, vol. 5082, pp. 1–12. Springer, Heidelberg (2008). https://doi.org/10.1007/978-3-540-85279-7_1
15. Maples, C.: Enterprise agile transformation: the two-year wall. In: Proceedings of the 2009 Agile Conference, pp. 90–95. IEEE, August 2009
16. Conboy, K., Carroll, N.: Implementing large-scale agile frameworks: challenges and recommendations. IEEE Softw. **36**(2), 44–50 (2019)
17. Uludağ, Ö., Kleehaus, M., Xu, X., Matthes, F.: Investigating the role of architects in scaling agile frameworks. In: Proceedings of the 21st International Enterprise Distributed Object Computing Conference, IEEE, pp. 123–132, October 2017
18. Diebold, P., Schmitt, A., Theobald, S.: Scaling agile: how to select the most appropriate framework. In: Proceedings of the 19th International Conference on Agile Software Development: Companion, pp. 1–4. ACM, May 2018
19. Linåker, J., Sulaman, S.M., Maiani de Mello, R., Höst, M.: Guidelines for conducting surveys in software engineering (2015)
20. Punter, T., Ciolkowski, M., Freimut, B., John, I.: Conducting on-line surveys in software engineering. In: International Symposium on Empirical Software Engineering, pp. 80–88. IEEE (2003)

21. Corbin, J.M., Strauss, A.L.: Basics of Qualitative Research: Techniques and Procedures for Developing Grounded Theory, 3rd edn. Sage Publications Inc., Los Angeles, Calif (2008)
22. Larman, C.: Scaling lean & agile development: thinking and organizational tools for large-scale Scrum. Pearson Education India (2008)
23. Larman, C., Vodde, B.: Practices for scaling lean & Agile development: large, multisite, and offshore product development with large-scale scrum. Pearson Education (2010)
24. Scaled Agile Inc.: PI Planning (2021). https://www.scaledagileframework.com/pi-planning/. Accessed 03 Oct 2021
25. Putta, A., Paasivaara, M., Lassenius, C.: Benefits and challenges of adopting the scaled agile framework (SAFe): preliminary results from a multivocal literature review. In: Kuhrmann, M., et al. (eds.) PROFES 2018. LNCS, vol. 11271, pp. 334–351. Springer, Cham (2018). https://doi.org/10.1007/978-3-030-03673-7_24
26. Scaled Agile Inc.: Reasons for SAFe Adoption (2021). https://www.scaledagileframework.com/reaching-the-tipping-point/. Accessed 03 Oct 2021
27. Paasivaara, M.: Adopting safe to scale agile in a globally distributed organization. In: Proceedings of the 12th International Conference on Global Software Engineering, pp. 36–40. IEEE, May 2017
28. Gustavsson, T.: Dynamics of inter-team coordination routines in large-scale agile software development. In: Proceedings of the 27th European Conference on Information Systems, pp. 1–6, June 2019
29. Heikkilä, V.T., Paasivaara, M., Rautiainen, K., Lassenius, C., Toivola, T., Järvinen, J.: Operational release planning in large-scale scrum with multiple stakeholders-a longitudinal case study at f-secure corporation. Inf. Softw. Technol. **57**, 116–140 (2015)
30. McMunn, D., Manketo, P.: Building strong foundations... underwriting fannie mae's agile transformation. In: International Conference on Agile Software Development, Agile Alliance, August 2017
31. Michelson, C., Adolph, S.: Bias from the bottom: A different way to bootup a safe train. In: International Conference on Agile Software Development, Agile Alliance (2019)
32. Putta, A., Paasivaara, M., Lassenius, C.: Benefits and Challenges of Adopting the Scaled Agile Framework (SAFe): preliminary results from a multivocal literature review. In: Kuhrmann, M., et al. (eds.) PROFES 2018. LNCS, vol. 11271, pp. 334–351. Springer, Cham (2018). https://doi.org/10.1007/978-3-030-03673-7_24
33. Putta, A., Paasivaara, M., Lassenius, C.: How are agile release trains formed in practice? a case study in a large financial corporation. In: Kruchten, P., Fraser, S., Coallier, F. (eds.) XP 2019. LNBIP, vol. 355, pp. 154–170. Springer, Cham (2019). https://doi.org/10.1007/978-3-030-19034-7_10
34. Kalenda, M., Hyna, P., Rossi, B.: Scaling agile in large organizations: Practices, challenges, and success factors. Journal of Software: Evolution and Process **30**, (2018)
35. Uludağ, Ö., Kleehaus, M., Dreymann, N., Kabelin, C., Matthes, F.: Investigating the adoption and application of large-scale scrum at a German automobile manufacturer. In: Proceedings of the 14th International Conference on Global Software Engineering, pp. 22–29. IEEE, May 2019

36. Wohlin, C., Runeson, P., Höst, M., Ohlsson, M.C., Regnell, B., Wesslén, A.: Experimentation in Software Engineering. Springer, Cham (2012)
37. Dingsøyr, T., Falessi, D., Power, K.: Agile development at scale: the next frontier. IEEE Softw. **36**(2), 30–38 (2019)

Open Access This chapter is licensed under the terms of the Creative Commons Attribution 4.0 International License (http://creativecommons.org/licenses/by/4.0/), which permits use, sharing, adaptation, distribution and reproduction in any medium or format, as long as you give appropriate credit to the original author(s) and the source, provide a link to the Creative Commons license and indicate if changes were made.

The images or other third party material in this chapter are included in the chapter's Creative Commons license, unless indicated otherwise in a credit line to the material. If material is not included in the chapter's Creative Commons license and your intended use is not permitted by statutory regulation or exceeds the permitted use, you will need to obtain permission directly from the copyright holder.

Coordination Strategies: Managing Inter-team Coordination Challenges in Large-Scale Agile

Marthe Berntzen[1]([✉]) [iD], Viktoria Stray[1,2] [iD], and Nils Brede Moe[2] [iD]

[1] University of Oslo, Gaustadalléen 23B, 0373 Oslo, Norway
{marthenb,stray}@ifi.uio
[2] SINTEF, Strindveien 4, 7465 Trondheim, Norway
{viktoria.stray,nils.b.moe}@sintef.no

Abstract. Inter-team coordination in large-scale software development can be challenging when relying on agile development methods that emphasize iterative and frequent delivery in autonomous teams. Previous research has introduced the concept of coordination strategies, which refer to a set of coordination mechanisms to manage dependencies. We report on a case study in a large-scale agile development program with 16 development teams. Through interviews, meeting observations, and supplemental document analyses, we explore the challenges to inter-team coordination and how dependencies are managed. We found four coordination strategies: 1) aligning autonomous teams, 2) maintaining overview in the large-scale setting, 3) managing prioritizations, and 4) managing architecture and technical dependencies. This study extends previous research on coordination strategies within teams to the inter-team level. We propose that large-scale organizations can use coordination strategies to understand how they coordinate across teams and manage their unique coordination situation.

Keywords: Coordination strategies · Coordination mechanisms · Dependency management · Large-scale agile · Inter-team coordination · Software development

1 Introduction

Digital transformation drives new sectors, such as the finance and transportation sectors, to make use of agile development methods, often in large-scale settings. Despite the popularity of agile, there are new and complex challenges associated with agile methods in large-scale settings due to the unavoidable coordination required when many development teams work together [1–3]. When many teams work simultaneously with large code bases, achieving technical consistency across teams, managing stakeholders, balancing a shortage of expert resources, and aligning autonomous teams can become problematic [3, 4]. Practitioners of large-scale agile need to understand how to organize for scale, select optimal large-scale practices, and enable inter-team knowledge sharing [1, 5]. Development teams need to manage dependencies between, for example, requirements, testing, integration, and deliverables, working together with requirement

© The Author(s) 2021
P. Gregory et al. (Eds.): XP 2021, LNBIP 419, pp. 140–156, 2021.
https://doi.org/10.1007/978-3-030-78098-2_9

engineers, architects, testers, other teams, and support and expert roles, all while keeping in line with the team's goals and prioritizations [3]. Many of these aspects represent coordination challenges, as several parts of the development organization depend on each other to align their efforts to deliver a software product.

Coordination is often defined as managing dependencies between activities [6], and effective coordination is considered a critical element for large-scale software development [5, 7]. Successful coordination is achieved by the use of appropriate coordination mechanisms, defined as organizational arrangements such as meetings, roles, tools, and artifacts associated with one or more dependencies that allow individuals or teams to realize collective performance [8]. When a set of coordination mechanisms are used to manage dependencies, it is known as a coordination strategy [9]. Moving to the inter-team level, coordination mechanisms, and potentially strategies, are directed at managing the dependencies between teams [2, 10]. Examples of mechanisms include Scrum-of-Scrum meetings and communities of practice, where representatives from each team are present [11], as well as tools and artifacts such as inter-team task boards and project backlogs. When mechanisms work together to address specific coordination issues, for instance managing inter-team prioritizations, they form coordination strategies.

While there is a vast literature on coordination in agile software development, research-based knowledge on inter-team coordination strategies is limited, as existing empirical studies have focused on coordination strategies within the team [9, 12]. To better understand the challenges to inter-team coordination and how they can be managed, we address the following research question: *How are coordination strategies used in large-scale agile to manage inter-team coordination challenges?*

We conducted a case study over six months in a large-scale program in the public transportation sector with 16 development teams. We analyzed data from interviews and field observations to identify the challenges. To guide our analysis, we applied concepts from the theory of coordination in co-located agile software development [9, 12], or the theory of coordination, for brevity [8]. This theory was developed in the context of co-located agile teams [9]. Of particular interest to further exploration is that the theory proposes one agile coordination strategy [9]. In large-scale contexts, there is likely to be a mix of typical agile software development practices and more traditional practices. Furthermore, as large-scale settings are characterized by complex dependencies [2, 3], there may be more than one strategy at play [10, 13].

2 Background and Related Work

2.1 Managing Dependencies in Large-Scale Agile Development

Dependencies are central to the study of coordination. A dependency is defined as when the progress of one action relies upon the timely output of a previous action or on the presence of a specific thing, such as an artifact, a person, or relevant information [12]. Moving to the large-scale level, an inter-team dependency occurs when the output of one team is required as input for another team's work [2, 10]. According to a dependency taxonomy for agile projects [12], there are eight types of dependencies, divided into three categories: knowledge, process, and resource dependencies. Table 1 summarizes the eight typxes of dependencies.

Prior research suggests that there are many and complex dependencies in large-scale agile, and that organizational context matters for large-scale coordination. Uludağ and colleagues [14] studied recurring development patterns and presented an iteration dependency matrix to visualize dependencies between teams. Sekitoleko et al. [15] investigated challenges associated with communication of technical dependencies in large-scale agile. They found challenges such as planning, task prioritization, code quality, and integration and suggested that these challenges can be addressed by practices such as Scrum-of-Scrum meetings, continuous integration, and working in an open space [15]. Dingsøyr et al. [5] explored coordination in a large-scale program with a high degree of task uncertainty and interdependencies and highlighted the importance of scheduled and unscheduled meetings for coordination by feedback. They also emphasized the need for changing coordination practices over time [5].

Further, Gustavsson [16] studied coordination in companies that had implemented the Scaled Agile Framework (SAFe) and found that SAFe provides several coordination mechanisms, such as product increment planning meetings, Scrum-of-Scrum meetings, and program task boards address inter-team dependencies. These, however, required tailoring to the specific contexts of each company [16]. Martini et al. [17] also highlighted the role of context for coordination between teams. They studied inter-group interaction speed in an embedded software development context, exploring how boundary-spanning roles, activities, and artifacts mitigate challenges, with interaction hindering speed between teams. Their findings highlight the need for boundary-spanning mechanisms across teams and organizational levels for software architecture, processes, shared responsibilities, and managing expectations [17].

Table 1. Types of dependencies that can affect agile project progress [24, 25]

Knowledge	A form of information is required for a project to progress	Requirement: Domain knowledge or a requirement is not known and must be located or identified.
		Expertise: Information about task is known only by certain persons or groups.
		Historical: Knowledge about past decisions is needed.
		Task Allocation: Who is doing what, and when, is unknown.
Process	A task must be completed before another task can process and this affects project progress	Activity: An activity is blocked until another activity is complete.
		Business process: Existing business processes cause a certain order of activities.
Resource	An object is required for a project to progress	Entity: A resource (person, place or thing) is not available.
		Technical: A technical aspect of development affects progress, such as when two software components must interact.

2.2 Coordination Strategies

One way to manage dependencies in software projects is to implement coordination strategies [9]. The idea that coordination mechanisms can be used together in the form of coordination strategies is not entirely new. Within software engineering, the concept has been explored conceptually in co-located [9, 12] and global software development settings [18]. However, empirical descriptions of the concept are scarce.

Xu [13] proposed eight coordination strategies for large agile projects for empirical exploration, focusing on decision-making, communication, and control as relevant dimensions of large-scale coordination and encouraging empirical exploration of these. Li and Maedche [18] conceptually explored coordination strategies within teams in a distributed setting, suggesting that increased communication within the team facilitates shared understandings within the distributed team. Scheerer and colleagues [10] described eight types of inter-team coordination strategies, from purely mechanistic to cognitive and organic, and suggested that future research further explore the concept. These studies recognize that situational factors influence coordination strategies, which should also be relevant to the large-scale inter-team context, where teams are often surrounded by complex organizational contexts [19].

In this paper, we apply concepts developed in the theory of coordination [9, 12]. We chose this theory as a lens for investigating inter-team coordination because it provides a framework for analyzing dependencies and coordination mechanisms specific to agile software development and captures both explicit (such as a Kanban board) and implicit forms of coordination (such as shared knowledge) [5, 9]. The theory, and in particular the coordination strategy concept, is relevant also to large-scale contexts because it takes into account that project complexity and uncertainty, as well as the organizational structure, influence coordination [9]. The theory of coordination proposes that coordination in agile software development results from a combination of various agile coordination mechanisms, such as daily stand-up meetings, product backlogs, and software demos, which address dependencies in different ways [9, 12, 20]. The theory further proposes that appropriate coordination strategies enable effective coordination [20].

A coordination strategy comprises three components: coordination mechanisms for synchronization, for structure, and for boundary spanning [9, 20]. Synchronization activities and artifacts refer to coordination mechanisms that promote shared understanding. Structure coordination mechanisms include the proximity, availability, and substitutability of personnel, whereas boundary spanning refers to mechanisms that involve interaction outside the boundaries of the development team [9, 20].

3 Method and Analysis

This study reports on a case study conducted in a Norwegian public sector organization. This organization has an ongoing development program, referred to as the PubTrans program. The data reported in this study was collected over six months during fall 2019. The case study design was chosen because the research-based knowledge on inter-team coordination of software development activities is limited, and case studies can provide detailed insights into the topic under investigation [21]. We took an ethnographic approach to the data collection, focusing on obtaining rich descriptions of the development process and the participants' experiences [22], complemented by in-depth interviews and document analyses.

3.1 Case Description

The PubTrans development program was established in 2016 following a public transportation reform and aims to develop a new micro-services-based platform. The new platform provides, among others, a sales platform for travel operators and a trip planner for travelers. Many languages and technologies were used across the program, and new technologies and tools were adopted as development needs arose. The new cloud-based platform ran on Google Cloud Platform with Kubernetes. Central languages and technologies in use included Kotlin and Java for back-end, and JavaScript (Node.js) and React-Native for front-end. They also used support tools such as Grafana, Prometheus, Slack, JIRA and Confluence. The development organization was mostly co-located with 16 teams, each responsible for their part of the overall software product.

Since the outset, PubTrans has worked with agile methods and autonomous teams. The agile values were largely embraced on the organizational level and the development management had top managements' support on working in agile ways of working. PubTrans did not subscribe to any specific agile methodology or large-scale agile framework, such as Scrum or SAFe. Rather, the development teams had the autonomy to choose which agile practices to use. Most teams had chosen to adopt practices from Scrum such as sprints, stand-up meetings and retrospectives with varying frequency. In addition to developers, all teams included a team leader, a tech lead (a form of team architect), and a product owner. In addition, there were several inter-team roles such as system-, cloud-, and security architects, as well as product and development managers.

Since the initial architecture and team organization was designed in 2016, PubTrans grew from five initial teams to the current large-scale set-up with 16 permanent teams. The teams were organized based on product areas, and the number of members per team varied from five to over fifteen team members. The program was initiated as a development project in 2016 but was transformed to an ongoing development program in 2018. Along the way, they went through several organizational phases and how to best align the team organization with the technical platform was an ongoing discussion.

While the new micro-services-based platform was being developed, PubTrans also delivered services both to their clients (typically public transportation operators) and to the general public through the old, monolithic system. More functionality was added to the new platform continuously and needed to be compatible also with the old system. Many dependencies existed between these systems, and all teams had dependencies to other teams. In addition, there were inter-team knowledge and process dependencies related to, for instance, the delivery sequences. Accordingly, the need for coordination across teams was high.

3.2 Data Collection and Analytical Procedures

During fall 2019, we spent a total of 24 full days at the PubTrans site. The observations consisted of more than 44 h of observation, including a total of 25 meetings. We conducted 12 interviews with team members and program managers. Additionally, we had

Table 2. Data sources

Data type	Description
Interviews	3 program architects, 3 tech leads, 1 product owner, 1 team leader, 4 program managers.
Observations	Twenty-four days on-site including observation of 6 tech lead forums, 6 stand-up meetings, 4 product owner meetings, 4 client meetings, 3 program demos, 2 retrospectives
Supplemental documents	Jira and Confluence documentation such as product backlog and prioritization documents, Slack channels; meeting agendas

frequent informal conversations with the program members. We also inspected documents, logs, and other textual sources for supplemental analysis. The data sources are specified in Table 2. All interviews were tape-recorded based on participants' consent and later transcribed by the first author. The duration was 62 min on average. All interviews were semi-structured, and although the conversations developed naturally, we used an interview guide with questions relating to participants' work habits and inter-team coordination practices. Questions included, *"What challenges do you face working with other teams or roles in the program?," "Can you describe how you interact with members of other teams?,"* and *"What may hinder teams from completing their tasks?"*.

When analyzing the data, we triangulated between sources to strengthen the accuracy and compellability of our findings [21]. By interviewing participants from different parts of the development organization, we gained access to participants' understanding of their work routines across teams and across levels of responsibility. By observing the development process as it unfolded over time and examining associated documents, we obtained context to the interview statements. Together, these data sources provided us with rich information for addressing our research question.

The data was coded in NVivo 12 by the first author, who knew the case in detail. To ensure validity, all emerging categories and concepts were negotiated during a series of discussions among the authors, and some of the material was coded by all authors before discussion. The analytical coding proceeded incrementally. During first-cycle coding, we used descriptive and holistic coding to understand "what is going on" in the data [23] and to identify the broad challenges observed and described by the participants. In the second stage, we categorized the challenges that were relevant across teams and identified the various dependencies and coordination mechanisms associated with inter-team challenges using focused coding [23]. Finally, we compared the challenges identified in the first stage with the dependencies and related mechanisms. We considered something a coordination mechanism if it was associated with one or more distinct dependencies, and a coordination strategy when the mechanisms addressed the same set of challenges [9]. As the mechanisms included operated at the inter-team level, we considered them all to be boundary-spanning [9].

3.3 Limitations and Threats to Validity

All empirical studies have limitations that might threaten the validity and reliability of the results. One limitation of this study is the reliance on a single case. As such, the general criticisms of single-case studies, including the replicability and generalizability to other settings, apply to our study [21]. However, there is theoretical generalizability in the concepts applied, as the challenges we report on are not expected to be unique to this setting [21]. A second limitation relates to the reliance on interviews as a major data source. However, we complemented the interviews with extensive on-site observations and supplemental documents. As such, data triangulation allowed us to obtain context for the interview statements and strengthen our findings [21]. A third limitation is related to the number and types of meetings we observed. If we had observed more and different meetings, such as more retrospectives, we might have found other challenges and mechanisms. However, our extensive on-site presence allowed us to observe many of the challenges in practice.

4   Findings

In this section, we present four coordination strategies that were used to manage challenges with inter-team coordination in the large-scale program. Below, we describe the challenges, dependencies, and corresponding coordination strategies in more detail. The coordination strategies were: 1) aligning autonomous teams, 2) gaining and maintaining overview across teams, 3) managing prioritization issues, and 4) managing architecture and technical dependencies. Table 3 provides an overview.

4.1   Strategy 1: Aligning Autonomous Teams

One set of challenges was related to aligning autonomous teams in the large-scale program. Providing the teams with a high degree of autonomy resulted in process dependencies such as teams blocking each other, as well as the surrounding organizational business processes, which could cause delays that slowed down the speed of the program. Additionally, lack of alignment resulted in technical dependencies not being sufficiently managed. PubTrans aimed to facilitate an agile environment and culture based on autonomous teams. For instance, the teams could choose whether they wanted to apply Scrum, Kanban, Scrumban, or any other agile method. Although autonomy was appreciated, there were challenges related to the freedom of choice when teams operated with different definitions of done, had different testing regimes, and different ways of updating their documentation. One informant stated, *"Here, one has chosen a model with autonomous teams that are allowed to define their own ways of working. If there are sixteen teams here, there are sixteen different ways of doing things"* [Manager 4].

The missing alignment was also observed when we examined the teams' Jira and Confluence pages; some had well-described processes and documentation, whereas others had little to none. In addition, missing alignment contributed to a lack of technical consistency across teams. *"We have allowed people to develop the new APIs team by team. That means they are not uniform"* [Manager 2]. Although team autonomy was

Table 3. Challenges and coordination mechanisms in the four strategies

	Challenge description	Coordination mechanisms
Strategy 1: Alignment	**Choice of agile methods result in different team routines:** - Different definitions of done - Different development routines - Different testing routines - Lack of technical consistency **Related dependencies:** Process: Activity and Business process dependencies Resource: Technical dependencies	**Synchronization activities**: Inter-team stand-ups and status meetings, tech lead forum **Synchronization tools and artefacts**: Shared routines for deliveries and documentation and testing, common definition of done, test team, platform team to support teams with shared technologies **Structure mechanisms**: Co-location, open office space
Strategy 2: Overview	**Large-scale makes it hard to maintain overview:** - Feeling out of sync with other teams - Problems with information flow - Task-related communication across teams - Locating people and information **Related Dependencies:** Knowledge: Expertise, Task allocation, Requirement dependencies	**Synchronization activities**: Inter-team stand-ups and status meetings, program demo **Synchronization tools and artefacts**: Slack, shared backlog in Jira, organization map on Confluence, program roadmap, Objectives and Key Results **Structure mechanisms**: Open office space, co-location
Strategy 3: Prioritization	**Hard deadlines and many clients lead to prioritization challenges:** - Stakeholder expectation management - Time and delivery pressure - Lack of time to prioritize quality work - Changing prioritizations - Lack of clarity in the prioritization process **Related Dependencies:** Process: Activity dependencies Resource: Entity and technical dependencies	**Synchronization activities**: Inter-team stand-up meetings, Product owner meetings **Synchronization tools and artefacts**: Prioritization task board, shared backlog **Structure mechanisms**: Temporary team arrangements (task force teams, taking on other teams' tasks)
Strategy 4: Architecture	**Complex technical dependencies:** - Two systems in use in parallel - Teams becoming bottlenecks - Large code bases of some teams - Risk of repeating old patterns - Vulnerability for errors **Related Dependencies:** Process: Activity dependencies, Resource: Technical dependencies	**Synchronization activities**: Tech lead forum **Synchronization tools and artefacts**: Objectives and Key Results, platform team **Structure mechanisms**: Temporary team arrangements
	Note. Some coordination mechanisms are recurring across the strategies as they address more than one dependency.	

appreciated, teams also saw the need for alignment across teams: *"It is great that the teams are free and have a lot of responsibility. But it is also essential to have arenas where we can discuss and share knowledge across teams so that it's not spinning out of control"* [Tech lead 2].

The challenges described above were addressed with several coordination mechanisms. PubTrans implemented shared documentation routines on Confluence, and shared delivery routines where a shared definition of done and common testing routines was central. Furthermore, they had established a platform team whose main responsibility was to support the development teams by *"developing functionality across teams, but also handling things like automatic builds, deploying, monitoring and logging overall across the teams"* [Team leader].

Other mechanisms included synchronization activities such as inter-team stand-ups for alignment of prioritizations, a test team that worked with testing across the teams, and a tech lead forum for addressing technical dependencies and architecture. Together, these mechanisms form a coordination strategy aiming to align the autonomous teams toward collective deliveries, while at the same time allowing the teams autonomy within appropriate boundaries.

4.2 Strategy 2: Gaining and Maintaining Overview Across Teams

Another major challenge to inter-team coordination was the difficulty of maintaining overview across teams. In the interviews, participants described challenges such as being out of sync with other teams; problems with the information flow; locating information concerning other teams; and insufficient communication about tasks across teams. One informant explained, *"Right now, it is a bit hard to know the status of any given team. I don't know where to find it. You need to play detective"* [Product owner]. Another said, *"It is an information problem. The technical state is not visible across teams and this is the greatest hindrance to addressing inter-team technical problems"* [Architect 2]. These challenges are examples of knowledge dependencies, such as expertise, task allocation, and requirement dependencies, because there is a need to know something about other teams in order to proceed on some action. In the team area, we observed expertise dependencies in practice when frustrated developers discussed whom they should talk to and who knew what in other teams.

The challenge with overview across teams was addressed by several coordination mechanisms. For instance, the office space supported overview and knowledge sharing by both providing open spaces for conducting inter-team stand-up meetings and supporting spontaneous informal coordination. A weekly program demo where the teams showcased their latest work was conducted in an open workspace (shown in Fig. 1). In addition, a program roadmap was visible to all in the open work space. To help team members identify each other, the program had a Confluence document with the names and photos of all members of each of the 16 teams, as well as other employees in the program, such as managers and program architects.

Furthermore, Slack channels and direct messages provided the developers with an easy way of sharing knowledge and reaching out to people they did not know. PubTrans also used Objectives and Key Results (OKRs), which is goal-setting framework where objectives and corresponding key results are defined for individual teams and at the organizational level to measure progress over a set time period, typically per quarter [24]. The company used OKRs as a mechanism to provide an overview of the increasingly complex development process. OKRs were formed for all teams during off-site quarterly workshops where product owners, team leaders, and program architects and managers

Fig. 1. The office space with the program's roadmap easily visible

worked iteratively with forming team-specific objectives and key results. Because of the many inter-team dependencies, it was important to compare and discuss OKRs across teams and adjust as needed. *"The goal of using OKRs is to get an overview and gain insight in the organization. OKR allows us to work more structured, and gain overview of 'this is where were we are now'. Then we can assess what to focus on and use it to take action."* [Architect 1]. Together, these activities and artifacts form a coordination strategy for gaining and maintaining overview across teams.

4.3 Managing Prioritization Issues

Because PubTrans was started as a result of a political reform, there were often hard deadlines the program needed to adhere to, causing time and delivery pressure. One tech lead explained how this impacted the prioritizations they could make: *"Because of these deadlines we are forced to make very hard prioritizations. And that is something I'm sure the clients feel. It's a bit painful from time to time"* [Tech lead 1]. PubTrans had many clients with different needs and the program sometimes overpromised what they were able to do. A manager explained, *"Things come up from different clients that they all expect us to solve. Sometimes we have not managed the expectations well enough, and we may simply not have finished on time"* [Manager 1]. Sometimes one team was forced to stop working on one task to prioritize something else with higher priority, which could cause delays for other teams. One tech lead illustrated a situation where three teams were working together: *"We were so close to finishing the feature! And then one of the teams had to prioritize something else"* [Tech lead 2].

Always chasing the nearest fixed deadlines had consequences for the overall product quality. Informants expressed the challenge of reducing technical debt and working on improvements: *"We need mechanisms that prevent us from always rejecting improvement work in favor of new features"* [Manager 3]. Another said, *"It's all about not overloading the team and setting aside time to prioritize improvement"* [Tech lead 1].

There was also a lack of clarity in the prioritization process. The product owners were in charge of the functional prioritizations and were given input from four account managers who were responsible for client communication. Furthermore, clients could communicate directly with the teams through Slack. Although frequent communication with the customers was important, this set-up led to some confusion. One manager related this to the scaling of the program: *"In the beginning, everything was clear. But now, as things are expanding, these considerations of prioritizations start to matter. Who are in charge of what is going to be prioritized? Right now, sitting in this chair, I still do not know how our overall prioritization mechanism works"* [Manager 3].

The prioritization challenges relate to process dependencies, as they impacted task completion when an activity was dependent on input from several teams. They also relate to resource dependencies as often both technical features and input from members of other teams or program experts, such as the architects, were required to proceed.

Managing prioritization across teams was addressed with mechanisms such as temporary task force teams. A tech lead explained how they had successfully assembled a task force team to implement a feature where multiple teams were involved: *"To get things done as soon as possible, we put together members from four teams. We sat together and held our own task force stand-ups, focusing only on what we needed to get through"* [Tech lead 2]. Furthermore, teams taking on tasks from other teams was described as a successful mechanism when prioritizations caused delays across teams. One team readjusted by implementing a feature for a team that had too much on their hands instead of waiting for them to do it. *"The payment solutions were implemented fully by another team, which was a great success and one of the smarter things we have done"* [Product owner]. To manage the prioritization process, PubTrans used inter-team status meetings for product owners and team leaders, where they discussed top priorities from the different teams toward the overall deliveries. These were conducted in front of a physical task board showcasing the most important inter-team prioritizations. The product owners also had weekly meetings discussing the prioritizations in more detail. Finally, a new and refined shared backlog was created to help with prioritizing across teams and clients. Together, these mechanisms form a coordination strategy for managing inter-team prioritization.

4.4 Managing Architecture and Technical Dependencies

The program scaled fast, growing from five teams in 2016 to 16 teams in 2019. In addition, new clients were constantly added. Scaling up meant that new technical and architectural dependencies arose; several software components from different teams needed to interact, knowledge dependencies arose as information was required across teams, as well as process dependencies, because development activities had to be completed across teams before they were integrated.

In developing the new micro-services-based application, it was hard to avoid developing copies of the old system, which, according to a team leader, left them at risk of developing a distributed monolith. *"Overall, we don't have any mechanism to protect us from repeating old patterns. We have some teams that have been able to create something entirely new, but we also have teams that simply re-implement what they have implemented in the past"* [Team leader]. After some time, two teams who developed key components became bottlenecks. At one point, one team's code base was seemingly large enough to constitute a mini version of the whole platform on which all teams depended. Furthermore, change in one part of the code could have a significant impact on other parts and make the platform vulnerable: *"One risk with developing a distributed monolith with poor error handling is that if one application goes down, the whole system goes down"* [Team leader].

Several coordination mechanisms were used to deal with these challenges. The architects formed specific OKRs to increase awareness of the technical state across teams and to identify constraints and bottlenecks that slowed down the delivery speed. The above-mentioned use of temporary team arrangements, the tech lead forum, as well as the platform team, also contributed to managing technical dependencies. Together, these coordination mechanisms form a coordination strategy for managing architecture and technical dependencies.

The tech lead forum was vital in this strategy because teams learned about each other's architectures and discussed their challenges in relation to each other. The forum was described as a community of practice aimed at sharing architecture-related knowledge and providing an overview of technical dependencies across all the teams. The forum met biweekly, facilitated by one of the program architects and accompanied by a Confluence page where meeting agendas and minutes were posted. One tech lead stated, *"I think the forum is great! It is very good to learn about other teams and what they do and what challenges they have. It's very helpful"* [Tech lead 2].

While valuable, such synchronization activities introduced new challenges, as all teams needed to be represented. Challenges included keeping the meetings relevant for all, engaging participants in discussions, and finding the optimal meeting size. Across the six tech lead forums we observed, between 20 and 25 people showed up, of whom several were managers who were interested in following the discussions. Being a popular meeting, there was a shortage of space, and at two meetings, some people had to stand because there were no more chairs available. Despite the many participants, there were mostly five or six people who talked. One tech lead reflected on why people did not speak up: *"It can be very quiet in tech lead forum. Maybe it is that we do not dare to use the time of all these important people who are here"* [Tech lead 2]. A final challenge with this forum was related to its dependency on a person (entity dependency): *"The tech lead forum is currently completely dependent on the architect facilitating it; it is not self-organizing in any way"* [Team leader].

5 Discussion

In this study, we explored the research question: *How are coordination strategies used in large-scale agile to manage inter-team coordination challenges?* We applied the theory of coordination as a guiding lens and extended the coordination strategy concept to the inter-team level. Our findings broaden the application of the theory of coordination beyond single co-located agile teams [9, 20] and answer calls for future research on coordination strategies [10, 13, 18].

According to the theory of coordination, a coordination strategy is a set of agile coordination mechanisms used to manage dependencies [9, 20]. This theoretical lens served to understand how PubTrans worked on solving their day-to-day coordination challenges among the 16 teams. These challenges are not unique to PubTrans, but rather are characteristics of scaling agile [4]. The four coordination strategies we identified from PubTrans' coordination challenges and mechanisms were 1) aligning autonomous teams, 2) maintaining overview in the large-scale setting, 3) managing prioritizations, and 4) managing architecture and technical dependencies. By extending the theory of coordination to the large-scale level, we show that the identified coordination strategies reflect the complex environment. In large-scale settings, agile practices are often used in combination with other organizational practices [2, 5]. We found that the four coordination strategies included both agile coordination practices, such as stand-up meetings, demos, and task-boards, as well as non-agile practices like OKRs, task force teams, and communities of practice.

Our findings further show that coordination mechanisms were used for several purposes to address challenges and dependencies in the program, which is reflected by their occurrence in several strategies. For instance, tools like Confluence and Slack supported both inter-team alignment (strategy 1) and overview of team members (strategy 2), by providing digital arenas for common documentation routines and gaining easy access to people. Inter-team stand-up meetings provided overview of what was going on in the teams (strategy 2) and served to manage prioritizations between teams (strategy 3). The use of temporary team arrangements supported both inter-team prioritizations (strategy 3), as well as technological dependency management (strategy 4).

Further, PubTrans had several coordinator roles [9, 25], such as the team leaders, product owners, and tech leads, as well as managers and program architects. Other studies highlight shared goals and knowledge enabled by high-quality communication between inter-team roles [3, 25, 26]. For instance, Sablis et al. [3] emphasize the importance of expert roles such as architects in supporting teams and that there is often a shortage of expertise in large-scale projects. In line with this research, we found that there were entity dependencies related to architects in facilitating the tech lead forum. Shastri and colleagues [26] found that project managers perform important coordinating activates such as facilitating, tracking, and negotiating project progress. This research relates to our findings in that program managers facilitated the use of OKRs and supported product owners and team leaders with inter-team prioritizations.

In large-scale software development, neither dependencies nor coordination needs are static. We found that the coordination strategies responded to coordination problems that emerged when the program scaled. Our findings are consistent with a study of two large-scale programs, where coordination mechanisms did not arise as ready-to-use procedures, but were formed during the coordination process [27].

5.1 Implications for Practice

Our findings generate a number of practical implications. While autonomous teams need to know what others are doing, solve technical dependencies, and align their prioritizations and processes with other teams [28], agile methods offer little specific advice on how this should be implemented in large-scale settings. In line with research on large-scale agile frameworks [16, 29] and hybrid settings [2], we found that coordination needs tailoring to the specific organizational context to cope with uncertainty, novelty, and complexity [6, 30]. Our results show that the coordination strategy concept is useful for dependency management at scale, and that large-scale agile programs benefit from adapting coordination mechanisms to their specific needs. We suggest that large-scale companies gather insights of their coordination challenges and dependencies across teams and use these to understand their own coordination strategies.

With respect to the first strategy, aligning autonomous teams, we find that while autonomous teams are central to agile, it appears important to strike a balance between autonomy and alignment and to be flexible across the large-scale development organization [2, 4, 31]. We suggest including shared documentation and testing routines and a common definition of done while still allowing the teams autonomy to choose development practices in an alignment strategy.

The second strategy, maintaining overview across teams, relates to typical challenges with knowledge dependencies as the number of teams grows so large that it is hard to keep track of who is working on what. For this strategy, we recommend including mechanisms such as keeping a team chart showcasing who does what in which teams, and using communication tools that provide easy access to members of other teams, such as Slack, and regular synchronization meetings to support overview [27].

Relating to the third strategy, managing prioritizations, PubTrans worked on establishing effective prioritization mechanisms. In line with previous studies [e.g., 5, 16, 27], we found that physical or digital prioritization boards highlight essential inter-team prioritizations and guided teams in adjusting to each other. Another successful practice in PubTrans was the ability of teams to take on the tasks of other teams. This flexibility appears core to an agile culture and mindset. We recommend such practices to make the most of a strategy for managing prioritizations. Concerning the fourth strategy, managing architecture and technical dependencies, we recommend the use of communities of practice, such as the tech lead forum, to support management of technical dependencies across teams [11], and establishing a platform team to support development teams [29].

6   Conclusion and Future Research

In this study, we explored the research question of how coordination strategies were used to manage challenges with inter-team coordination in a large-scale agile program with 16 teams. We found the coordination strategy concept useful for studying inter-team coordination in large-scale settings. The concept provides practitioners with an approach that is highly context-specific and flexible and thus suitable for the volatile, complex, and ambiguous large-scale development setting. From our analysis, we found four coordination strategies: 1) aligning autonomous, 2) gaining and maintaining overview across teams, 3) managing prioritization issues and, 4) managing architecture and technical dependencies. We extend the coordination strategy concept to include more practices beyond agile coordination mechanisms, as we found that the mechanisms included in the strategies consisted of both agile practices, such as stand-up meetings and demos, and other practices such as OKRs and a community of practice. Future research could further explore how coordination mechanisms fit together to form coordination strategies, and how to tailor them to contribute to effective coordination in large-scale settings. We also encourage future research to explore coordinator roles in relation to inter-team coordination strategies. Finally, our on-site access allowed us to explore coordination in a co-located setting. Since then, the workplace has changed, and we encourage empirical research on coordination strategies in distributed settings.

Acknowledgements. This research was supported by the Research Council of Norway through the research project Autonomous teams (A-teams) project, under Grant Number 267704.

References

1. Bass, J.M., Salameh, A.: Agile at scale: a summary of the 8th International Workshop on Large-Scale Agile Development. Presented at the Agile Processes in Software Engineering and Extreme Programming–Workshops (2020)
2. Bick, S., Spohrer, K., Hoda, R., Scheerer, A., Heinzl, A.: Coordination challenges in large-scale software development: a case study of planning misalignment in hybrid settings. IEEE Trans. Softw. Eng. **44**, 932–950 (2018)
3. Sablis, A., Smite, D., Moe, N.: Team-external coordination in large-scale software development projects. J. Softw. Evol. Process. e2297 (2020)
4. Dikert, K., Paasivaara, M., Lassenius, C.: Challenges and success factors for large-scale agile transformations: a systematic literature review. J. Syst. Softw. **119**, 87–108 (2016)
5. Dingsøyr, T., Moe, N.B., Seim, E.A.: Coordinating knowledge work in multi-team programs: findings from a large-scale agile development program. Proj. Manage. J. **49**, 64–77 (2018)
6. Malone, T.W., Crowston, K.: The interdisciplinary study of coordination. ACM Comput. Surv. (CSUR). **26**, 87–119 (1994)
7. Faraj, S., Sproull, L.: Coordinating expertise in software development teams. Manage. Sci. **46**, 1554–1568 (2000)
8. Okhuysen, G.A., Bechky, B.A.: 10 coordination in organizations: an integrative perspective. Acad. Manag. Ann. **3**, 463–502 (2009)
9. Strode, D.E., Huff, S.L., Hope, B., Link, S.: Coordination in co-located agile software development projects. J. Syst. Softw. **85**, 1222–1238 (2012)
10. Scheerer, A., Hildenbrand, T., Kude, T.: Coordination in large-scale agile software development: a multiteam systems perspective. Presented at the 2014 47th Hawaii international conference on system sciences (2014)
11. Smite, D., Moe, N.B., Levinta, G., Floryan, M.: Spotify guilds: how to succeed with knowledge sharing in large-scale agile organizations. IEEE Softw. **36**, 51–57 (2019)
12. Strode, D.E.: A dependency taxonomy for agile software development projects. Inf. Syst. Front. **18**(1), 23–46 (2015). https://doi.org/10.1007/s10796-015-9574-1
13. Xu, P.: Coordination in large agile projects. Rev. Bus. Inf. Syst. (RBIS). **13**, (2009)
14. Uludağ, Ö., Harders, N.-M., Matthes, F.: Documenting recurring concerns and patterns in large-scale agile development. Presented at the Proceedings of the 24th European Conference on Pattern Languages of Programs (2019)
15. Sekitoleko, N., Evbota, F., Knauss, E., Sandberg, A., Chaudron, M., Olsson, H.H.: Technical dependency challenges in large-scale agile software development. In: Presented at the International Conference on Agile Software Development (2014)
16. Gustavsson, T.: Dynamics of inter-team coordination routines in large-scale agile software development. In: Proceedings of the 27th European Conference on Information Systems (ECIS), pp. 1–16, Uppsala (2019)

17. Martini, A., Pareto, L., Bosch, J.: A multiple case study on the inter-group interaction speed in large, embedded software companies employing agile. J. Softw. Evol. Process. **28**, 4–26 (2016)

18. Li, Y., Maedche, A.: Formulating effective coordination strategies in agile global software development teams (2012)

19. Mikalsen, M., Næsje, M., Reime, E.A., Solem, A.: Agile autonomous teams in complex organizations. In: Hoda, R. (ed.) XP 2019. LNBIP, vol. 364, pp. 55–63. Springer, Cham (2019). https://doi.org/10.1007/978-3-030-30126-2_7

20. Kanaparan, G., Strode, D.: A theory of coordination: from propositions to hypotheses in agile software development. In: Presented at the Proceedings of the 54th Hawaii International Conference on System Sciences (2021)

21. Yin, R.K.: Case Study Research and Applications: Design and Methods. Sage Publications, Thousand Oaks (2018)

22. Sharp, H., Dittrich, Y., de Souza, C.R.B.: The role of ethnographic studies in empirical software engineering. IEEE Trans. Softw. Eng. **42**, 786–804 (2016)

23. Saldaña, J.: The Coding Manual for Qualitative Researchers. Sage, Thousand Oaks (2012)

24. Niven, P.R., Lamorte, B.: Objectives and Key Results: Driving Focus, Alignment, and Engagement with OKRs. John Wiley & Sons, Hoboken (2016)

25. Berntzen, M., Moe, N.B., Stray, V.: The product owner in large-scale agile: an empirical study through the lens of relational coordination theory. In: Presented at the International Conference on Agile Software Development (2019)

26. Shastri, Y., Hoda, R., Amor, R.: The role of the project manager in agile software development projects. J. Syst. Softw. **173**, 110871 (2021)

27. Moe, N.B., Dingsøyr, T., Rolland, K.: To schedule or not to schedule? An investigation of meetings as an inter-team coordination mechanism in large-scale agile software development (2018)

28. Martini, A., Stray, V., Moe, N.B.: Technical-, social-and process debt in large-scale agile: an exploratory case-study. In: Presented at the International Conference on Agile Software Development (2019)

29. Paasivaara, M.: Adopting SAFe to scale agile in a globally distributed organization. In: Presented at the 2017 IEEE 12th International Conference on Global Software Engineering (ICGSE) (2017)

30. Jarzabkowski, P.A., Lê, J.K., Feldman, M.S.: Toward a theory of coordinating: creating coordinating mechanisms in practice. Organ. Sci. **23**, 907–927 (2012)

31. Moe, N.B., Smite, D., Paasivaara, M., Lassenius, C.: Finding the sweet spot for organizational control and team autonomy in large-scale agile software development. Empirical Softw. Eng. (2021)

Open Access This chapter is licensed under the terms of the Creative Commons Attribution 4.0 International License (http://creativecommons.org/licenses/by/4.0/), which permits use, sharing, adaptation, distribution and reproduction in any medium or format, as long as you give appropriate credit to the original author(s) and the source, provide a link to the Creative Commons license and indicate if changes were made.

The images or other third party material in this chapter are included in the chapter's Creative Commons license, unless indicated otherwise in a credit line to the material. If material is not included in the chapter's Creative Commons license and your intended use is not permitted by statutory regulation or exceeds the permitted use, you will need to obtain permission directly from the copyright holder.

Challenges of Adopting SAFe in the Banking Industry – A Study Two Years After Its Introduction

Sara Nilsson Tengstrand[1], Piotr Tomaszewski[2]([⊠]) [iD], Markus Borg[1,2] [iD], and Ronald Jabangwe[2] [iD]

[1] Lund University, Lund, Sweden
[2] RISE Research Institutes of Sweden, Lund, Sweden
`{piotr.tomaszewski,markus.borg,ronald.jabangwe}@ri.se`

Abstract. The Scaled Agile Framework (SAFe) is a framework for scaling agile methods in large organizations. We have found several experience reports and white papers describing SAFe adoptions in different banks, which indicates that SAFe is being used in the banking industry. However, there is a lack of academic publications on the topic, the banking industry is missing in the scientific reports analyzing SAFe transformations. To fill this gap, we present a study on the main challenges with a SAFe transformation at a large full-service bank. We identify the challenges in the bank under study and compare the findings with experience reports from other banks, as well as with research on SAFe transformations in other domains. Many of the challenges reported in this paper overlap with the generic SAFe challenges, including management and organization, education and training, culture and mindset, requirements engineering, quality assurance, and systems architecture. However, we also report some novel challenges specific to the banking domain, e.g., the risk of jeopardizing customer relations, stability, and trust of external stakeholders. This study validates several SAFe-related challenges reported in previous work in the banking context. It also brings up some novel challenges specific to the banking industry. Therefore, we believe our results are particularly useful to practitioners responsible for SAFe transformations at other banks.

Keywords: Large-scale agile · Scaled agile framework · Banking · Interview study

1 Introduction

Even though agile methods have become popular among all kinds of companies, the methods were initially created for small teams and organizations. This often causes challenges when large organizations want to go agile [1]. Several frameworks guide a large-scale agile adoption, such as Large Scale Scrum, Disciplined Agile Delivery, and the Scaled Agile Framework (SAFe) [2]. According to a yearly survey by VersionOne, a company specializing in agile solutions, SAFe is the most popular framework for scaling

© The Author(s) 2021
P. Gregory et al. (Eds.): XP 2021, LNBIP 419, pp. 157–171, 2021.
https://doi.org/10.1007/978-3-030-78098-2_10

agile in large enterprises [3]. SAFe is a set of principles and practices that aims at scaling agile methods for large organizations.

Scaled Agile, the company behind SAFe, publishes experience reports from companies that have introduced SAFe. The financial sector, and the banking industry specifically, are represented there [2]. At the time of writing, several actors from the banking industry are in the middle of a SAFe-transformation. Scaled Agile quotes experience reports from SAFe introductions at banks such as Nordea, Standard Bank, and Capital One [4], showing that SAFe is actively used in the banking industry.

As it can be expected, there are numerous challenges for both large-scale agile transformations in general and SAFe transformations specifically [1, 2, 5]. Despite that fact, Putta et al. [2] report a lack of scientific research on the challenges of SAFe adoptions in general. The banking industry is no exception in this matter.

Our study aims to fill that gap by identifying the challenges for a SAFe transformation in the banking industry. We seek an answer to the following research question:

RQ: What are the main challenges for adopting SAFe in the banking industry?

To answer this question, we conduct a qualitative survey at a large full-service bank. The study consists of several interviews with people representing key roles involved in the SAFe transformation. To establish how our findings fit into the existing body of knowledge and how much they can be generalized, we compare them to the existing research on challenges with general agile transformations and to the aforementioned SAFe introduction experience reports.

The rest of the paper is organized as follows: Sect. 2 introduces theory on large-scale agile software development and the Scaled Agile Framework. Section 3 presents related work and Sect. 6 describes the research method. Section 5 presents the results of the study; Sect. 6 discusses the results. Section 7 concludes the findings.

2   Large Scale Agile Software Development

Dikert et al. [1] define large-scale agile software development as software development organizations with 50 or more people or at least six teams. Agile methods were originally created with small and isolated teams in mind. Scaling up agile practices to larger organizations with multiple teams poses certain difficulties. Software development in large companies often means larger projects that span over a long period. Moreover, there is often a need to coordinate multiple teams in the software development process. To be able to meet the needs of large organizations, agile practices need to be applied to the entire organization. There have been a number of scaled agile frameworks proposed and, as mentioned, the most popular amongst them is SAFe [3].

SAFe is a set of principles and practices that make it possible to apply an agile way of working throughout the entire organization. SAFe can be configured in different ways and can be adapted to the specific needs of the company. The framework is built on core values and principles and has an implementation roadmap to guide organizations on how to go through the transformation. SAFe is suitable for companies ranging from medium-sized, with roughly 50 employees, to large with thousands of people [6].

SAFe offers several different configurations. In the most extensive configuration, there are guidelines for four defined levels of the organization: team, program, value stream/solution, and portfolio. Figure 1 shows some examples of roles and activities. At the Team level, the Scrum master, agile teams, and the product owner are operating and delivering working systems at least every two weeks. The development is primarily based on user stories and enabler stories. At the Program level, the agile teams are coordinated by an Agile Release Train (ART). ART consists usually of five to twelve teams that work together coordinated by the Release Train Engineer. This level focuses on creating artifacts such as a vision, roadmaps, and features. The Value stream level, sometimes called the solution level, is for organizations that require additional roles to integrate the work of complex systems that are dependent on each other. At this level, release management roles work with economic frameworks to coordinate multiple ARTs and value streams. The Portfolio level has the purpose of aligning the value streams from the lower levels to meet the business goals and financial goals of both the portfolio and the organization's overall business goals by program portfolio management. At this level, there are so-called Epics, which are initiatives that transcend all levels of the organization, i.e., from the visions of the upper levels to concrete development projects in the lower levels [7].

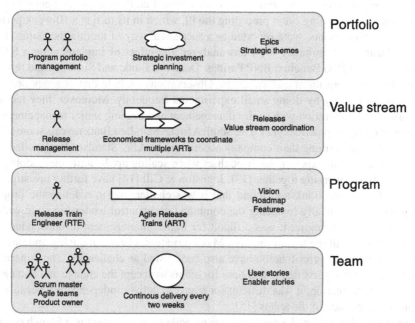

Fig. 1. Examples of roles and activities included at each level of SAFe

3   Related Work

This section presents individual studies on SAFe transformations from the literature, followed by three secondary studies.

3.1 Individual Case Studies

Although there is little research on SAFe transformations in the banking industry, there are studies on large-scale agile transformations in other industries. Laanti et al. [8] have made a case study on the organization-wide transformation at Nokia and found that the main group of challenges is related to the deployment of agile methods and the second largest group of challenges is managing and planning requirements according to agile methods. Paasivaara et al. [9] have made a case study on Ericsson's large-scale agile transformation and experienced challenges such as change resistance, lack of training and coaching, and that the surrounding organization was still in "waterfall mode". Paasivaara et al. [10] have further made a case study on the SAFe transformation at Comptel, a globally distributed software development company. In the case of Comptel, challenges such as lack of early training sessions and change resistance are reported.

Several white papers reporting challenges from SAFe transformations in full-service banks are available on the Scaled Agile website. Nordea introduced SAFe in 2014. One challenge that was reported is that different teams in the same Agile Release Train were frustrated because the delivery streams were not in unison, meaning it was not clear what was supposed to be delivered. However, the so-called Program Increment (PI) sessions, which is a planning event preceding the PI, which in its turn is a 10-week period consisting of five sprints, were reported as a successful way of uniting the teams [11]. Initio, a business consultancy firm, has analyzed the effect of implementing a SAFe transformation at ING Benelux, BNP Paribas, Deutsche Bank, and SimCorp and reports lessons learned from the transformations. Observations include that changes need to happen incrementally by doing small experiments frequently. Moreover, they recommend a close collaboration with senior management and training senior management in SAFe principles and practices [12]. The South African Standard Bank reveals some challenges when transforming their company according to SAFe. Standard Bank rolled out a few agile teams but experienced difficulties when scaling up the agile methodologies and having teams working together [13]. Johnston & Gill [14] have further investigated the case of Standard Bank and found that it was challenging to redefine the project manager role, specifically replacing the command-and-control leadership style with a coaching one. Furthermore, it was difficult for higher management to understand the long term benefits of the transformation. Making tradeoffs between quality and time as well as requirements prioritization have also been listed as challenges. The American Bank Capital One reports that it was hard for teams to accept the change and that early on in the transformation, it was difficult for teams to deliver independently because of dependencies outside of the teams [15].

Berkani et al. conducted a case study on an agile transformation in a French central bank [16]. The study is motivated by the research gap on how a company goes from experimenting with agile methods to establishing agile methods as a natural part of the organization. The study lists factors for a successful implementation in a large organization such as a reorganization of the Project Management Office and IT projects department, and generalizations of internal agile methods from a top management perspective. However, the study does not describe challenges related to the transformation.

3.2 Systematic Literature Reviews

We have identified three different systematic literature reviews that summarize and categorize findings from studies on large scale agile transformations [1, 2, 5]. Figure 2 summarizes the categories of challenges found in these studies. The first two studies focus on large-scale agile transformations in general, while the third study focuses on SAFe transformation in particular. In the first study by Dikert et al., the category where most challenges are reported is "agile difficult to implement" and an example of a challenge in that category is that agile is customizable poorly [1]. The second study by Uludag et al. reports most challenges with coordinating multiple agile teams that work on the same product, which is a challenge in the "communication and coordination" category [5]. In the third study by Putta et al., which focuses specifically on SAFe transformations, the most common challenge is change resistance, found in the "organizational and cultural" category [2].

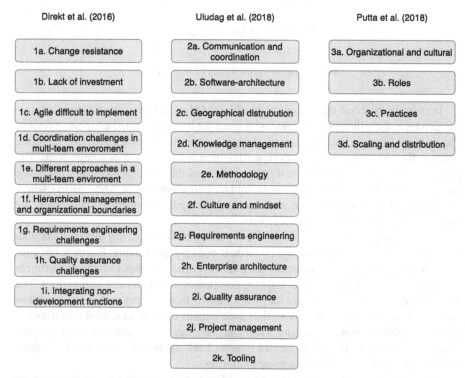

Fig. 2. Categories of challenges presented in three different systematic literature reviews. Note that the ordering within each column does not convey any particular meaning.

4   Method

Figure 3 shows the research strategy. The study is exploratory since it seeks new insights into the SAFe transformation challenges in the case company and the banking industry in general.

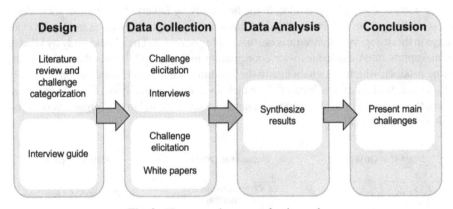

Fig. 3. The research strategy for the study

In order to establish the current body of knowledge with regards to the agile transformations and challenges associated with them we have performed a literature review. The findings from the literature review, primarily from the existing systematic literature reviews, formed a base for an interview study that we conducted in a large bank. The purpose of the study was to identify the challenges the bank faced during the SAFe transformation. On top of that we have looked into a number of white papers where other banks described their own experiences from agile transformations. Finally, we have compared and synthesized the results.

The company where the interviews were performed is a large full service bank with services such as consumer banking, investment banking and trading. Examples of consumer banking services are customer saving accounts and mortgages whereas investment banking includes services such as assisting companies in mergers and acquisitions. The bank has physical branches where they offer face-to-face services to their customers as well as online presence. Furthermore, the case company operates in several countries and has over 12,000 employees globally. The bank has a large IT department that is responsible for customer facing products, like internet banking, but also products facilitating internal operations, like digital meeting platforms.

The goal of the SAFe transformation under study is to make the entire company operate in an agile manner. The bank has been transforming according to SAFe since 2018 and has a handful Agile Release Trains in operation. The bank chose SAFe as it was considered to have the highest chance to be accepted and trusted by decision-makers. Another reason for selecting SAFe was the standardization of roles and practices, that makes it easier to both educate employees and recruit new ones. The company has previous experience with agile on a smaller scale, and some individual teams apply agile practices in their daily work.

Prior to the interviews, we created a list of categories where the challenges have been previously identified based on the input from literature reviews [1, 2, 5]. To assure completeness, we ensured that all categories identified by the three systematic literature reviews fit into the proposed categories. On top of that, we added a "Banking specific" category to capture the challenges that are specific to the domain under study. Figure 4 shows the resulting categories. These categories were used as a base for each interview. During the interviews, the interviewees were asked if the category was relevant for their transformation, and to provide examples of challenges they faced.

Management and Organization	Requirements Engineering	Education and Training	Quality Assurance	Mindset on Change	System Architecture	Banking Specific
1d, 1e, 1f, 1i, 2a, 2c, 2d, 2e, 2h, 2j, 3a, 3b	1g, 2g	1b, 1c, 2k, 3c	1h, 2i	1a, 2f	2b, 3d	

Fig. 4. The different categories of challenges in a SAFe transformation used as a foundation in the study. The references relate to the challenges reported in previous secondary studies, see Fig. 2.

The interviews were performed with four representatives from the bank. The sampling of the interviewees was motivated by their experience and expertise in the SAFe transformation in the bank. They all belong to the selected group of individuals who were driving the agile transformation in the company. As such, they are expected to have wide knowledge of obstacles and challenges not only in their respective areas, but also in the bank in general. Dealing with such challenges is an important part of their daily work.

A semi-structured interview is common to use in such studies, as such interviews are exploratory and descriptive [17]. The use of interviews with both open-ended and specific questions allows for answers with unforeseen information but still makes sure that the interview stays on topic. Since the respondents have different roles in the transformation, they were not asked the exact same questions. However, each interview followed the same pattern. We started with establishing some background information about the interviewees and their roles in the agile transformation. After that we went through the categories from Fig. 4. For each category the interviewees were asked to provide information about the challenges that the bank faced in the respective area.

To ensure that the responses were interpreted correctly, the transcript was sent to the interviewees for validation. Based on the transcripts, each of the three involved researchers (authors 1–3) performed an independent identification and categorization of the challenges. Later, a workshop was arranged to agree on a joint list of categorized challenges. The final list was compared to the findings from other studies.

5   Results

The results are summarized in Table 1 and further elaborated in this chapter.

Table 1. The resulting list of challenges

Management and organization
A1. Difficult to adapt existing internal processes to the agile development practices
A2. Difficult to define and adapt to new roles
A3. Difficult to create a shared vision and align the entire organization around common goals
A4. Challenge to make the entire organization to work agile
A5. Hard to coordinate and align agile development in a distributed organization
Education and training
B1. Competency gap between old and new roles
B2. Difficult to achieve optimal time planning for the training activities
B3. Need for tailoring of training to meet different needs in the organization
Culture and mindset
C1. Individual resistance to change
C2. Change is discouraged in the banking industry
C3. Banking values traditions and stability, implies difficulties for transformation
Requirements engineering
D1. Difficult to prioritize requirements
D2. Difficult to break down requirements
D3. Hard to find a balance between specificity and time
D4. Requirements in SAFe defined differently, new way of dealing with requirements
Quality assurance
E1. Difficult to balance speed and quality
E2. Challenge to increase test automation
Systems architecture
F1. Legacy systems are not easily adopted to agile ways of working
F2. Complexity and interdependencies between legacy systems are hard to deal with
Banking specific
G1. External rules and regulations complicate transformations in the banking industry
G2. Big transformations may adventure the external stakeholder trust

Management and Organization (A): In general, software development teams are more likely to have the knowledge or even previous experience with agile methods and the transformation might therefore not be as challenging for them as it is for other departments. The challenge is instead to integrate and engage every unit that are in a large organization in the SAFe transformation, especially if they have traditionally been working in non-agile ways. This challenge is exacerbated when developers are not collocated.

Education and Training (B): The case company faces a competency gap in profiles of old and new roles as the transformation is taking place. But despite the positive attitude on employees' competency, there are difficulties with bridging the competency gap that the SAFe transformation requires. This highlights that there is need for better training when adopting SAFe. To be able to adopt SAFe successfully, it is important to educate all Scrum masters of the purpose and the principles behind SAFe for them to, in turn, be ambassadors within their teams. However, the case company faced difficulties in providing effective training activities. The main issues relate to the need for tailoring training to the companies' and needs, and also finding optimal time for training and minimizing impact on productivity.

Culture and Mindset (C): The main challenge of adopting SAFe is that the employees are not used to making changes. It was reported that there is no company infrastructure for supporting change and transformation management, which leads to people not wanting or expecting change. One interviewee mentioned that the banking industry in general values traditions and that many people are used to working in a way where it is easier to predict outcomes and to make long-term planning, in contrast to agile methods. The case company has a successful business, and it is then hard for some employees to understand why a transformation as big as adopting SAFe should be made.

Requirements Engineering (D): The traditional requirements engineering role has faced one of the most significant changes in the transformation. One interviewee mentioned that it is a challenge to change the requirements process to instead begin with expressing high-level business needs that the development team should build from, rather than begin with a complete list of requirements as in the previous way of working. In addition, rationale for requirement prioritization from upper management is not clearly communicated to developments. The reason for this might be, according to one interviewee, that the SAFe transformation was started at the bottom of the organization.

An interviewee revealed that there is a problem with teams viewing agile epics as just a high-level requirement that should be broken down into smaller requirements when it should instead be viewed as a placeholder for communication. An epic should be tied to a story so that everyone involved understands what is desired to be achieved. By communicating the epic as a story instead of through conventional documentation, the chance of success increases, as stated by the interviewee. In the case company, this has shown to be a long process, taking up to three years before the new way of dealing with requirements has become universally accepted.

Quality Assurance (E): In a more traditional development process, software testing occurs primarily towards the end of the process. On the other hand, agile methods strive for built-in-quality where testing takes place continuously in the process. One interviewee reported that when changing the way of working with testing, the case company faces several challenges. One reported challenge is building a foundation for automated testing, and another one was the challenge of balancing quality and time.

Systems Architecture (F): One challenge mentioned in the interviews is that the complexity of the systems makes it difficult to work according to SAFe. Dependencies between systems and having many systems are all impediments for the SAFe transformation. The complexity of the systems makes it harder for the case company to deliver customer value for every sprint (i.e., every two weeks), e.g., compared to a fast-moving small startup. However, according to the interviewees, it will never be relevant to increase the sprint length.

Banking Specific (G): The case company's reputation is dependent on releasing reliable products and services that people can trust. However, balancing reliability and frequent releases is a delicate issue. The interviewees mentioned the risk of adventuring external stakeholders' trust when working with more frequent releases. Simultaneously, new and sometimes unpredictable regulations and quickly changing demands in the market put pressure on the case company's ability to be flexible. In an industry where more niche banks take market shares, the competitive landscape puts pressure on the large full-service banks to become fast and flexible while not jeopardizing the trust and loyalty of external stakeholders that are more used to stability and a slow pace of changes.

6 Discussion

The challenges of adopting SAFe can vary between different banks. We believe that by comparing the study result with other experience reports some common challenges can be identified. All the challenges that were found in the case company are listed in Table 1. We have found that many of them are also mentioned in experience reports from other banks, or even in other industries.

We show that the case company faced several challenges in the "management and organization" category. Some of them are also reported by other banks. Capital One [15] reports dependencies outside of the teams as a challenge, similar to our findings at the case company. This suggests that organizational boundaries in companies affect the SAFe transformation. Here, an interesting dilemma appears. It is a common practice not to deploy the transformation all at once but instead introduce changes incrementally, as mentioned in the cases of ING Benelux, BNP Paribas, Deutsche Bank, and SimCorp [12]. At the same time, dependencies between departments are an issue for a successful transformation, implying that changes need to occur at many departments at once. Not surprisingly, the challenge to transform the entire organization into an agile way of working is not unique to the banking industry. Ericsson also reports a challenge with surrounding organizations being in "waterfall mode" when scaling the agile methods [9]. Furthermore, the challenge of redefining roles is also reported at Standard Bank [13], confirming that is evident across banks transforming according to SAFe.

Experience reports from other banks also cover challenges identified in the "education and training" category. One of them is the need for tailoring of training to meet different needs in the organization. Standard Bank reports difficulties for uniting teams when scaling up the transformation [13], and Nordea reports a challenge with aligning different agile teams [11]. This emphasizes the need to align knowledge and competency about agile practices across all teams. The challenge of aligning agile teams could also be a challenge related to management and organization since a lack of shared vision and optimization targets might be a reason why teams are not synchronized.

For the challenges in the "culture and mindset" category, we show that the general characteristics of the banking industry culture pose particular difficulties for making changes in general. This has also been found in another bank, where accepting change is reported as a challenge in the case of Capital One [15].

There are also some challenges reported in the "requirements engineering" category. One of the challenges is reported by Standard Bank. The report states that having transparent requirements prioritization is difficult [13]. This challenge further shows a need for management to formulate and communicate goals in the teams. Previous research suggests that effective communication can facilitate the prioritization of requirements [18]. The requirements engineering-related challenges in SAFe transformation generalize beyond the banking industry as managing and planning requirements are also mentioned as challenges at Nokia [8].

When it comes to "quality assurance," the issue of balancing quality and speed of delivery found in this study is also found in the experience report from Standard Bank [14]. The challenge of managing more frequent releases is also related the "systems architecture" category, where the complexity of the systems and dependencies between the systems are found challenging for the SAFe transformation in the case company.

The case company faces challenges originating from the external stakeholders, as reported in the "banking specific" category. The company operates in an industry where every product has to undergo rigorous testing procedures before releasing due to external regulations. The testing process can be hard to align with agile methods. Similar issues with agile methods and regulated development are discussed in safety-critical contexts [19]. In the banking domain, the characteristics of the services necessitate instilling high levels of trust, which can be difficult when having to work with incremental updates and frequent releases, as recommended by agile principles.

To summarize, Table 2 maps the challenges identified in our study to other studies and experience reports reporting similar findings. The distinction is made between findings from within and outside of the banking industry. We find that some of the challenges are found in other banks, and that a majority of the challenges is common with SAFe transformations in other industries. The challenges that do not appear in previous customer stories or research are:

- C3. Banking values traditions and stability, implies difficulties for transformation
- G1. External rules and regulations complicate transformations in the banking industry
- G2. Big transformations may adventure the external stakeholder trust

All these challenges are very specific to the banking industry, and can be considered sensitive, which may explain why they have not been reported previously. As these challenges seem not to have been obvious from the beginning, we believe that they are one of the unique contributions of our study and can be of particular interest for other actors in the banking industry.

Table 2. Mapping between challenges found in this study and related work

Challenge in our study	Challenge found in other banks	Challenge found in other industries
A1	[15]	[2]
A2	[13]	[2]
A3		[5]
A4		[9]
A5		[2]
B1		[2]
B2		[10]
B3	[13]	[9]
C1		[5]
C2	[15]	[10]
C3		
D1	[13]	[2]
D2		[5]
D3		[5]
D4		[5]
E1	[14]	[5]
E2		[2]
F1		[2]
F2		[5]
G1		
G2		

7 Threats to Validity

This section discusses threats to the validity of our conclusions. The discussion is organized into construct validity, external validity, and reliability issues. We do not discuss internal validity, as our conclusions include no causal claims.

Construct validity reflects how well the phenomenon under study is captured. The researchers have substantial pre-understanding of agile transformations and combined experience of almost two decades of large-scale agile transformations at five different companies. Regarding the constructs under study, we rely on standard SAFe concepts that were well understood by all interviewees. Thus, we consider the threats to construct validity as minimal.

External validity is related to the generalization of the findings outside the studied setting. We claim that our conclusions are relevant for other large banks. To mitigate the threats to external validity, we selected interviewees with broad experience and insights in various units within the bank – some of them also had worked with other banks in the past. We have also identified an overlap between our findings and what other banks undergoing similar transformation report in white papers, as well as an overlap between our findings and the general body of knowledge with respect to agile transformations. We believe that strengthens the generalizability claim. Further studies may reveal that our findings, at least in part, also generalize to smaller challenger banks [20] and other FinTech businesses such as insurance companies.

The reliability of a study is related to the dependence on specific researchers. We mitigate the threats to research bias by applying established research practices. The interview guide was co-developed iteratively by the first three authors. The interviews were conducted, recorded, and transcribed by the first author. Three authors independently analyzed the transcripts, and a joint workshop was organized to summarize the results. The few findings that deviated were discussed until a common understanding was reached. We maintained a chain of evidence from the conclusions to individual interview statements through fine-granular traceability during the study. However, for confidentiality and anonymity reasons, we agreed with the case company and with the interviewees not to reveal exact mappings between statements and interviewees in this paper. Nevertheless, it is possible that another set of researchers would emphasize other aspects of SAFe transformations. However, as the reported findings are presented on a high-level of detail, we consider the threats to the reliability of the study as minor.

8   Conclusions

The goal of this study was to identify challenges of a SAFe transformation in the banking industry. To address the research question, we have performed a study at a large full-service bank. In the study, we have identified several challenges belonging to seven categories, ranging from technical challenges related to the system architecture to banking specific issues. Significant challenges include the alignment of goals and optimization targets within the entire organization. Our findings considerably overlap with experience reports from similar transformations, both in the banking industry and in other industries. Consequently, we believe that the findings are interesting for the banking industry and, therefore, are relevant to other banks that are about to embark upon their SAFe transformation journeys. As a natural next step we would like to investigate how the challenges have been addressed at the bank to be able to provide actionable recommendations.

References

1. Direkt, K., Paasivaara, M., Lassenius, C.: Challenges and success factors for large-scale agile transformations: a systematic literature review. J. Syst. Softw. **119**, 87–108 (2016)
2. Putta, A., Paasivaara, M., Lassenius, C.: Benefits and challenges of adopting the Scaled Agile Framework (SAFe): preliminary results from a multivocal literature review. In: Proceedings of the International Conference on Product-Focused Software Process Improvement, pp. 334–351 (2018)
3. Version One (2020): 14th Annual State of Agile Report. https://stateofagile.com/#ufh-i-615 706098-14th-annual-state-of-agile-report/7027494
4. Scaled Agile, (n.d.): SAFe customer stories, 2020–08–25. https://www.scaledagile.com/cus tomer-stories/

5. Uludag, Ö., Kleehaus, M., Caprano, M., Matthes, F.: Identifying and structuring challenges in large-scale agile development based on a structured literature review. In: Proceedings of the 22nd International Enterprise Distributed Object Computing Conference, pp. 191–197 (2018)
6. Scaled Agile: Achieving business agility with SAFe® 5.0 December 2019. https://www.sca ledagile.com/?ddownload=47510
7. Knaster, R., Leffingwell, D.: SAFe 4.0 distilled: applying the Scaled Agile Framework for lean software and systems engineering, Boston: Addison-Wesley Professional (2017)
8. Laanti, M., Salo, O., Abrahamsson, P.: Agile methods rapidly replacing raditional methods at Nokia: a survey of opinions on agile transformation. Inf. Softw. Technol. **53**, 276–290 (2011)
9. Paasivara, M., Behm, B., Lassenius, C., Hallikainen, M.: Large-scale agile transformation at Ericsson: a case study". Empir. Softw. Eng. **23**, 2550–2596 (2018)
10. Paasivaara, M.: Adopting SAFe to scale agile in a globally distributed organization. In: Proceedings of the 12th International Conference on Global Software Engineering, pp. 36–40 (2017)
11. Scaled Agile: (2015) SAFe Case Study: Nordea, 2020–08–30. https://www.scaledagile.com/ case_study/nordea/
12. Everaerts, S.: Initio (2018), 2020–08–30. https://www.initio.eu/blognavigation/2018/12/3/ embracing-scaled-agile-framework-in-banking-amp-investment-industry
13. Scaled Agile, (n.d.): SAFe Case Study: Standard Bank, 2020–08–30. https://www.scaledagi leframework.com/standard-bank-case-study/
14. Johnston, K.A., Gill, G.: Standard Bank: The Agile Transformation, vol. 6, no. 1 (2017)
15. Scaled Agile, (n.d.): SAFe Case Study: Capital One, 30/8, 2020. https://www.scaledagilef ramework.com/capital-one-case-study/
16. Berkani, A., Causse, D., Thomas, L.: Triggers analysis of an agile transformation: the case of a central bank. In: Procedia Computer Science, pp. 449–456 (2019)
17. Runeson, P., Höst, M.: Guidelines for conducting and reporting case study research in software engineering. Empirical Softw. Eng. **14**(2), 131–164 (2009)
18. Bjarnason, E., Wnuk, K., Regnell, B.: Requirements are slipping through the gaps – a case study on causes & effects of communication gaps in large-scale software development. In: Proceedings of the 19th International Requirements Engineering Conference, pp. 37–46 (2011)
19. Steghöfer, J.-P., Knauss, E., Horkoff, J., Wohlrab, R.: Challenges of scaled agile for safety-critical systems. In: Proceedings of the International Conference on Product-Focused Software Process Improvement, pp. 350–366 (2019)
20. Blakstad, S., Allen, R.: New standard models for banking. In: FinTech Revolution, Palgrave Macmillan, Cham, pp. 147–166 (2018). https://doi.org/10.1007/978-3-319-76014-8_9

Open Access This chapter is licensed under the terms of the Creative Commons Attribution 4.0 International License (http://creativecommons.org/licenses/by/4.0/), which permits use, sharing, adaptation, distribution and reproduction in any medium or format, as long as you give appropriate credit to the original author(s) and the source, provide a link to the Creative Commons license and indicate if changes were made.

The images or other third party material in this chapter are included in the chapter's Creative Commons license, unless indicated otherwise in a credit line to the material. If material is not included in the chapter's Creative Commons license and your intended use is not permitted by statutory regulation or exceeds the permitted use, you will need to obtain permission directly from the copyright holder.

Benefits and Challenges of Adopting SAFe - An Empirical Survey

Abheeshta Putta[1]([✉]), Ömer Uludağ[2], Maria Paasivaara[1,3],
and Shun-Long Hong[2]

[1] Aalto University, Espoo, Finland
{abheeshta.putta,maria.paasivaara}@aalto.fi
[2] Technische Universität München, München, Germany
{oemer.uludag,shunlong.hong}@tum.de
[3] LUT University, Lappeenranta, Finland
maria.paasivaara@lut.fi

Abstract. During the last two decades, turbulent business environments tempted firms to adopt agile methods to cope with the ever-changing customer demands. The success of agile methods in small and co-located teams inspired companies to apply them to large-scale endeavors. Agile scaling frameworks, such as the Scaled Agile Framework (SAFe), have been proposed by practitioners to scale agile practices to large projects and enterprises. Companies are increasingly taking these frameworks into use. However, the number of quantitative empirical studies assessing the benefits and challenges of adopting the agile scaling frameworks is still limited. This paper starts filling in this gap by presenting the results from a survey of 100 industry participants around the world on their perception of the benefits and challenges of adopting the SAFe framework. Our results show that the SAFe adoption improves transparency, as well as collaboration and dependency management between agile teams. The most commonly mentioned challenges of the SAFe adoption are organizational politics, difficulties in establishing an agile mindset, change resistance, and team formation challenges.

Keywords: Agile scaling frameworks · Large-scale agile software development · Scaled agile framework · Survey

1 Introduction

Agile software development methods were originally designed for small and co-located teams. The realized benefits in small organizations led to an increased interest in agile across large-scale organizations [1]. Transformation to agile is not an easy undertaking; several studies have reported significant challenges while adopting agile in large-scale settings, e.g., change resistance, coordination challenges in multi-team environment, and challenges in involving non-development units [1]. Agile adoption is more than just implementing practices; it is about

© The Author(s) 2021
P. Gregory et al. (Eds.): XP 2021, LNBIP 419, pp. 172–187, 2021.
https://doi.org/10.1007/978-3-030-78098-2_11

changing the mindset, and culture [2]. Several agile scaling frameworks, e.g., Scaled Agile Framework (SAFe) [3], Large Scale Scrum (LeSS) [4], Disciplined Agile Delivery (DAD) [5] were designed by practitioners and consultants to support scaling of agile to large organizations. Out of all scaling frameworks, SAFe has been the most popular according to the most recent State of Agile survey by VersionOne, with 35% of the respondent organizations reporting its usage [6].

The popularity of SAFe and successful marketing of its benefits by the Scaled Agile Inc. has encouraged companies to take SAFe into use [7]. Over one hundred companies have reported about their SAFe usage via case studies and short stories [8]. According to the official SAFe website [3], 70% of Fortune 100 companies have certified SAFe professionals, and 700,000 practitioners have been trained in SAFe. Despite the popularity of SAFe in industry, scientific research exploring SAFe usage is still limited; nevertheless, there is a slight increase in scientific studies published after 2018. However, the majority of reported experiences on SAFe still comes from grey literature [7], most of which is published on the SAFe official website, which may lead to biased information. The SAFe adopters have reported several benefits [7]. However, we do not have much research-based evidence of these benefits. Therefore, it would be essential to identify whether the SAFe framework can mitigate the challenges of scaling agile, bring the promised benefits, and determine whether it brings in new challenges [9].

A few quantitative studies have already reported the benefits and challenges of SAFe usage [10–12]. However, we need more quantitative studies to capture the state-of-practice of SAFe adoption, as the limitations of the existing surveys prevent generalization, e.g., in [10], out of 111 respondents, only 5% were pure SAFe users, and [11] studied only three organizations. As many researchers have expressed the need for better understanding the SAFe usage and adoption [13,14], in this paper, we investigate the state-of-practice of SAFe adoption by conducting an empirical survey of companies that have taken SAFe into use. We report the contextual factors of companies, as well as the benefits and challenges of SAFe usage.

The remainder of this paper is structured as follows. In Sect. 2, we present the background and related work of our paper. Section 3 describes the underlying research method of this paper. Section 2 presents our results and provides a discussion of our main findings. Section 5 concludes our study with a summary of our results and remarks on future research.

2   Background and Related Work

This section gives an overview of SAFe and presents the previous empirical studies on SAFe.

2.1   SAFe

Dean Leffingwell established SAFe in 2011. The latest version, 5.0, was released in 2020 [3]. SAFe incorporates practices from agile and lean [3]. It has four different configurations: Essential, Large Solution, Portfolio, and Full SAFe. Each configuration has set of practices, artifacts, and roles to deliver solutions to the end user. SAFe has four core values: built-in quality, transparency, alignment, and program execution [15].

SAFe claims that the most common benefits of its adoption are: employee engagement, productivity, time to market, and quality [3]. Challenges of implementing SAFe are not mentioned.

2.2 Previous Studies

In this section, we present the benefits and challenges of SAFe adoption reported in the previous studies.

Putta et al. [7] conducted a multivocal literature review (MLR) and reported a total of 23 benefits and 15 challenges of SAFe adoption. The most common benefits were: transparency, alignment, and quality. The most often mentioned challenges were: resistance to change, moving away from agile, and controversies within the framework. The study's limitation is the use of grey literature from the SAFe website that might lead to the results being biased towards the benefits of SAFe.

Laanti and Kettunen [10] conducted an empirical survey on SAFe adoptions in Finland. They analyzed data from 111 respondents. As the most significant benefits of SAFe they reported: transparency, co-operation, and common cadence. The most commonly mentioned challenges were: old mindset and culture, the model not fitting correctly to own organization, and missing fluency when using the model. The limitation is that only 5% of the respondents were pure SAFe users.

Gustavsson and Bergkvist [11] surveyed SAFe in three different organizations: automotive, financial, and public sector. They reported increased visibility, overview, and transparency as the most common benefits and the lack of productivity, focus, and efficiency as the most common drawbacks of SAFe adoption. As the study had only three organizations participating, it makes it hard to transfer the results to other organizational settings.

Salikhov et al. [12], surveyed 16 organizations that had adopted SAFe and received answers from 21 respondents. Their preliminary results indicate improved productivity, better handling of dependencies, improved coordination between levels, and better vision of the big picture as the most often mentioned benefits. The most common drawbacks include: requires more resources, complex structure, lack of autonomy, and decreased productivity.

The existing surveys are few, and they are limited to selected locations and organizations, which reduces their external validity. In this paper, we present the benefits and challenges of SAFe by conducting an empirical survey with respondents from various geographical locations, domains, roles, and differing length of experience with SAFe, which helps to understand SAFe usage more broadly in the industry and improves the external validity of the findings.

3   Research Methodology

This section describes the research design by presenting the research questions, survey design, data collection, and data analysis.

3.1   Research Questions

We aim to answer the following research questions:

- **RQ1:** *What benefits are realized after the adoption of SAFe?*
- **RQ2:** *What challenges are witnessed during and after the adoption of SAFe?*

3.2   Survey Design

In order to answer the research questions, we created a survey following the guidelines suggested by Linåker et al. [16]. The survey questionnaire consisted of six sections with a total of 25 questions[1]. In the first section, we presented our research goals and information on who should answer the survey (only practitioners having experience in one or several of the scaling frameworks were asked to answer the survey). The second section included questions on the organizations' transformation background, such as how long they had used a specific framework. In the subsequent three sections, we asked the participants to assess their agreement regarding their own organization on lists of reasons, benefits, and challenges, which were compiled based on three previous studies on agile and large-scale agile development [17–19]. Additionally, in each of the three sections described above, we included an open-ended question for the respondents to add other reasons, benefits, or challenges experienced/witnessed respectively to reduce the anchoring effect. In the fifth section, we captured the participants' background information, such as their company's domain, respondent's primary role in the organization, and the location of the organization. The last section provided closing remarks on the survey and a thank you message.

Survey Validation. The questionnaire was first carefully reviewed by first three authors. Then, we asked for comments from an academic subject matter expert. Next, two survey experts helped to make sure that the questionnaire adhered to the best practices of survey research. Finally, an industry expert on large-scale agile reviewed the questionnaire and suggested, e.g., reducing the questionnaire's length. After incorporating all suggestions, we conducted a pilot survey with three respondents and asked for their feedback on the questionnaire's length, understandability, and readability. After final modifications, the survey was ready to be submitted to the target audience.

Sampling and Target Audience. In this context, we used non-probabilistic convenience sampling, which involves *"getting responses from the individuals who are willing and are available"* [20]. The target audience for the survey included

---

[1] Link to the questionnaire: https://figshare.com/s/abd8810840a3fe514db6.

software professionals from various roles, e.g., developers, managers, coaches, who use agile scaling frameworks in their organizations.

Data Collection. The data collection took place between May and September 2019 using a third-party, online tool *"LimeSurvey"*[2]. To reach our target population, we promoted the survey in: (1) conferences, (2) meetup groups, (3) social media groups, and (4) via personal networks.

We promoted the survey in three conferences: the 20th International Conference on Agile Software Development (XP 2019)[3], the 14th International Conference on Global Software Engineering (ICGSE 2019)[4], and the Agile 2019[5].

Two researchers promoted the survey at the XP 2019 conference. They spoke to people during the breaks and mailed the link to those interested in answering the survey. A link to the survey was distributed among all XP 2019 participants in a conference news post. At the ICGSE 2019 conference, two researchers promoted the survey in the same way as at the XP 2019. At the Agile 2019 conference, one researcher promoted the survey by handing out cards containing survey information and a QR code to the online survey. The survey link was also sent out to all participants via email in the daily conference news letters during the conference, as well as one week after the conference.

The survey link was also published on selected social media platforms, promoted at Agile Meetups, and distributed to professionals. In June 2019, the survey link was posted in the worldwide LinkedIn group *"Lean and Agile Software Development"*[6], which is the largest online community of Lean and Agile practitioners with more than 157.000 members from all over of the world. We promoted the survey in two Agile Meetups, where practitioners share their experiences, ideas, and knowledge on issues regarding agile software development. One was held in Helsinki, Finland, in August 2019 with 32 participants and one in Copenhagen, Denmark, in June 2019 with 30 participants. The survey leaflets, containing the link and QR code, were distributed to all Meetup participants. Finally, professionals from different organizations worldwide were approached via email, LinkedIn, and other social media channels and asked to fill in the survey. By snowballing of contacts we aimed to find new contacts, i.e., the personal networks of existing contacts were leveraged.

3.3   Data Analysis

We imported the collected survey data from LimeSurvey to the SPSS Statistics tool[7]. We conducted a two-day workshop among all authors to clean the data, e.g., removed incomplete responses and agreed on how to conduct the statistical analysis.

---

[2] https://www.limesurvey.org/, last accessed on: 03-11-2021.

[3] https://www.agilealliance.org/xp2019/, last accessed on: 03-11-2021.

[4] https://conf.researchr.org/home/icgse-2019, last accessed on: 03-11-2021.

[5] https://www.agilealliance.org/agile2019/, last accessed on: 03-11-2021.

[6] https://www.linkedin.com/groups/37631, last accessed on: 03-11-2021.

[7] https://www.ibm.com/products/spss-statistics, last accessed on: 03-11-2021.

Descriptive Statistics. We started the data analysis by running the basic descriptive statistics for contextual information, benefits, and challenges of SAFe, such as frequencies, to get an overview of the data and insights on how to proceed with inferential statistics. Then, we calculated the mean values for both benefits and challenges.

Inferential Statistics. To test the normality of data, we conducted the *Kolmogorov-Smirnov test* [21], which showed that our data had a non-normal distribution. Thus, we adopted non-parametric tests to conduct inferential statistics. We used the *Mann-Whitney U* [22] to compare the differences between two independent groups, e.g., duration of the agile scaling framework usage, when the dependent variable is either ordinal or interval/ratio, e.g., benefits and challenges. In the case of more than two groups, we used *Krusal-Wallis H test* [22].

4   Results and Discussion

In this section, we present an overview of contextual information of our respondents and answer our research questions on the benefits and challenges of adopting the SAFe framework, as well as compare to previous findings. Finally, we discuss the limitations of our study.

4.1   Overview of the Contextual Information

In total, we received 204 responses to our survey. 100 respondents had adopted SAFe as their primary framework that was predominantly used in their organization, while the rest of the respondents had adopted other scaling frameworks as their primary frameworks. We separated the data of SAFe respondents and analyzed them to answer our research questions. Next, we present the contextual and descriptive information of the SAFe respondents.

Geographic Distribution of Respondents. The respondents that adopted SAFe were distributed to all continents except South America. As shown in Fig. 1, the highest number of respondents were from the USA (24% of respondents), followed by Germany (16%), and Denmark (11%). The geographical distribution of our respondents matches the information on the SAFe web page, as most organizations using the SAFe framework are reported to be located in the USA [8]. Another plausible explanation that most of our respondents are from the USA is that we approached participants in conferences that took place in the USA (Agile 2019) and Canada (XP 2019, ICGSE 2019). The next highest response rates were from Germany and Denmark, as two authors were located in these countries leading to more responses from those locations.

Roles of Respondents. The highest number of our respondents (see Fig. 2) had a process related role (57% of the respondents), such as Scrum Master or agile coach, followed by the management roles (26%), such as project and

Fig. 1. Geographical distribution of the respondents

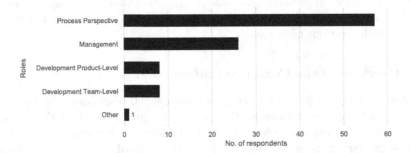

Fig. 2. Roles of the respondents

line managers. Roles from development team level (8%) included developers and team leaders and roles from product level included Product Owners and requirement engineers (8%).

Duration of Usage. Most of our respondents had started their SAFe adoption either 1–2 years ago (40% of the respondents) or 3–5 years ago (40%), while 13% had less than one year of SAFe experience and only 7% had more than five years of experience in implementing SAFe (see Fig. 3).

Previously used Development Approaches. The majority of our respondents used plan-driven methods before adopting SAFe (52%) (see Fig. 4).

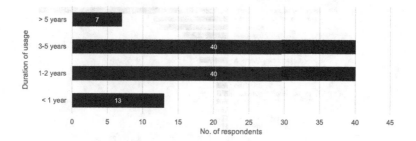

Fig. 3. The number of years of experience since SAFe adoption

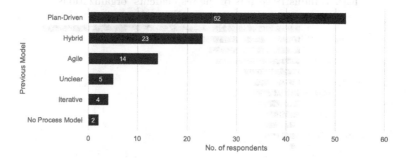

Fig. 4. Previously used software development approaches before SAFe adoption

Industry Sector. Our respondents' organizations that had adopted SAFe came from several different domains. As shown in Fig. 5, the highest percentage of respondents came from the financial sector (33% of the respondents), followed by the public sector (13%) and technology domain (12%). The distribution of the domains matches with the results from a prior MLR on SAFe [7], that indicated that many organizations adopting SAFe were from the finance and technology sectors.

Organizational Areas in which Framework was Applied. The inventors of SAFe have designed it to scale agile and lean practices to whole enterprises, indicating that the adoption of SAFe is not only limited to software development, but can also be used at higher organizational levels or in other organizational units, such as marketing or human resources [3]. However, our survey data shows that the majority of our respondents have adopted SAFe primarily in the IT (74 responses[8]), and product development (59 responses) areas (see Fig. 6).

---

[8] Here the respondents were able to choose multiple options. Thus, the number of responses exceeds the total number of 100 respondents.

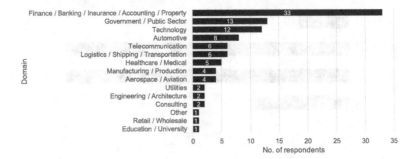

Fig. 5. Industry sectors of the respondents' organizations

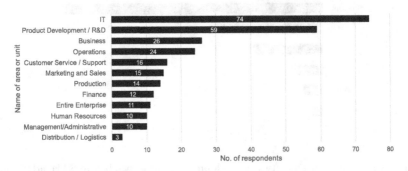

Fig. 6. Organizational areas in which SAFe has been adopted

4.2   Benefits of Adopting SAFe

Based on the previously published survey [17], we identified eleven benefits that the adoption of agile entails (see Fig. 7). Our respondents were asked whether their organizations realized these benefits after adopting SAFe. To better understand the respondents' agreement on the realized benefits of adopting SAFe, we calculated the mean values for each benefit. In Fig. 7 the benefits have been arranged from highest to lowest mean values.

Our respondents provided the highest level of agreement (sum of strongly agree and agree) that the adoption of SAFe has *improved collaboration between agile teams* (71% of the respondents), followed by the statements that the adoption of SAFe has resulted in *improved dependency management between teams* (68%) and *improved transparency* (66%). Our findings on the most realized benefits were also the most frequently cited benefits in previous SAFe surveys and literature reviews [7,10,11]. These benefits also align with the two core values of SAFe: *alignment* and *transparency* [15]. Furthermore, the other benefits we found were also identified in a prior MLR on SAFe [7].

According to the SAFe website, organizations using SAFe have reported that its adoption improved their software quality by 50% [3]. However, in our survey, software quality received the least agreement and had the lowest mean value, indicating that a big part of our respondents disagreed with the statement that

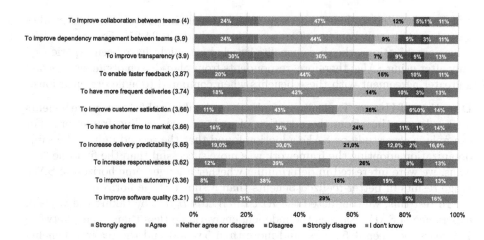

Fig. 7. Agreement of the Benefits of SAFe, arranged according to the Mean Values

the adoption of SAFe has improved the software quality. This finding also contradicts with one of the core values of SAFe: *built-in quality* [15]. However, we did not measure the actual increase or decrease of software quality in this survey. Thus, we believe that further research on actual measurements is needed. Other benefits claimed by SAFe are related to improved engagement, productivity, and time to market [3]. However, we did not investigate the first two benefits claimed by SAFe in our survey, as the survey was designed to capture general benefits that would be common to several frameworks. Nevertheless, we identified a faster time to market in our survey, with 50% of our respondents agreeing on this benefit after adopting SAFe.

Previous Development Methodology. A systematic mapping study of Uludağ et al. [23] showed that the most organizations transforming to large-scale agile development by adopting agile scaling frameworks, used before the transformation either plan-driven or traditional agile methods, such as Scrum. Thus, we wanted to determine whether previous experiences in agile methods resulted in better-realized benefits compared to those having previous experience in plan-driven methods. We conducted the *Man-Whitney U test* to identify a possible difference between those two groups. We took the previous development methods (plan-driven and agile) as the independent variable while the dependent variable was each of the benefits.

We did not identify any statistically significant difference between the two groups for any of the benefits[9]. However, mean ranks for all the benefits, except for *to enable faster feedback*, *to have more frequent deliveries*, and *to have shorter time to market*, were higher for agile organizations when compared to plan-driven organizations. This might indicate that the agile organizations experienced these

---

[9] The results of the tests can be found here: https://figshare.com/s/c589fc84ffbed853e723.

benefits more due to their longer experience in agile in general. Previous studies have reported such benefits of using agile methods [6,24,25]. For many plan-driven organizations, the three benefits listed above might have been experienced only after using SAFe; therefore, respondents from plan-driven organizations had a greater agreement with these benefits when compared to agile organizations.

Duration of Usage. Typically, organizations should be able to see more benefits after a longer time from the adoption of agile or agile scaling framework. For example, a case study on SAFe adoption found that the second unit in the same organization adopting the framework was more successful than the first one [26]. Thus, we were interested in determining whether a longer time horizon of SAFe usage results in better-realized benefits than a shorter time horizon.

To test this, we conducted the *Kruskal-Wallis H test* by taking the years of experience of SAFe usage as the independent variable (less than 1 year, between 1–2 years, between 3–5 years, and more than 5 years) and the realized benefits of SAFe adoption as the dependent variable.

We found a statistically significant difference for the following benefits: *to improve team autonomy* (Kruskal-Wallis H = 10.49, p = 0.015), *to have more frequent deliveries* (Kruskal-Wallis H = 14.244, p = 0.003), *to have shorter time to market* (Kruskal-Wallis H = 12.028, p = 0.007), and *to enable faster feedback* (Kruskal-Wallis H = 11.407, p = 0.01) meaning that companies with longer experience of SAFe reported experiencing more of these benefits. We also observed that mean ranks for most of the benefits increased with an increase in SAFe adoption duration. These results seem to indicate that organizations may realize the full extent of the benefits of adopting SAFe only after a longer time horizon. Our results are in line with previous studies [24,27]. For instance, Laanti et al. [24] concluded that years of experience with agile methods may positively influence their usefulness.

4.3   Challenges of Adopting SAFe

Figure 8 shows the results for the sixteen challenges identified in the literature, arranged from highest to lowest mean values.

The challenge that received the highest agreement (sum of agree and strongly agree) among the respondents was *organizational politics* (72% of the respondents) which also has the highest mean value. This challenge was also reported as a significant challenge during a SAFe transformation in a case study conducted in a financial organization [28]. The next most agreed challenges were *difficulties in establishing an agile mindset* (68%), *change resistance* (67%), and *team formation challenges*. As the majority of our respondents transformed to SAFe from plan-driven methods, the difficulties in establishing an agile mindset and overcoming change resistance are understandable. These aforesaid challenges were also frequently identified in large-scale agile endeavours [1,6] as well as in SAFe adoptions [7,28].

The challenge, *framework does not help in resolving problems with dependencies between development teams* (14%) received the least agreement among the respondents and the smallest mean value. While challenges related to dependency management between agile teams were quite commonly mentioned in large-scale agile endeavours [1,6] and SAFe adoptions [7], by disagreeing this statement (69% disagreed) our respondents indicate that adopting SAFe might actually help in managing dependencies between agile teams. This is further conformed by our survey results on SAFe benefits, as the *improved dependency management between teams* received second highest agreement by our respondents.

Other challenges, such as *difficulties in including non-development units* (63% agreed), and *difficulties in staffing new roles* (56% agreed) have also been reported by an MLR on SAFe [7].

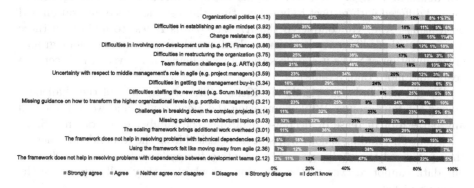

Fig. 8. Agreement of the Challenges of SAFe, arranged according to the Mean Values

Previous Development Methodology. We tested whether the agreement on challenges faced differed between organizations using previously plan-driven methods and those using previously agile methods by conducting the *Mann-Whitney test*.

We found statistically significant differences[10] regarding the following challenges: *uncertainty with respect to middle management's role in agile* (Mann-Whitney U = 102.5, p = 0.0046) and *difficulties in getting the management buy-in* (Mann-Whitney U = 88, p = 0.0018), meaning that previously plan-driven organizations agreed to these challenges more than agile organizations. These results match previous findings that plan-driven organizations struggle to clarify the new roles of managers in agile environments compared to organizations having already experience with agile methods [28]. Similarly, getting the management buy-in in plan-driven organizations is more complicated than in agile organizations due to power struggles and politics [28].

The mean rank for most of the challenges for respondents coming from plan-driven organizations was higher than for respondents from agile organizations,

---

[10] The results of the tests can be found here: https://figshare.com/s/69852ec3b24dd73406e4.

which indicates that previous agile experience may ease SAFe adoption. Only for the following challenges: *the scaling framework brings additional work overhead, using the framework felt like moving away from agile,* and *missing guidance on architectural topics* had a higher mean rank among the organizations that had already used agile, indicating that already agile organizations felt these more problematic than plan-driven organizations, which could be expected. For example, a case study on SAFe transformation from the Scrum model reported these same challenges and mentioned that long fixed increments of SAFe (e.g., a 8-week Program Increment cycle) may look like a step back to the plan-driven world for an organization that is already used to the fast agile planning cycle [26].

Duration of Usage. We tested whether the agreement on the challenges experienced differed with respect to how long time the respondent's organization had been using SAFe. We conducted the *Kruskal-Wallis H test* to find out if there was a statistical difference between each of the challenges and the four groups of the duration of SAFe usage (less than 1 year, between 1–2 years, between 3–5 years, and more than 5 years).

We did not find statistically significant difference for any of the challenges among the four groups. While comparing the mean ranks, and we did not find any pattern of increase or decrease regarding the number of years since SAFe adoption. This finding is not surprising as we asked from the respondents whether they perceived the challenges *when adopting the agile scaling framework,* thus our data cannot answer to the question on whether they still experience the same problems.

4.4   Threats to Validity

Although we employed a rigorous survey design and paid attention to data collection and analysis, there are limitations that are discussed next and organized as suggested by Wohlin et al. [29].

Internal Validity. This threat concerns factors that can influence the relationship between the research process and the obtained results, e.g., respondent bias. We mitigated the respondent bias by collecting data from reliable sources: most of the responses came from people we met during the conferences and Meetups, and we knew they were using the agile scaling frameworks, which helped us to avoid unreliable or unauthentic responses. As the questionnaire consisted of separate sections investigating the benefits and challenges of adopting agile scaling frameworks, respondents could not overemphasize the positive elements of the SAFe adoption.

External Validity. This threat is related to the generalizability of our results. We counteracted this limitation by having respondents with different roles, working in different domains, coming from various countries, and having different length of SAFe experience. This helped us to improve to external validity of our survey when compared to previous quantitative studies (e.g., [10,11]).

Construct Validity. This treat concerns whether the questions asked in the questionnaire represent the attributes being measured. We formulated the survey statements on the benefits and challenges based on earlier findings in the literature. However, as we had to limit the questionnaire length, we could not include all the benefits and challenges we identified from the literature. Therefore, were not able to fully address this threat, which is a prevalent problem in survey research [16]. We validated the questionnaire with a domain expert, survey experts, and tested it by conducting a pilot study. This helped to make the questionnaire as clear and understandable to the respondents as possible.

Conclusion Validity. This threat is concerned with the ability to draw the right conclusion from the collected data. The survey data was mostly Likert data, and we conducted appropriate non-parametric tests for identifying differences between independent groups. We also compared the results with the existing literature for validating our results.

5   Conclusions and Future Work

This study provided empirical evidence on the adoption of SAFe in industry. We analyzed data from 100 practitioners using SAFe as their primary scaling framework. Our results show that the three topmost realized benefits of adopting SAFe are: *improved collaboration between teams, improved dependency management between teams,* and *improved transparency. Improved software quality* is the least agreed benefit, even though the SAFe founders claim it to be a common benefit from SAFe. It is important to note that we did not measure the actual increase or decrease of the benefits. However, our contribution to practitioners is to provide objective information on the SAFe benefits as experienced by SAFe user organizations. We encourage the researchers to collect actual metrics used to quantify the benefits of SAFe usage.

Our results further revealed that the most common challenges of adopting SAFe were *organizational politics, difficulties in establishing an agile mindset, change resistance,* and *team formation challenges.* The last two challenges were also frequently reported in previously conducted reviews and surveys in large-scale agile development. As the present literature on large-scale agile development is mostly problem-centric [23], we encourage researchers to investigate what types of solutions have been adopted by organizations to address the challenges witnessed during transformation.

References

1. Dikert, K., Paasivaara, M., Lassenius, C.: Challenges and success factors for large-scale agile transformations: a systematic literature review. J. Syst. Softw. **119**, 87–108 (2016)
2. Klünder, J., Hohl, P., Schneider, K.: Becoming agile while preserving software product lines: An agile transformation model for large companies. In: Proceedings of the 2018 International Conference on Software and System Process, pp. 1–10. ACM, May 2018

3. Scaled Agile Inc.: Description about SAFe. https://bit.ly/3dsqEPr. Accessed 03 Nov 2021
4. Larman, C., Vodde, B.: Practices for Scaling Lean & Agile Development: Large, Multisite, and Offshore Product Development with Large-Scale Scrum. Pearson Education (2010)
5. Ambler, S.W., Lines, M.: Disciplined Agile Delivery: A Practitioner's Guide to Agile Software Delivery in the Enterprise. IBM Press (2012)
6. Agile Version One: 14th Annual State of Agile Survey (2020). https://bit.ly/3usL0y6. Accessed 03 Nov 2021
7. Putta, A., Paasivaara, M., Lassenius, C.: Benefits and Challenges of Adopting the Scaled Agile Framework (SAFe): preliminary results from a multivocal literature review. In: Kuhrmann, M., et al. (eds.) PROFES 2018. LNCS, vol. 11271, pp. 334–351. Springer, Cham (2018). https://doi.org/10.1007/978-3-030-03673-7_24
8. Scaled Agile Inc.: SAFe Case Studies. https://bit.ly/2NGa2J8
9. Putta, A.: Scaling agile software development to large and globally distributed large-scale organizations. In: Proceedings of the 13th International Conference on Global Software Engineering, pp. 141–144. ACM, May 2018
10. Laanti, M., Kettunen, P.: SAFe adoptions in Finland: a survey research. In: Hoda, R. (ed.) XP 2019. LNBIP, vol. 364, pp. 81–87. Springer, Cham (2019). https://doi.org/10.1007/978-3-030-30126-2_10
11. Gustavsson, T., Bergkvist, L.: Perceived impacts of using the scaled agile framework for large-scale agile software development. In: Proceedings of the 28th International Conference on Information Systems Development, August 2019
12. Salikhov, D., Succi, G., Tormasov, A.: An empirical analysis of success factors in the adaption of the scaled agile framework-first outcomes from an empirical study. arXiv preprint arXiv:2012.11144 (2020)
13. Moe, N.B., Olsson, H.H., Dingsøyr, T.: Trends in large-scale agile development: a summary of the 4th workshop at xp2016. In: Proceedings of the Scientific Workshop Proceedings of XP2016, pp. 1–4. ACM, May 2016
14. Moe, N.B., Dingsøyr, T.: Emerging research themes and updated research agenda for large-scale agile development: a summary of the 5th international workshop at xp2017. In: Proceedings of the XP2017 Scientific Workshops, pp. 1–4. ACM (2017)
15. Scaled Agile Inc.: Core Values. https://bit.ly/3kb1yG7. Accessed 03 Nov 2021
16. Linåker, J., Sulaman, S.M., Maiani de Mello, R., Höst, M.: Guidelines for conducting surveys in software engineering (2015)
17. Version One: 13th State of Agile Survey. https://bit.ly/3sadydS. Accessed 03 Nov 2021
18. Uludağ, Ö., Kleehaus, M., Xu, X., Matthes, F.: Investigating the role of architects in scaling agile frameworks. In: 2017 IEEE 21st International Enterprise Distributed Object Computing Conference (EDOC), IEEE (October 2017) 123–132
19. Uludag, Ö., Kleehaus, M., Caprano, C., Matthes, F.: Identifying and structuring challenges in large-scale agile development based on a structured literature review. In: IEEE 22nd International Enterprise Distributed Object Computing Conference. IEEE 2018, pp. 191–197 (2018)
20. Kitchenham, B., Pfleeger, S.L.: Principles of survey research: part 5: populations and samples. ACM SIGSOFT Softw. Eng. Notes 27(5), 17–20 (2002)
21. Lilliefors, H.W.: On the kolmogorov-smirnov test for normality with mean and variance unknown. J. Am. Stat. Assoc. 62(318), 399–402 (1967)
22. Conover, W.J.: Practical Nonparametric Statistics, vol. 350. Wiley, New York (1998)

23. Uludag, Ö., Philipp, P., Putta, A., Paasivaara, M., Lassenius, C., Matthes, F.: Revealing the state-of-the-art in large-scale agile development: A systematic mapping study. arXiv preprint arXiv:2007.05578 (2021)
24. Laanti, M., Salo, O., Abrahamsson, P.: Agile methods rapidly replacing traditional methods at nokia: a survey of opinions on agile transformation. Inf. Softw. Technol. **53**(3), 276–290 (2011)
25. Begel, A., Nagappan, N.: Usage and perceptions of agile software development in an industrial context: an exploratory study. In: Proceedings of the First International Symposium on Empirical Software Engineering and Measurement, pp. 255–264. IEEE, September 2007
26. Paasivaara, M.: Adopting safe to scale agile in a globally distributed organization. In: Proceedings of the 2017 IEEE 12th International Conference on Global Software Engineering, pp. 36–40. IEEE, May 2017
27. Salo, O., Abrahamsson, P.: Agile methods in European embedded software development organisations: a survey on the actual use and usefulness of extreme programming and scrum. IET Softw. **2**, 58–64 (2008)
28. Putta, A., Paasivaara, M., Lassenius, C.: How are agile release trains formed in practice? a case study in a large financial corporation. In: Kruchten, P., Fraser, S., Coallier, F. (eds.) XP 2019. LNBIP, vol. 355, pp. 154–170. Springer, Cham (2019). https://doi.org/10.1007/978-3-030-19034-7_10
29. Wohlin, C., Runeson, P., Höst, M., Ohlsson, M.C., Regnell, B., Wesslén, A.: Experimentation in Software Engineering. Springer Science & Business Media (2012)

Open Access This chapter is licensed under the terms of the Creative Commons Attribution 4.0 International License (http://creativecommons.org/licenses/by/4.0/), which permits use, sharing, adaptation, distribution and reproduction in any medium or format, as long as you give appropriate credit to the original author(s) and the source, provide a link to the Creative Commons license and indicate if changes were made.

The images or other third party material in this chapter are included in the chapter's Creative Commons license, unless indicated otherwise in a credit line to the material. If material is not included in the chapter's Creative Commons license and your intended use is not permitted by statutory regulation or exceeds the permitted use, you will need to obtain permission directly from the copyright holder.

Short Contributions

Using a Low Code Development Environment to Teach the Agile Methodology

Mary Lebens[(✉)] [iD] and Roger Finnegan [iD]

Metropolitan State University, Saint Paul, MN 55106, USA
{mary.lebens,roger.finnegan}@metrostate.edu

Abstract. The Agile development methodology is soaring in popularity in the business world. Companies are turning to Agile to develop products quickly and to achieve digital transformation of their organization. Because of this push, companies need employees who understand Agile. Therefore, higher education is obligated to provide an understanding of Agile to students as they enter the workplace. Providing Agile experience to students who are new to programming is difficult because they are so worried about the coding aspects of the assignment, they cannot take time to think about the methodology they are using. The coding crowds out the time needed to get an understanding of how Agile actually works. One remedy for this is to use a low or no-code development platform. With this type of platform students spend less time learning to create apps, freeing them to experience the rituals and roles of Agile. This study examines using the Agile methodology along with the Microsoft Power Apps platform to provide an Agile experience to students. Two course sections were surveyed to learn if students perceived that they acquired a better understanding of Agile and to learn their perceptions of a no-code platform experience. The students completed surveys to ascertain their comfort with the Agile methodology and whether the no-code environment increased their comfort level. The results showed students perceived the no-code platform increased their comfort with using the Agile methodology. The implication is that no-code platforms can be used broadly to help students to gain experience with Agile.

Keywords: Agile methodology · No-code · Experiential learning

1 Introduction

Although the Agile software development methodology is now ubiquitous in the business world, it is not common in beginning software development courses due to the difficulty in teaching Agile. Agile is best learned in the context of a software development project. However, students who are new to programming often need the entire semester to learn the programming structures and syntax, leaving no time for completing an Agile project. In addition, the normal challenges of a group project are still present in Agile student projects, such as getting students to work effectively together and avoiding free riders who do not complete their fair share of the work.

© The Author(s) 2021
P. Gregory et al. (Eds.): XP 2021, LNBIP 419, pp. 191–199, 2021.
https://doi.org/10.1007/978-3-030-78098-2_12

One approach to freeing up class time to teach Agile is using a low- or no-code development environment in place of teaching a traditional programming language. Low- and no-code environments allow students to develop applications through a Graphical User Interface (GUI), reducing time spent on coding. This paper examines using the Agile software development methodology in conjunction with a no-code environment in a beginning application development course. Two course sections of students were surveyed to learn if they perceived that they acquired a deeper understanding of Agile, as well as to learn their perceptions of the no-code platform. Both course sections were taught in an online, asynchronous format.

2   Related Work

Although the *Agile Manifesto* [1] was written over twenty years ago, few University courses cover more than a mention of Agile and its general characteristics [2]. Part of the difficulty in teaching Agile is that it is best taught through student projects, but the complexity of projects and the lack of sufficient time during the academic calendar make this difficult [3]. In addition, textbooks provide only cursory coverage of the Agile methodology, exacerbating the time crunch by requiring professors to spend more class time discussing Agile in order to make up this deficit [4].

Despite the difficulty of teaching Agile, there are proven benefits to using Agile practices with students [5]. Agile projects featuring feedback after each iteration increase students' software development skills more than traditional group projects [6]. Students find Agile practices such as pair programming beneficial [7]. College students in asynchronous online courses reported that using Agile led to a more effective learning experience and allowed them to produce deliverables of a higher quality [8]. Additionally, using small teams and timeboxed iterations overcomes some of the hurdles of traditional group projects, like free-riding students who do not complete their fair share of the work [9].

Due to the difficulty in teaching students coding along with Agile practices in a single course, some college faculty have tried alternative no-code approaches, such as assigning students to build a wiki, solve an IT business case, or construct a building using Legos [10–12]. In addition to these no-code approaches in college courses, the no-code environment Scratch has been used to successfully teach middle school students Agile practices [13]. No-code software development environments are not only becoming more popular for teaching, but for use by business professionals as well, with Microsoft PowerApps as one of the leading platforms [14]. Combining a no-code environment with Agile practices provides benefits students and teaches skills that employers desire.

2.1   Microsoft PowerApps

The low-code development platform Microsoft PowerApps was used during this research. PowerApps was chosen in part because it is freely available to students. Power-Apps is part of the Office 365 suite used by Metropolitan State University. The University supplies students with Office 365 free of charge. PowerApps is a subscription-based platform to create applications. It is used to create browser-based apps that connect to a data source. Students can create screens to view and edit data for business processes [15]. Gartner has recognized PowerApps as a leader in enterprise low-code platforms [16].

2.2 Course Background

The course targeted for this study is MIS 328-Applications Development I, an introductory software development course that is part of the MIS major at Metropolitan State University. The course curriculum assumes that the students do not have any previous programming experience. The learning outcomes include students experiencing the process, tools and methodologies used to create and revise computer applications. In addition, the students experience the existing and future paradigms of application development with the Agile framework currently being the most important paradigm. The course is at the junior level and is required for all MIS majors. Due to its historic reliance on teaching a programing language, such as C#, Visual Basic, or even Cobol in an early iteration, it carried the reputation of being the hardest course in the program. Many students avoided taking the course until their last year or even their last semester.

The course was redesigned to give students the experience of being on an Agile development team while reducing the stress of learning a development language. That is, the development language was deemphasized in order to allow the students the time to better learn the Agile methodology. It was surmised that the gain that the students achieved with the Agile experience would more than offset the reduction in the experience with a programming language. This gain in Agile methodology knowledge is expected to help students in their job search.

The course, MIS 328, is Application Development I. As the name implies it was developed to teach students how applications are created in organizations. In years past the waterfall methodology would have been emphasized, but since the Agile framework is becoming more and more important in organizations [17] it is now being taught. The course includes the opportunity to write user stories, create prototypes, develop a product, participate in sprint planning meetings, participate in standup meetings, and interact with a development team.

2.3 Hypothesis

As a result of reviewing the literature and related work, the following hypothesis was developed.

- H_0: Students do not perceive they have a better understanding of the Agile methodology after using a low-code development environment to experience participating in an Agile team.
- H_1: Students perceive they have a better understanding of the Agile methodology after using a low-code development environment to experience participating in an Agile team.

3 Research Methods

3.1 Participants

To gauge the students' reactions to the no-code platform teaching method for Agile we conducted a survey across two sections in the fall semester of 2020. The students involved were undergraduates majoring in Management Information Systems (MIS). Fifty-seven students participated in the survey across the two sections.

3.2 Materials

The goal of the survey was to determine how the students felt about their familiarity and comfort with the Agile methodology after using it as part of a no-code development team. The specific things that the authors wanted to learn from the survey were the students' comfort level with the Agile framework and if our reliance on a no-code platform was the correct decision. The authors realized that students would not have any firsthand experience with the way in which the course had been previously taught with its use of a programming language but were confident that students would be able to gauge if they would be overwhelmed as they needed to learn both the Agile framework and a new programming language at the same time. The survey instrument used the following questions:

1. I feel that I have an understanding of the Agile software development methodology.
2. I feel that I have more comfort with the Agile methodology after experiencing it in MIS 328.
3. Going through the development process with Power Apps helped me better understand the Agile methodology.
4. It would have been harder to learn the Agile methodology if I had also been required to learn how to write computer code at the same time.
5. I feel that I will be a more effective employee for companies with my new knowledge of the Agile methodology.

The possible responses were recorded on a Likert scale:

- Strongly agree
- Agree
- Neither agree nor disagree
- Disagree
- Strongly disagree

3.3 Procedure

The survey was administered at the end of the course. At this point in the course the students had completed the second sprint in their development team final project. It was felt that they would have sufficient experience with the Agile methodology at this point in the course to express an opinion. The students were given extra credit points as an incentive to complete the survey. It was administered anonymously through Survey Monkey. Survey Monkey was chosen to get more candid answers than might have been possible using the learning management system.

4   Results

The results of the survey strongly demonstrated that the students felt that learning Agile by using a no-code platform increased their understanding of the methodology. One hundred percent of students strongly agreed or agreed that they understood the Agile methodology. This affirmed hypothesis H_1 that students will perceive they have a better understanding of the Agile methodology after using a low-code development environment to experience participating in an Agile team. Agile has been described as a culture [18]. Giving the students the ability to experience that culture as part of their learning was an important part of the planned experience.

As shown in Fig. 1, ninety-eight percent of students strongly agreed or agreed that they were comfortable with using the Agile methodology. This helped with the goal of increasing their comfort with Agile in order to better prepare the students for careers with companies that are making strong use of the method. This comfort level is expected to be very important to student's career success [19].

Ninety-six percent of students strongly agreed or agreed that using the Power Apps no-code platform helped them get a better understanding of the development platform, as shown in Fig. 1. Power Apps was selected as the platform since it is already part of the Office 365 suite. The University supplies the students access to Office 365 so there was no additional cost to the students to access the platform. The Mendix platform had been used in previous semesters but the migration to Power Apps was seen as advantageous to the students' careers since it is more popular in industry. Power Apps is also seen as becoming more important by Gartner [20].

Eighty-four percent of the students strongly agreed or agreed that learning the Agile methodology would have been more difficult if they also had been required to learn to write computer code, as shown in Fig. 1. This corroborated the authors assumption that having to learn a programming language and the Agile methodology at that same time would be difficult and stressful for students. The course was already known for its difficulties and adding the additional requirements for Agile could have increased the apprehension regarding it. The need to teach Agile [21] outweighed the need to teach coding.

Figure 1 shows ninety-six percent of students strongly agreed or agreed that they will be better employees with their knowledge of the Agile methodology. Providing the students the skills that they need to be productive employees and competitive in the job market was the most important factor in the decision to emphasize the Agile method over programming skills. Companies that use the Agile framework have a 30 percent higher project success rate than companies using the traditional waterfall methodology [22].

The results of the survey gave the authors the sense as well as the metrics to show that their decision to use the no-code platform and emphasize the Agile methodology increased students' confidence with the methodology. Additionally, the survey results showed students felt confident in their ability to use the knowledge to become valuable employees and be successful in the job market.

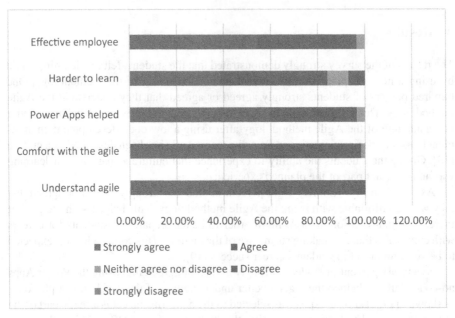

Fig. 1. Survey results for the five questions posed to the students.

5 Discussion

This study expands on previous research which found other types of no-code approaches were useful for teaching Agile, such as building a wiki, solving an IT business case, or constructing a building using Legos [10–12]. A key contribution of this study is that this course design not only teaches students Agile, but also teaches them software development using a popular and common no-code platform [14]. The combination of no-code with Agile allowed students in this study to gain valuable skills as a part of an Agile development team while simultaneously gaining experience with a leading application development platform, Microsoft PowerApps [14].

Another key contribution of this study is that it demonstrates a no-code environment allows students to learn Agile in a short timeframe. Using a no-code environment to teach the Agile methodology allowed students to grow their Agile skills and successfully develop fully functioning mobile apps in a single semester. This short timeframe is a boon for college professors who are seeking to teach students career-boosting Agile skills under the constraints of the academic calendar.

The implication of these findings for the Information Technology (IT) and Information Systems (IS) disciplines is that no-code platforms can be used more broadly to allow students to gain experience with Agile, without the added stress and time requirements of learning a traditional programming language. This approach to teaching Agile methodology will be helpful for college programs which only require a single software development course, such as IT, IS, or networking, since the course time devoted to programming is extremely limited in that case. Additionally, this approach may be valuable for business programs, since this approach could also help non-technical students learn the Agile methodology and later apply it to projects in their careers.

5.1 Limitations and Further Research

A key limitation of this study is the sample was limited to two course sections, since the University only offers two sections of MIS 328. Further research on additional sections is needs to determine if the results hold true over a larger sample. In addition, further research is needed to determine if this approach works in programs outside of IS, particularly in more narrowly focused IT programs such as networking and in non-technical programs such as business. The two course sections used for this study were both held in an asynchronous online format, so additional research into the effectiveness of teaching a no-code or low-code environment in different types of formats is warranted. The asynchronous format does not include course meetings, so further research on face-to-face, hybrid, and synchronous online courses would be useful to determine if the students' perceptions remain the same across formats.

6 Conclusion

In this study, the authors examined using the Agile methodology in conjunction with a no-code environment to provide students with the experience of participating in an Agile development team. The results overwhelmingly showed students perceived the no-code platform increased their comfort with using the Agile methodology. The stressors and time constraints of teaching both application development and Agile in a single semester was overcome using the no-code development environment. The implication is that no-code platforms can be used broadly to allow students to gain experience with Agile across the IT and IS disciplines.

References

1. Agile Alliance: Agile manifesto and principles (2001). http://agilemanifesto.org/principles.html
2. Devedžić, V., Milenković, S.R.: Teaching agile software development: a case study. IEEE Trans. Educ. **54**(2), 273–278 (2011). https://doi.org/10.1109/TE.2010.2052104
3. Fitsilis, P., Lekatos, A.: Teaching software project management using agile paradigm. In: Proceedings of 21st Pan-Hellenic Conference on Informatics, Larissa, Greece, (2017). https://doi.org/10.1145/3139367.3139413
4. May, J.: Play ball: Bringing scrum into the classroom. J. Inf. Syst. Educ. **27**(2), 87–92 (2016)
5. Missiroli, M., Russo, D., Ciancarini, P.: Learning agile software development in high school: An investigation. In: Proceedings - International Conference on Software Engineering, pp. 293–302, ACM, Austin, Texas (2016). https://doi.org/10.1145/2889160.2889180

6. Yang, J., Zhang, X.L., Su, P.: Deep-learning-based agile teaching framework of software development courses in computer science education. Procedia Comput. Sci. **154**, 137–145 (2018). https://doi.org/10.1016/j.procs.2019.06.021

7. Monett, D.: Agile project-based teaching and learning. In: Proceedings of the 11th International Conference on Software Engineering Research and Practice, pp. 377–383. (2013)

8. Hulshult, A.R., Krehbiel, T.C.: Using eight agile practices in an online course to improve student learning and team project quality. J. High. Educ. Theor. Pract. **19**(3), 55–68 (2019). https://doi.org/10.33423/jhetp.v19i3.2116

9. Stapel, K., Lübke, D., Knauss, E.: Best practices in extreme programming course design. In: Proceedings - International Conference on Software Engineering, pp. 769–775 (2008). https://doi.org/10.1145/1368088.1368197

10. Cubric, M.: Agile learning & teaching with wikis: building a pattern. In: Proceedings of the 2007 International Symposium on Wikis, pp. 11–24 (2008). https://doi.org/10.1145/1296951.1296953

11. Rush, D.E., Connolly, A.J.: An agile framework for teaching with scrum in the IT project management classroom. J. Inf. Syst. **31**(3), 196–207 (2020)

12. JSteghöfer, J.P., Knauss, E., Alégroth, E., Hammouda, I., Burden, H., Ericsson, M.: teaching agile: addressing the conflict between project delivery and application of agile methods. In: 2016 IEEE/ACM 38th IEEE International Conference on Software Engineering Companion, pp. 303–312 (2016). https://doi.org/10.1145/2889160.2889181

13. Fronza, I., El Ioini, N., Corral, L.: Teaching computational thinking using agile software engineering methods: a framework for middle schools. ACM Trans. Comput. Educ. **17**, 4 (2017). https://doi.org/10.1145/3055258

14. Rymer, J.R., Koplowitz, R.: The Forrester Wave^{TM}: Low-code development Platforms for AD&D professionals. Technical report, Forrester (2019)

15. Leung, T.: Beginning PowerApps. Apress, Berkeley (2017)

16. Vincent, P., et al.: Magic Quadrant for Enterprise Low-Code Application Platforms (2020). https://www.gartner.com

17. Brower, T.: Why agile is the mindset to get us through the Covid Crisis: 4 lessons from agile for today and the new normal. Forbes (2020). https://www.forbes.com/sites/tracybrower/2020/04/12/why-agile-is-the-mindset-to-get-us-through-the-covid-crisis-4-lessons-from-agile-for-today-and-the-new-normal/?sh=4f350a3631d3

18. Prieto, R.: The agile classroom: Embracing an agile mindset in education. Medium (2016). https://medium.com/laboratoria/the-agile-classroom-embracing-an-agile-mindset-in-education-ae0f19e801f3

19. Nikolova, Z.: 3 things that you should know about career development in an agile context. Leanify (2016). http://leanify.com/3-things-about-agile-career/

20. Cunningham, R.: Gartner magic quadrant names Microsoft Power Apps a leader for low code application platforms. Microsoft (2020). https://powerapps.microsoft.com/en-us/blog/gartner-magic-quadrant-names-microsoft-power-apps-a-leader-for-low-code-application-platforms/

21. Zenagile: Agile training: What it is and why you should adopt it. (2020). https://www.zenagile.com/agile-training/

22. Keita, B.: Top 5 benefits of agile certification. Invensis Learning (2020). https://www.invensislearning.com/blog/benefits-of-agile-certifications/

Open Access This chapter is licensed under the terms of the Creative Commons Attribution 4.0 International License (http://creativecommons.org/licenses/by/4.0/), which permits use, sharing, adaptation, distribution and reproduction in any medium or format, as long as you give appropriate credit to the original author(s) and the source, provide a link to the Creative Commons license and indicate if changes were made.

The images or other third party material in this chapter are included in the chapter's Creative Commons license, unless indicated otherwise in a credit line to the material. If material is not included in the chapter's Creative Commons license and your intended use is not permitted by statutory regulation or exceeds the permitted use, you will need to obtain permission directly from the copyright holder.

Comparing Participants' Brainwaves During Solo, Pair, and Mob Programming

Makoto Shiraishi(✉), Hironori Washizaki(✉) [iD], Daisuke Saito(✉) [iD], and Yoshiaki Fukazawa(✉) [iD]

Waseda University, Okubo, Shinjuku City, Tokyo, Japan
{makwhitestone,d.saito}@fuji.waseda.jp,
{washizaki,fukazawa}@waseda.jp

Abstract. Participants' feelings and impressions utilizing electroencephalography (EEG) and the effectiveness of code are compared for different types of programming sessions. EEG information is obtained as an alternate viewpoint during three programming sessions (solo, pair, and mob programming). Mind-Wave Mobile 2 (brainwave detector) is equipped to collect the attention levels, meditation levels, and EEG brainwaves. These data are utilized to distinguish efficiencies, weaknesses, and points of interest by programming session. The results provide preliminary information to distinguish between the three sessions, but further studies are necessary to make firm conclusions. Additionally, alternative methods or systems are required to analyze the collected data.

Keywords: Mob programming · Pair programming · Programming · Brainwaves · EEG · Meditation · Attention

1 Introduction

Mob programming is becoming more prevalent, especially in the field of agile development. Mob programming is a method to learn programming in a group. Although it is becoming popular, its effects and limitations remain unclear.

Herein analysis is conducted from a different perspective: EEG (electroencephalography). This new information is used to analyze participants' EEG brainwaves to identify efficiencies, shortcomings, and advantages of different types of programming sessions (solo, pair, mob programming). Pair programming is a method to learn programming with another individual, it has similar concepts to mob programing. Here, four hypotheses (RQs) are investigated.

- RQ1: Do pair and mob programming induce lower levels of concentration (attention) compared to solo programming?

© The Author(s) 2021
P. Gregory et al. (Eds.): XP 2021, LNBIP 419, pp. 200–209, 2021.
https://doi.org/10.1007/978-3-030-78098-2_13

Often tasks requiring high concentration levels are performed individually, suggesting that sessions involving multiple people will lower concentration levels. Working alone may be better for tasks that require high fixation and core interest. An investigation known as the Coding War Games found that software engineers worked more efficiently alone [2]. Another benefit of working alone is that the individual may become completely immersed in their work. However, a drawback is that the person is solely responsible for the performance and output. In contrast, people working in a group may find motivation and inspiration throughout the whole session because it is the group's responsibility to produce results and there is peer pressure to not disappoint the group. This research question examines the difference in attentiveness in groups vs. individual programming work.

- RQ2: Do group sessions induce higher levels of calmness (meditation) compared to solo programming?

The psychological benefits of collaborative learning are increased participants' self-esteem and reduced anxiety [3]. Thus, we approximate that group work is calmer than solo programming sessions. Typically, participants working in a larger group are more comfortable with an unfamiliar problem because other people are around to assist. They are more mentally assured and less worried about solving the task because someone else in the group may know the answer. It is important to understand the difference in calmness in these sessions to be able to create an environment that can be continued for a prolonged/maintained period of time. As an increase in calmness/meditation can lead to less tension and stress.

- RQ3: Does difficulty decrease when working in a group?

Previous research found that groups of three to five individuals perform best when solving complex problems, suggesting that groups are better suited than those working alone to address challenging problems [4]. Additionally, those in a group tend to retain more information, especially since the group can work together and share knowledge. Finally, working with others provides new insight and perspectives. If a significant difference can be seen within individual/group size, we will be able to assign tasks to groups or individuals according to the difficulty of the task. Thus, making it much easier for participants to program a task.

Here, task difficulty is measured using EEG brainwaves such as the frequency of low β and low α. An increase of $low\,\beta/low\,\alpha$ denotes an increasing difficulty [5].

- RQ4: What are the significant differences between pair and mob programming sessions?

Although solo and group work should have clear differences, the impact of group work in pairs or a larger group may also result in differences in attention and concentration. This question compares group work in teams of two to that in larger groups. It is possible that working in a larger group will decrease how the participants feel on the difficulty of solving problems/tasks.

A comparison between the roles (driver, navigator) is necessary to compare pair and mob programming. In both sessions, the driver's attention level and the navigators' meditation levels should be highest because the driver will be coding and perhaps more focused, while the navigator is more relaxed as no coding is actually done.

2 Background

Mob programming is an agile software development practice where a group works together on the same screen and changes roles at set time intervals. This approach began with Woody Zuill's programming ventures at Hunter Industries [6]. Assigned roles assigned the productivity and efficiency. During a mob programming session, one software engineer (the driver) codes for the entire group by utilizing a console and mouse. Other software engineers (navigators) audit the code and ensure that the driver's work is free from logical or syntactical errors. Mob programming sessions aim to complete specific programming improvement assignments while working together with the client [7]. Advantages include an organized cycle for utilizing distributed information and a greater code fulfillment due to the inherent sharing of information and experience among the participants [8].

A systematic literature review (SLR) revealed [14] that (1) experimentation with controls is vital and (2) most mob programming sessions are finished during working hours, but the eventual outcomes are rarely investigated. Participant surveys show definite impacts such as improved code quality and expanded profitability, but the results are subjective and lack scientific evidence. Logical proof from an expert's viewpoint confirms that mob and pair programming have logical confirmation [9–12]. Performing coding tests (which have been recognized by experts) during mob programming sessions can monitor the effects on code quality. Furthermore, the influence of the mob programming session length on the coding speed should be investigated.

The SLR highlights the importance of investigating and analyzing the impacts of mob programming. This study uses a new perspective (brainwaves) to discover empirical evidence.

3 Collection and Analysis of Brainwaves

In this study, we employed a new method, which is similar to a preliminary study of pair programming on brainwaves [13], to collect empirical evidence and answer our four RQs. Participants' brainwaves were used to understand and compare the mental state from a scientific viewpoint. We collected three main datasets: attention, meditation, and difficulty. We compared the numerical values of how the participants mentally feel in each programming session. Surveys, code testing time, code quality, and personal options are conventionally used to analyze mob programming. However, these methods do not provide clear logical proof or analysis. On the other hand, our new method provides a clear psychological view. Although this study could simply investigate the differences in code testing time and code quality after several mob programming sessions, herein we assess mental states using attention, meditation, and difficulty values.

A brainwave detector, called the MindWave Mobile 2, was used, and NeuroView software collected and analyzed the EEG.

MindWave Mobile 2 (Brainwave Device). The device measures and outputs the EEG (0–127.75 Hz) power spectra (alpha, beta waves, etc.). Additionally, it monitors attention and meditation. The device consists of a headset, an ear-clip, and a sensor arm [1].

EEG. EEG was performed to assess the electrical activity of the brain. Brain cells communicate with each other via electrical impulses. The MindWave Mobile 2 tracks and records brainwave patterns. Small flat metal discs called electrodes are attached to the scalp with wires. The electrodes analyze the electrical impulses in the brain and send signals to a computer that records the results [1].

Attention. The eSense Attention meter (0–100) indicates the intensity of a user's level of mental "focus" or "attention" during intense concentration or directed mental activity. Distractions, wandering thoughts, lack of focus, or anxiety lowers the meter level. Thus, the concentration levels during programming sessions can be measured [1].

Meditation. The eSense Meditation meter (0–100) indicates the level of a user's mental "calmness" or "relaxation." Meditation is a measure of a person's mental state not physical levels. Meditation is related to reduced activity for active mental processes in the brain. Distractions, wandering thoughts, anxiety, agitation, and sensory stimuli lower the meditation meter levels [1].

Difficulty. Difficulty felt by participants during a certain task can be calculated using

$$low\,\beta\,waves / low\,\alpha\,waves \tag{1}$$

collected from the MindWave Mobile 2 [5]. A previous study involving ten high school students used a typing practice with two difficulty levels (basic & advanced). The study proposed that **an increase of** $(low\,\beta / low\,\alpha)$ **indicates a higher difficulty** (low β wave (13–16.75 Hz) and low α wave (7.5–9.25 Hz)) [5]. In this paper, we used this approach to evaluate the third RQ.

4   Experimental Method

We evaluated three types of sessions: solo, pair, and mob. Nine subjects (E1–E9), who were university or graduate students over 18 years old and with a certain level of programming skills (i.e., completed basic programming), participated in each experiment. Each experiment was repeated twice. The flow of the experiment was as follows:

1. Subjects were divided into six groups: 3 Solo groups, 3 Pair groups and 3 Mob groups. Each participant was involved in two sessions: Solo & Mob or Pair & Mob (Table 1).

Table 1. Participant overview

Session	E1	E2	E3	E4	E5	E6	E7	E8	E9
Solo programming	Sa			Sb			Sc		
Pair programming		Pa1	Pa2		Pb1	Pb2		Pc1	Pc2
Mob programming	Ma1	Ma2	Ma3	Mb1	Mb2	Mb3	Mc1	Mc2	Mc3

2. We asked the participants to wear an EEG on their heads and to meditate for 1 min to obtain EEG data during a neutral state. That is, we asked the participants to close their eyes and relax. This data was used to compare with the EEG data obtained during the programming period.
3. The two sessions were conducted consecutively with a 15-min break in between them. Each group was asked to answer up to three programming questions with varying degrees of difficulty.

Example Question: Given an integer number n, return the difference between the product of its digits and the sum of its digits. Input: n = 234 Output: 15 Explanation: Product of digits = 2 * 3 * 4 = 24 Sum of digits = 2 + 3 + 4 = 9, Result = 24 − 9 = 15

---

4. The time limit was 30 min. Subjects were not required to finish questions. A new question was given once the previous question was completed. EEG brainwaves were recorded using the MindWave Mobile 2 while the subjects answered the questions.
5. For the Solo programming session, the participant coded alone, and was not allowed to communicate with anybody. However, for pair and mob programming sessions, participants could communicate with group members. For pair and mob programming sessions, there were two roles (driver and navigator). There was only one driver at a time, and the other participants were navigators. The participants switched roles after 15 min for pair programming and 10 min for mob programming sessions. Each participant performed both roles. The groups were assigned as shown in Table 1.

5 Evaluation of Results

The experiments assessed the RQs. Figures 1–2 show the data to answer the first two research questions, while Fig. 3 shows that for the third research question.

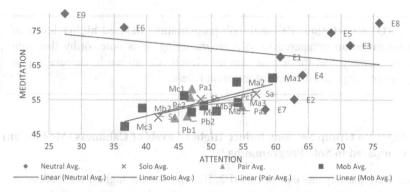

Fig. 1. Comparison of meditation and attention levels by programming state.

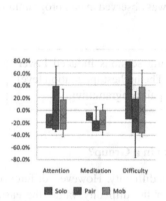

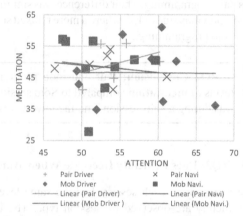

Fig. 2. Box and whisker of participants' aver-age percentage in change of attention, medita-tion, and difficulty from the neutral state by programming session.

Fig. 3. Attention vs. meditation for participants in driver & navigator roles during pair and mob programming

5.1 RQ1: Do Pair and Mob Programming Induce Lower Levels of Concentration (Attention) Compared to Solo Programming?

In many situations, tasks requiring high concentration are often worked on alone. In Fig. 1, concentration (attention) levels were highest in the neutral state. Therefore, the average percentage change in each programming session (Fig. 2) decreased concentration. Pair programming showed the highest percentage of attention level change. However, both group programming sessions (pair and mob) had higher concentration levels than the individual programming session.

> **RQ1 Conclusion:** Pair and mob programming induced **higher** levels of **concentration** compared to solo programming. It is noteworthy that solo programming had the lowest attention levels. Group work, especially pair programming, had the highest attention levels.

5.2 RQ2: Do Group Sessions Induce Higher Levels of Calmness (Meditation) Compared to Solo Programming?

In Fig. 1, all participants except two (E2, E7) showed the highest meditation level in the neutral state. Overall, a decrease was observed in the average for all three types of programming sessions. The highest average meditation level was solo, and the lowest was pair programming. Their difference was significant (around 13%). This result differs from a previous study [13], where a more relaxed state was observed in pair programming than solo programming.

> **RQ2 Conclusion:** Pair and mob programming sessions induced **lower** levels of **meditation** compared to Solo sessions. The highest meditation level was during a solo session, and the lowest was in pair programming.

5.3 RQ3: Does Difficulty Decrease When Working in a Group?

The questions in each session had the same level of difficulty. However, differences in difficulty are observed by session type. The lower the difficulty value, the easier a task feels. Figure 2 shows the average change in difficulty by group relative to the neutral state. The solo experiment showed a 36% increase in difficulty, whereas the mob programming group had a 1% increase in difficulty compared to the neutral state. On the other hand, pair programming showed a decreased difficulty of around −14%. These results imply that working in a group setting is less difficult than working alone.

> **RQ3 Conclusion:** Participants' difficulty **decreased** as the group became larger. The difference between working in a group and working alone was significant.

5.4 RQ4: Are there the Significant Differences Between Pair and Mob Programming Sessions?

Attention and Meditation. Both pair and mob programming sessions were positively correlated with attention and meditation, but the correlation was not significant (Fig. 1). **Only pair programming had a positive percent change** compared with the neutral value (Table 2). There was a somewhat **positive correlation (Pearson's Correlation**

Table 2. Comparison of the average percentage change from neutral state

Role	Attention (Rank)	Meditation (Rank)	Difficulty (Rank)
Pair Driver	2.4% (1)	−22.9% (3)	−49% (4)
Pair Navigator	4.6% (2)	−24.9% (4)	−44% (3)
Mob Driver	−4.9% (3)	−4.9% (1)	−4% (1)
Mob Navigator	−17.6% (4)	−21.4% (2)	−5% (2)

Coefficient [15]) **only for the driver in pair programming** (Fig. 3), but the rest (pair navigator and mob) had a negative or close to zero correlation. For **mob programming**, a **significant difference** was observed **between the roles** (driver and navigator). The attention and meditation levels decreased **more than 10%** from the **navigator to the driver**, suggesting that participants concentrate less and are more relaxed when they are navigators.

Difficulty. Participants had an easier time in a group than when working alone (Fig. 2). Pair programming and mob programming showed a significant difference. Participants in pair programming found it easier to tackle problems, but there was not a significant difference between the roles (Table 2).

RQ4 Conclusion: Our small experiment suggested that pair programming is more beneficial for participants. The largest factor was the difference in the roles during a programming session. The difference by role was smaller in the pair session, indicating that both roles were exerting similar amounts of effort.

---

6 Discussion

Four RQs were examined to obtain a deeper knowledge of mob programming and pair programming compared to solo programming. MindWave Mobile 2 was used to collect brainwave data from a new research perspective. The results indicate that group programming can realize more efficient learning than individual programming. As shown in the results, the meditation levels were lowest in solo work which suggests working alone may lead to less stress and tension compared to group work. Additional research is necessary to identify patterns. First, a larger dataset is necessary since this study involved only six participants. Due to time limitations, two programming sessions were conducted in a row. If the programming sessions occurred on different days, the participants would be more refreshed, which may affect the concentration and meditation results. Second, the EEG results have yet to be fully analyzed. The results here should be compared with other brainwave data.

7   Conclusion and Future Work

We preliminarily identify the differences between the brainwaves of programmers under different sessions (solo, pair, and mob). MindWave Mobile2 collected the levels of meditation, concentration, and EEG signals. Although differences between the participants in each session were distinguished, it is too early to yield conclusions. It is unclear whether the apparent differences between these programming methods are sustained by scientific and empirical evidence. Consequently, future research should investigate appropriate systems to look at brainwaves and summarize noteworthy quantities of data.

References

1. EEG - Ecg – Biosensors. http://neurosky.com/
2. DeMarco, T., Lister, T.R.: Peopleware: Productive Projects and Teams. Addison-Wesley, Upper Saddle River (2014)
3. Laal, M., Ghodsi, S.M.: Benefits of collaborative learning. Procedia. Soc. Behav. Sci. **31**, 486–490 (2012). https://doi.org/10.1016/j.sbspro.2011.12.091
4. Laughlin, P.R., Hatch, E.C., Silver, J.S., Boh, L.: Groups perform better than the best individuals on letters-to-numbers problems: effects of group size. J. Pers. Soc. Psychol. **90**(4), 644–651 (2006). https://doi.org/10.1037/0022-3514.90.4.644
5. Umezawa, K., Saito, T., Ishida, T., Nakazawa, M., Hirasawa, S.: An Electroencephalograph-Based Method for Judging the Difficulty of a Task Given to a Learner. In: 2017 IEEE 17th ICALT (2017). https://doi.org/10.1109/icalt.2017.18
6. Zuill, W.: Mob Programming - A Whole Team Approach. Agile Alliance (13 June 2019). https://www.agilealliance.org/resources/experience-reports/mob-programming-agile2014/
7. Kattan, H.M., Soares, F., Goldman, A., Deboni, E., Guerra, E.: Swarm or pair? In: Proceedings of the 19th International Conference on Agile Software Development: Companion (2018). https://doi.org/10.1145/3234152.3234169
8. Kattan, H.M., Oliveira, F., Goldman, A., Yoder, J.W.: Mob programming: the state of the art and three case studies of open source software. In: Santos, V.A.D., Pinto, G.H.L., Serra Seca Neto, A.G. (eds.) WBMA 2017. CCIS, vol. 802, pp. 146–160. Springer, Cham (2018). https://doi.org/10.1007/978-3-319-73673-0_12
9. Dybå, T., Arisholm, E., Sjoberg, D.I.K., Hannay, J.E., Shull, F.: Are two heads better than one? on the effectiveness of pair programming. IEEE Softw. **24**(6), 12–15 (2007). https://doi.org/10.1109/ms.2007.158
10. Hanks, B.: Empirical evaluation of distributed pair programming. IJHCS **66**(7), 530–544 (2008). https://doi.org/10.1016/j.ijhcs.2007.10.003
11. Radermacher, A., Walia, G.: Investigating student-instructor interactions when using pair programming: An empirical study. In: 2011 24th IEEE-CS CSEE&T (2011). https://doi.org/10.1109/cseet.2011.5876117
12. Salleh, N., Mendes, E., Grundy, J.: Empirical studies of pair programming for CS/SE teaching in higher education: a systematic literature review. IEEE Trans. Software Eng. **37**(4), 509–525 (2011). https://doi.org/10.1109/tse.2010.59
13. Busechian, S., et al.: Understanding the impact of pair programming on the minds of developers. In: Proceedings of the 40th ICSE: NIER (2018). https://doi.org/10.1145/3183399.318 3413

14. Shiraishi, M., Washizaki, H., Fukazawa, Y., Yoder, J.: Mob programming: a systematic literature review. In: 2019 IEEE 43rd Annual Computer Software and Applications Conference (COMPSAC) (2019). https://doi.org/10.1109/compsac.2019.10276
15. Pearson's Correlation Coefficient. (n.d.). Springer Reference. https://doi.org/10.1007/springerreference_83937

Open Access This chapter is licensed under the terms of the Creative Commons Attribution 4.0 International License (http://creativecommons.org/licenses/by/4.0/), which permits use, sharing, adaptation, distribution and reproduction in any medium or format, as long as you give appropriate credit to the original author(s) and the source, provide a link to the Creative Commons license and indicate if changes were made.

The images or other third party material in this chapter are included in the chapter's Creative Commons license, unless indicated otherwise in a credit line to the material. If material is not included in the chapter's Creative Commons license and your intended use is not permitted by statutory regulation or exceeds the permitted use, you will need to obtain permission directly from the copyright holder.

Author Index

Printed in the United States
by Baker & Taylor Publisher Services

Printed in the United States
by Baker & Taylor Publisher Services